For Richard
with my love

When the ocean of My presence hath ebbed
and the Book of My Revelation is ended,
turn your faces toward Him Whom God hath purposed,
Who hath branched from this Ancient Root.
Bahá'u'lláh

We have made Thee a shelter for all
mankind, a shield unto all who are in heaven
and on earth, a stronghold for whosoever hath
believed in God, the Incomparable, the All-Knowing.
Bahá'u'lláh

Contents

Author's Note on Sources and Acknowledgements

My intention in writing this book has been to provide a clear and straightforward historical account of the life of 'Abdu'l-Bahá. The writings of Bahá'u'lláh, 'Abdu'l-Bahá and Shoghi Effendi are the foundation of this work.

I owe a very considerable debt to Hasan M. Balyuzi. His book *'Abdu'l-Bahá, The Centre of the Covenant of Bahá'u'lláh* is the first full-length biography of 'Abdu'l-Bahá. I acknowledge myself greatly indebted to Adib Taherzadeh whose books *The Covenant of Bahá'u'lláh* and *The Revelation of Bahá'u'lláh*, volumes 1 to 4, have so greatly enriched our knowledge and understanding of Bahá'í history.

I have also drawn on the work of Myron H. Phelps whose book *The Master in 'Akká* contains so many of the vivid recollections of Bahíyyih <u>Kh</u>ánum, the Master's beloved sister.

We are fortunate that so many of the early Bahá'ís took the time to record their memories of their meetings and times spent with 'Abdu'l-Bahá. I acknowledge a special debt of gratitude to Ḥájí Mírzá Ḥaydar-'Alí, Lady Blomfield, Juliet Thompson, Howard Colby Ives, May Maxwell, Lua Getsinger, Corinne True, Thornton Chase, John Esslemont and all those who have enabled us all to glimpse the Master through their eyes.

It is my hope that, once a clear outline of 'Abdu'l-Bahá's life is obtained, readers will be able to read, with increased enjoyment and appreciation, the numerous works listed in the bibliography.

It was a special challenge to find material that would bring to life those places associated with the early childhood of 'Abdu'l-Bahá. In this area I am indebted to the work of Nabíl-i-A'ẓam and Dr David Ruhe. I would like to draw the reader's attention to two books which may not be well-known. The first is a novel by Gina Barkhordar Nahai called *Cry of the Peacock* which tells of the experience of the Jewish community in Iran from the late 18th century to the present day. The second is *Daughter of Persia* by Sattareh Farman Farmaian, a remarkable personal memoir which helps us to understand the nature of life in a large household in Ṭihrán in the early decades of the present century.

I would like to thank Jeannie and Buzz Damarell for the generous gift of their copy of *The Master in 'Akká*. My warm thanks to Cindy Pacileo for reading the manuscript and providing helpful suggestions. My deepest gratitude to my husband Richard who has provided constant support and loving encouragement and with infinite patience has helped this techno-peasant move towards a measure of computer literacy.

Preface

This is the third volume of a brief historical account of the lives of the three central figures of the Bahá'í Faith.

The first volume, *Hour of the Dawn*, relates the life of the Báb, the Martyr-Herald of the new Faith, who gave up His own life to proclaim the coming of Bahá'u'lláh. *Day of Glory* tells of the life of Bahá'u'lláh, the Founder-Prophet of the Bahá'í Faith. This present volume examines the life of 'Abdu'l-Bahá, the eldest son of Bahá'u'lláh, appointed by His Father as the Centre of the Bahá'í Covenant.

On the evening of the 22nd of May, in the year 1844, in the city of Shíráz, in southern Persia, the Bahá'í Era began, when the Báb declared His mission to Mullá Ḥusayn, His first disciple. Near midnight on that same luminous night, some four hundred miles to the north, in the city of Ṭihrán, the Qájár capital of Persia, 'Abdu'l-Bahá was born.

The title 'Abdu'l-Bahá, which was given to Him by Bahá'u'lláh while He was still a child and which He preferred above all others, means 'the Servant of the Glory'.

'Abdu'l-Bahá was not a manifestation of God as were the Báb and Bahá'u'lláh but He occupies a unique position in the Bahá'í Faith and, indeed, His station is without parallel in the whole of recorded religious history. He is the Centre of Bahá'u'lláh's Covenant, the Perfect Exemplar of Bahá'u'lláh's teachings, the unerring interpreter of His Father's word and the embodiment of every Bahá'í virtue.

'Though not invested with the rank of the Manifestation of God,' Adib Taherzadeh explains, 'the authority which

Bahá'u'lláh has conferred on Him is such that His words have the same validity as those of Bahá'u'lláh and the Báb.'[1]

Adib Taherzadeh further explains:

> God has in this day vouchsafed to humanity two price-less gifts. One is the Revelation itself, supreme over all things; the other is an instrument to shield the Revelation. The one is manifested through Bahá'u'lláh, the other fulfilled through 'Abdu'l-Bahá.[2]

This book attempts to provide a concise and straightforward historical account of the remarkable life of 'Abdu'l-Bahá.

Section I
1844–68

*Bahá'ís in
Adrianople*

1

Earliest Years

The birth of a child in May 1844 was a cause of particular joy to Bahá'u'lláh and Ásíyih Khánum for two children born to them earlier had both died in infancy. They named this newborn son 'Abbás after His paternal grandfather, Mírzá Buzurg, the distinguished vizier of Núr who had passed away five years earlier. At the time of His birth, Bahá'u'lláh and His family were living in a rented house near the Shimrán Gate, not far from the splendid mansion that Mírzá Buzurg had himself earlier occupied.

It was the Qájár rulers who first made Ṭihrán their power base. Áqá Muḥammad Khán, a eunuch chieftain of Turkish origin, coldly calculating and utterly ruthless, fought his way to power for 15 brutal years. In 1794 he captured and savagely murdered the last young ruler of the Zand dynasty and seized the crown. Three years later, in 1797, he himself died at the hands of assassins and was succeeded by his nephew Fatḥ-'Alí Sháh. The Zand kings had ruled from Shíráz. The Qájár monarchs, determined to make their own distinctive mark on the history of the country, chose Ṭihrán as their capital city.

Though unsurpassed in its natural setting beneath the mighty Alburz range, Ṭihrán was, at the opening of the 19th century, no more than a large, remote and disease-ridden village. The new rulers built a deep moat around the area where they intended their city to grow and raised behind the moat a four-mile long, tile-decorated mud wall, pierced by six arched gateways and punctuated by 18 towers. In a central square the main thoroughfares leading in from the main gates intersected. Along these dusty roads came camel-trains, mules and donkeys, heavily-laden, and large flocks of poultry and geese.

Close to the central square the Qájárs built their palaces and their main government buildings. They adapted for their use as a prison the former cistern of a nearby public bath. Here, near the square, rose the mosques and the great roofed bazaar, the shops of the potters, metal-smiths, cloth merchants and the homes of the new capital's more prosperous citizens. Here, too, outside the mosques, the government offices and the homes of the wealthy, gathered the poor and the professional beggars, the destitute, the maimed, the blind, the crippled and the mentally deranged.

'Abbás, who became known as 'Abdu'l-Bahá, was barely three months old when Mullá Husayn brought to Tihrán a scroll of the Báb's writing and presented it to Bahá'u'lláh. Bahá'u'lláh's acceptance of the Báb's message was immediate and unconditional. At once He began to promote the new teachings both in His home province of Núr and in Tihrán. Thus, from the earliest months of infancy, 'Abdu'l-Bahá was raised in the light and the shelter of a fresh revelation of God's grace to humankind.

His early childhood was a very happy one for His parents were devoted to each other and they presided over a well-ordered and harmonious household. In 1847 a daughter was born to them. She is known to us by the title Bahíyyih Khánum, given to her by her father. Two years later a son was born, a delicate child, named Mihdí after a dearly-loved brother of Bahá'u'lláh who had died a year earlier. He is known to us by the title 'The Purest Branch', also given to him by Bahá'u'lláh.

In much later years Bahíyyih Khánum recalled for Lady Blomfield her memories of those distant, peaceful days of her early childhood, of her father, whom they all adored, and of her gentle mother.

'I always think of her', she said,

> in those earliest days of my memory as queenly in her dignity and loveliness, full of consideration for everybody, gentle, of a marvellous unselfishness . . . her very presence seemed to make an atmosphere of love and happiness wherever she came, enfolding all comers in the fragrance of gentle courtesy.[3]

Theirs was a hospitable home where the doors were always open to the poor and from which no one in need was ever turned away. The lifestyle of Bahá'u'lláh and Ásíyih Khánum stood in stark contrast to the pattern of life indulged in by many of their noble contemporaries. A certain E.C. Bailey, working in the colonial administration of India in the latter part of the 19th century, described the upper classes of Persia as being 'as individuals, almost without exception, corrupt, selfish, debased and shamelessly unprincipled to a degree which it is scarcely possible to conceive'.

Bahá'u'lláh and Ásíyih Khánum cared little for the customary pursuits of the nobility and instead spent their very considerable wealth on feeding the hungry and in helping the oppressed and downtrodden, earning from those they aided the titles 'Father of the Poor' and 'Mother of Consolation'.

The steward of Bahá'u'lláh's large household was an African servant named Isfandíyár. His reputation for honesty, loyalty and hard work was well-established in Ṭihrán. Many prominent people, ministers and other high government officials frequently attempted to secure Isfan-

díyár's services for their own households but his devotion
to Bahá'u'lláh and His family was complete and he refused
all offers. Isfandíyár was a close and trusted friend of
Bahá'u'lláh's children and held a very special place in their
affections.

When the searing summer heat and the fear of cholera
emptied the great houses of Ṭihrán, Bahá'u'lláh often took
His family to a villa on the cool and wooded slopes above
the city. Here the air was fresh and cool, mountain streams
tumbled down the steep hillsides and here the wealthy of
Ṭihrán had built themselves villas and pavilions set in
fragrant flower gardens and orchards.

But whenever they could, Bahá'u'lláh and Ásíyih Khánum took their children to Bahá'u'lláh's ancestral home
in the village of Tákur in the province of Mázindarán. Both
Bahá'u'lláh and Ásíyih Khánum's family roots were deeply
entwined in that province for their ancestors had lived
there for many generations. The north of Mázindarán,
along the Caspian Sea, was then thickly wooded with
ancient forests. Further south, where the Alburz range
begins to rise, steep hillsides, where sheep farmers wrest
a living, soar above deep green valleys. Tákur, a small
village of perhaps 60 households, is situated in a long
green valley, two hard days' ride over the mountains from
Ṭihrán.

In Tákur, on a fertile platform of land near a tumbling
stream, Mírzá Buzurg, 'Abdu'l-Bahá's grandfather, had
built a magnificent house and surrounded it with a beautiful garden filled with flowers, fruit trees and flowering
shrubs. Here the young 'Abdu'l-Bahá, His sister, Bahíyyih
Khánum, and Mírzá Mihdí spent many happy hours. Ásíyih
Khánum's home was in nearby Yálrúd so the children had
numerous relatives to visit and many visited them during
those halcyon summer days. The ties of family were strong

and their parents' joy in visiting their home must have been shared by their children.

On the slopes above Ṭihrán and in Tákur Bahá'u'lláh shared with His children His own deep delight in the countryside and His love for the beauties of the natural world. It was probably during these summer visits that 'Abdu'l-Bahá learnt to ride, a sport in which He delighted and at which He excelled. In Tákur Bahá'u'lláh took His young son with Him on horseback across the hills and through the villages that formed part of the extensive family estate.

Bahá'u'lláh was an exemplary landlord, concerned for and considerate of all who depended on His land for their livelihood. A story is recorded that 'Abdu'l-Bahá went one day, without His father, to see the thousands of sheep which Bahá'u'lláh then owned. The story is told thus:

> The shepherds, wishing to honour their young Guest, gave Him a feast. Before 'Abbás was taken home at the close of the day, the head shepherd advised Him that it was customary under the circumstances to leave a present for the shepherds. 'Abbás told the man that He had nothing to give. Yet the shepherd persisted that He must give something.[4]

In much later years, 'Abdu'l-Bahá Himself recounted the rest of the story in these words:

> I was indeed in a dilemma but after thinking a moment the idea came to me to give each shepherd a few sheep from our own flocks. I communicated the idea to the overseer who was rather pleased with it; and it was announced in a solemn tone, and immediately acted upon. When at last we reached home, and my act of generosity was related to the Blessed Perfection, he laughed very much over it and said: 'We must appoint

a guardian to protect Aga – master – from his own liberality; else, some day, he may give himself away.'[5]

2

A Season of Terror

In Ṭihrán Bahá'u'lláh's prestige in court circles and in the city enabled Him to act as a shield for the other, less prominent Bábís of the city. His home soon became a haven for the local Bábís and for those travelling through it. While she was under house arrest in Ṭihrán, Ṭáhirih was a frequent visitor to Bahá'u'lláh's home.

'She used often, during her short visit, to take me on her knee,' 'Abdu'l-Bahá recalled, 'caress me, and talk to me. I admired her most deeply.'[6]

One visit of Ṭáhirih's He remembered with especial clarity. He was sitting on her knee in the private parlour of His mother. As the door of this room was open, they could all hear, from behind the curtain, the voice of Vaḥíd who was talking and 'arguing with my Father'.[7]

Nabíl-i-A'ẓam, an early believer and noted chronicler of the early history of the new Faith, recorded 'Abdu'l-Bahá's own description of this event in these words:

Ṭáhirih was listening from behind the veil to the utterances of Vaḥíd, who was discoursing with fervour and eloquence on the signs and verses that bore witness to the advent of the new Manifestation. I was then a child and was sitting on her lap, as she followed the recital of the remarkable testimonies which flowed ceaselessly from the lips of that learned man. I well remember how she suddenly interrupted him and, raising her voice, vehemently declared: 'O Yaḥyá! Let deeds, not words, testify to thy faith, if thou art a man of true learning. Cease idly repeating the traditions of the past, for the day of service, of steadfast action, is come. Now is the time to show forth the true signs of God, to rend asunder the veils of idle fancy, to promote the Word of God, and to sacrifice ourselves in His path. Let deeds, not words, be our adorning.'[8]

Ṭáhirih's radiant enthusiasm as she spoke these words made a deep and lasting impression on the young 'Abdu'l-Bahá.

A vivid pen-portrait of 'Abdu'l-Bahá in these years also comes to us in *Nabíl's Narrative*. Nabíl writes of a visit to Bahá'u'lláh's house when he was asked to accompany 'Abdu'l-Bahá to the school He attended:

> I gladly consented, and as I was preparing to leave, I saw the Most Great Branch, a child of exquisite beauty . . . emerge from the room which His Father occupied, and descend the steps leading to the gate of the house. I advanced and stretched forth my arms to carry Him. 'We shall walk together,' He said, as He took hold of my hand and led me out of the house. We chatted together as we walked hand in hand in the direction of the madrisih known in those days by the name of Pá-Minár. As we reached His classroom, He turned to me and said: 'Come again this afternoon and take me back to my home, for Isfandíyár is unable to fetch me. My Father will need him to-day.' . . . [I] returned to the madrisih in time to conduct the Most Great Branch to His home.[9]

In July 1850 the Báb was executed. At Zanján, Ḥujjat and his fellow-believers kept up a stubborn resistance against overwhelming odds but by early 1851 they too were forced into submission. For some months the authorities sought evidence that would link Bahá'u'lláh with the Bábí resistance but they failed to find the evidence they sought. In July 1851 Bahá'u'lláh left for Iraq on a journey of pilgrimage to the holy shrines of Najaf and Karbilá. He did not return to Ṭihrán until the early summer of 1852.

Sometime in 1851 'Abdu'l-Bahá contracted tuberculosis. While in Paris in 1911 He spoke of this event:

> While I was a child in Ṭihrán, seven years of age, I contracted tuberculosis. There was no hope of recovery. Afterwards the wisdom of and the reason for this became evident. Were it not for that illness I would have been in Mázindarán [the province where Bahá'u'lláh's ancestral home was]. But because of it I remained in Ṭihrán and was there when the Blessed Perfection was imprisoned.[10]

In Bahá'u'lláh's absence, in their great grief and despair, a handful of Bábís hatched a plot to assassinate the Sháh, seeing in him the origin of all their troubles. On His return from Iraq, as soon as He heard of this, Bahá'u'lláh vehemently denounced the scheme and urged its immediate abandonment. His warning and counsel went unheeded.

On the morning of 15 August 1852 three of the Bábí plotters shot at the Sháh as he set out on a hunting trip from his summer palace at Níyávarán. This misguided act gave the authorities just the excuse they were looking for to launch a pogrom against the Bábís. Bábís high and low, rich and poor, men, women and children were seized, imprisoned, tortured and killed. Bahá'u'lláh's noble rank, great wealth and considerable prestige at court could not save Him.

At the time, Bahá'u'lláh was a guest of the brother of the Grand Vizier and was staying on an estate which His host owned at Lavásán, above Ṭihrán. Orders for His arrest went out. His host urged Him to go into hiding but He rode out, unafraid, towards the army camp at Níyávarán, to meet His captors. He was stripped of His outer garments and His turban, the emblem of His noble rank. His shoes were removed and He was bastinadoed, severely beaten with rods on the soles of His feet. Accompanied by a jeering mob, He was hustled, barefoot and in chains, for about fifteen kilometres, to prison in Ṭihrán.

Ásíyih Khánum and her children were in their town mansion when a servant burst in, anguished, breathless, with the news:

> The master, the master, he is arrested – I have seen him! He has walked many miles! Oh, they have beaten him! They say he has suffered the torture of the bastinado! His feet are bleeding! He has no shoes on! His turban has gone! His clothes are torn! There are chains upon his neck![11]

'Abdu'l-Bahá, Bahíyyih Khánum and Mírzá Mihdí saw their mother's face whiten in shock and terror. They clung to her, weeping bitterly. Then the roar of the approaching mob reached them. Drums throbbed, bugles sounded and cymbals clashed. In an instant, friends, relatives and all but one African woman servant fled the house. The mob broke down the doors and burst in like an angry wave. Yelling, shouting and cursing the detested Bábís, they swept through the house, pillaging and looting as they went.

Ásíyih Khánum could not turn to Isfandíyár for help for he was not there. He was out in the town attending to some household business. She just had time, with the help of the one servant who had dared to remain, to snatch up a few valuable possessions, gather Mírzá Mihdí into her arms, instruct the other two to follow closely behind her and lead them away from further assault. 'They threw so many stones into our house', 'Abdu'l-Bahá later recounted, 'that the courtyard was crammed with them . . .'[12]

When the mob surged out as wildly as they had surged in, nothing whatsoever of value remained, the property was a wrecked and desolate ruin.

Ásíyih Khánum hurried her children away from the dangerous central section of the town into the dim alley-ways of the great bazaar. On the far side of the bazaar they were obliged to emerge from its shadowy shelter and cross another crowded and menacing open area where religious meetings were frequently held. Safely past this hazard, she sought shelter and obscurity in a section of the town named Sangilaj. Here, with the help of Bahá'u'lláh's brother Mírzá Músá, she rented a small house.

When Isfandíyár returned to the pillaged house, he sought the family out, even though he risked his own life in so doing. The Sháh had already sent people out to search the streets for him for they hoped to extract from him the names of Bábís who had gathered in his master's house. Trusting in God to guide his steps, Isfandíyár walked unmolested through the streets. No one recognized him and he found those he sought.

The children were overjoyed to see him.[13] Years later, during His journeys to the West, 'Abdu'l-Bahá spoke thus of Isfandíyár:

> If a perfect man could be found in the world, that man was Isfandíyár. He was the essence of love, radiant with sanctity and perfection, luminous with light. Whenever I think of Isfandíyár I am moved to tears although he passed away fifty years ago.[14]

Ásíyih Khánum now managed, with the help of a relative, to obtain two small rooms near to the prison, the Síyáh-Chál, where Bahá'u'lláh and the other Bábí prisoners were held. From here she was able, with the help of this same relative, to get food to Bahá'u'lláh. This was critical, for prisoners whose families could not manage to send food into the prison died of starvation and their corpses were dumped unceremoniously at the prison entrance.

Ásíyih Khánum and her children remained in close hiding in the two little rooms while around them in the streets Bábís were hunted down, tortured and killed.

Bahíyyih Khánum has left us a vivid account of those agonizing days.

> The mob crowded to these fearful scenes, and yelled their execrations, whilst all through the fiendish work, a drum was loudly beaten.
>
> These horrible sounds I well remember, as we three children clung to our mother, she not knowing whether the victim was her own adored husband. She could not find out whether he was still alive or not until late at night, or very early in the morning, when she determined to venture out, in defiance of the danger to herself and to us, for neither women nor children were spared.
>
> How well I remember cowering in the dark, with my little brother, Mírzá Mihdí, the Purest Branch . . . in my arms, which were not very strong, as I was only six. I was shivering with terror, for I knew of some of the horrible things that were happening, and was aware that they might have seized even my mother.
>
> So I waited and waited until she should come back. Then Mírzá Músá, my uncle, who was in hiding, would venture to hear what tidings my mother had been able to gather.
>
> My brother 'Abbás usually went with her on these sorrowful errands.[15]

Myron Phelps, an early biographer of 'Abdu'l-Bahá, includes in his book an incident related by Bahíyyih Khánum

which explains why it was that Ásíyih Khánum took 'Abdu'l-
Bahá with her when she went out:

> At first, on going to her aunt's, my mother would take
> me with her; but one day, returning unusually late, we
> found 'Abbás Effendi surrounded by a band of boys
> who had undertaken to personally molest him. He was
> standing in their midst as straight as an arrow – a little
> fellow, the youngest and smallest of the group – firmly
> but quietly *commanding* them not to lay their hands
> upon him, which, strange to say, they seemed unable
> to do. After that, my mother thought it unsafe to leave
> him at home, knowing his fearless disposition, and that
> when he went into the street, as he usually did to watch
> for her coming, eagerly expectant of news from his
> father for whom, even at that early age, he had a pas-
> sionate attachment, he would be beset and tormented
> by the boys. So she took him with her . . .[16]

To venture out into Ṭihrán late at night or early in the
morning demanded considerable courage even in more
normal times, for every night, at four hours past sunset,
a bugle sounded for the closing of all shops and streets.
Only a privileged few, who had access to the night's pass-
word, were allowed to remain outside. A pack of wild dogs,
which lived on the roofs of the bazaar by day, was nightly
let loose inside the bazaar to guard the shops against any
attempt at robbery.

Ásíyih Khánum had scarcely any money and very little
food. 'Abdu'l-Bahá recounts:

> . . . one day our means of subsistence were barely ade-
> quate, and mother told me to go to my aunt's house,
> and ask her to find us a few qiráns [a silver coin] . . . I
> went and my aunt did what she could for us. She tied
> a five-qirán piece in a handkerchief and gave it to me.
> On my way home someone recognized me and shouted:

'Here is a Bábí'; whereupon the children in the street
chased me. I found refuge in the entrance to a house
. . . There I stayed until nightfall, and when I came out,
I was once again pursued by the children who kept
yelling at me and pelted me with stones . . . When I
reached home I was exhausted. Mother wanted to know
what had happened to me. I could not utter a word and
collapsed.[17]

Bahá'u'lláh was kept in the prison for four months. 'Abdu'l-
Bahá, grieving at this cruel separation, asked to be taken
to the dungeon. He later recalled:

They sent me with a black servant to His blessed presence in the prison. The warders indicated the cell, and
the servant carried me in on his shoulders. I saw a dark,
steep place. We entered a small, narrow doorway, and
went down two steps, but beyond those one could see
nothing. In the middle of the stairway, all of a sudden
we heard His blessed voice: 'Do not bring him in here',
and so they took me back. We sat outside, waiting for
the prisoners to be led out. Suddenly they brought the
Blessed Perfection out of the dungeon. He was chained
to several others. What a chain! It was very heavy. The
prisoners could only move it along with great difficulty.
Sad and heart-rending it was.[18]

Bahá'u'lláh was so ill that He could hardly walk. His hair
was unkempt, His neck galled and swollen by a cruel steel
collar. His body was bowed down by the weight of an
appallingly heavy chain. This sight of His beloved father
so 'haggard, dishevelled, freighted with chains',[19] pierced
the tender heart of 'Abdu'l-Bahá. Overcome with shock and
grief, He fainted and was carried away unconscious.

When Bahá'u'lláh was eventually released He came to
His family in the two little rooms still dressed in His prison
garb. They could all see how the steel collar had cut into

His neck, how His feet, so long untended, bore evidence
of the torture of the bastinado. They could not nurse Him.
He needed far more care than they could possibly provide
in their cramped quarters. He moved into the house of His
half-brother Mírzá Riḍá-Qulí and there was able to regain
a little strength for the arduous journey that lay just ahead,
for Bahá'u'lláh and His family were banished from Persia.

No sooner was the reunion with Bahá'u'lláh achieved
than the family suffered another cruel separation. They
could not risk taking the delicate Mírzá Mihdí, only four
years old, with them on a long midwinter journey. They left
him with Ásíyih Khánum's maternal grandmother and she
was the only one of all their relatives who dared come out
to bid them a final sad farewell.

This was 'Abdu'l-Bahá's first departure from His homeland. He was never to return.

3

Exile and Separation

The small party of exiles who left Ṭihrán on that bitter winter morning consisted of Bahá'u'lláh's two wives and their children, His two brothers Mírzá Músá and Mírzá Muḥammad Qulí together with their wives, their young children and a number of servants. Three months of exhausting travel now lay ahead over bleak terrain and through mountain passes in a cold which Bahá'u'lláh Himself described as 'so intense that one cannot even speak, and ice and snow so abundant that it is impossible to move'.[20] Bahíyyih Khánum later related:

> My father was very ill. The chains had left his neck galled, raw, and much swollen. My mother, who was pregnant, was unaccustomed to hardships, and was worried and harassed over our recent trials and the uncertainty of our fate . . . We were all insufficiently clothed, and suffered keenly from exposure. My brother in particular was very thinly clad. Riding upon a horse, his feet, ankles, hands, and wrists were much exposed to the cold, which was so severe that they became frost-bitten and swollen and caused him great pain.[21]

The effects of that frost-bite 'Abdu'l-Bahá was to feel for the rest of His life.

In April 1853, exhausted, the exiles reached Baghdád. 'We arrived in Baghdad', Bahíyyih Khánum recalled, in a state of great misery, and also of almost utter destitution . . . My father was still very ill; my mother and other women in delicate health; small children needed care, while our means were insufficient to procure even the usual necessities of life . . .

In short, our sufferings – at least those of our own family – were indescribable. However, we struggled through this period as bravely as we could, until after a time, occasional remittances came to us from Tehran . . .[22]

Ásíyih <u>Kh</u>ánum had managed to arrange, before leaving Ṭihrán, for a few valuable items from her dowry which had escaped the pillaging of their house, to be sold. The money sent to Ba<u>gh</u>dád from the sale of these items enabled the exiles to purchase basic necessities.

'Abdu'l-Bahá had left Ṭihrán still suffering from tuberculosis. Remarkably though, in spite of this serious illness and despite the ordeal of the winter journey, once in Ba<u>gh</u>dád, suddenly and against the opinions of the doctors who had pronounced His condition incurable, He made a full recovery.

Sometime during the first year in Ba<u>gh</u>dád 'Abdu'l-Bahá perceived through His own spiritual insight the meaning of the mystery that had occurred in the Síyáh-<u>Ch</u>ál. He was only nine years old but, though still a child, He alone understood the cause of the 'new radiance' which, in the words of Bahíyyih <u>Kh</u>ánum, seemed to enfold their father 'like a shining vesture'.[23] He recognized the station of Bahá'u'lláh as a Manifestation of God, and though still so young in years, threw Himself at Bahá'u'lláh's feet and begged to be allowed to offer up His own life in His pathway.

Hand of the Cause Hasan Balyuzi has written of this event:

> The Báb states that the first one to believe in a Manifestation of God is the essence of the achievement of the preceding dispensation; and so, 'Abdu'l-Bahá, the first to believe with His whole being in the Mission of His Father, was the most eminent representative of the virtues called forth by the Báb.[24]

It is certain that so gifted and perceptive a child would have been all too well aware of the bitter jealousy of His father felt by Mírzá Yaḥyá, Bahá'u'lláh's half-brother, and of the deep enmity in the heart of Siyyid Muḥammad, the fomenter of division in the small Bábí community in Iraq. When, on account of this poison of envy, Bahá'u'lláh abruptly left Baghdád in April 1854, telling no one where He was going or even whether He intended to return, 'Abdu'l-Bahá grieved long and deeply.

Already in His young life 'Abdu'l-Bahá had experienced bitter persecution, homelessness and utter impoverishment. But while His beloved father was with them, these things had been bearable. Now, so suddenly bereft of One whose mission He alone had fully recognized and without any idea where His father had gone, He was desolate.

The trials brought upon His family by their most difficult house-guest, Mírzá Yaḥyá, the death of His own infant brother, the constant and ever-widening intrigues of Mírzá Yaḥyá and Siyyid Muḥammad, the responsibility He assumed as head of a household in exile in His father's absence, the acute loneliness and uncertainty of those days and the agony of a second seemingly endless separation from His adored father, aged 'Abdu'l-Bahá far beyond His years. He confided to Nabíl at the time that He felt that He had grown old while still a child. Bahíyyih Khánum later remembered:

. . . my brother was deeply attached to his father; this attachment seemed to strengthen with his growth. After our father's departure he fell into great despondency. He would go away by himself, and, when sought for, be found weeping, often falling into such paroxysms of grief that no one could console him. His chief occupation at this time was copying and committing to memory the tablets of the Báb. The childhood and youth of my brother was, in fact, in all respects unusual . . . Horseback riding was the only diversion of which he was fond; in that he became proficient . . .[25]

Though desolated by His father's absence, in the company of the believers who had emigrated with His family 'Abdu'l-Bahá was calm and serene. Mírzá Músá took Him regularly to the meetings of the friends where His eloquence and sagacity astonished all. It was the strength and consolation that 'Abdu'l-Bahá found in the writings of the Báb that sustained Him.

A year and more dragged by. Ásíyih Khánum and Mírzá Músá made every possible inquiry but without result. 'Abdu'l-Bahá spent many entire nights in earnest prayer.

'My brother's distress at the prolonged absence,' Bahíyyih Khánum later recounted to Lady Blomfield, 'was pathetic.'

On one occasion he prayed the whole night a certain prayer with the one intention, that our father might be restored to us.

The very next day, he and our uncle, Mírzá Músá, overheard two people speaking of a marvellous one, living as a dervish in the wild mountain district of Sulaymáníyyih; they described him as 'The Nameless One', who had magnetized the countryside with his love. And they immediately knew that this must be our Beloved.[26]

It was at the request of 'Abdu'l-Bahá and Mírzá Músá that Shaykh Sulṭán and Javád the woodcutter at once set out for the mountains to search for the dervish.

Shaykh Sulṭán was a devoted Bábí who had learnt of the new Faith through Ṭáhirih. He had no ties in Baghdád and told Ásíyih Khánum and her children that he desired no greater happiness than to be allowed to seek for Him whom all loved so much and that he would not return without Bahá'u'lláh. 'He was, however,' Bahíyyih Khánum relates,

> very poor, not being able even to provide an ass for the journey; and he was besides not very strong, and therefore not able to go on foot. We had no money for the purpose, nor anything of value by the sale of which money could be procured, with the exception of a single rug, upon which we all slept. This we sold and with the proceeds bought an ass for this friend, who thereupon set out upon the search.
>
> Time passed; we heard nothing, and fell into the deepest dejection and despair. Finally, four months having elapsed since our friend had departed, a message was one day received from him saying that he would bring my father home on the next day. The other members of the family could not credit the truth of this news, but it seemed to electrify my brother. He minutely questioned and examined the messenger, and became much excited. He quite believed that his father would return, but no one else did.
>
> During the night following the next day, however, my father walked into the house. We hardly knew him; his beard and hair were long and matted – he really was a dervish in appearance. The meeting between my brother and his father was the most touching and pathetic sight I have ever seen. 'Abbás Effendi threw himself on the floor before him and kissed and embraced his feet, weeping and crying, 'Why did you

leave us, why did you leave us?' while the great uncouth dervish wept over his boy. The scene carried a weight not to be expressed in words.[27]

4

'The Mystery of God'

On His return from Kurdistán Bahá'u'lláh began the task of reviving and revitalizing the Bábí community which had, in His absence, fallen to the uttermost depth of degradation. 'Abdu'l-Bahá was present at most of the meetings which His father held with the believers. In addition to this very considerable task, Bahá'u'lláh was sought out by many others in Baghdád and beyond. Bahíyyih Khánum relates that:

> After his return the fame which he had acquired in the mountains reached Baghdad, and not only Bábís but many others came to hear his teachings; and many, also, merely out of curiosity to see him. As he wished for retirement these curiosity seekers were a great trouble and annoyance to him. This aroused my brother and he declared that he would protect his father from such intrusions . . . he himself would first see those who came. If he found that they were genuine truth-seekers he admitted them to his father's presence; otherwise he did not permit them to see him.[28]

On many occasions when visitors were present 'Abdu'l-Bahá played a part in answering their questions and solving their difficulties. He had a profound grasp of academic and theological concepts. His insight and keen intelligence, His modest bearing and gentleness of manner aroused general admiration in the local mosques and amongst the learned theologians with whom He came in daily contact.

'Abdu'l-Bahá's days of formal schooling had ended abruptly with the arrest and exile of Bahá'u'lláh and He did not attend any school in Baghdád. In the early years in Baghdád He received lessons sometimes from His mother, at other times from Mírzá Músá and occasionally from Bahá'u'lláh. Bahá'u'lláh also arranged for a certain imám of good character and sound education to discuss academic questions with 'Abdu'l-Bahá on certain mornings and afternoons. This man, whose name was 'Abdu's-Salám Effendi, told Bahá'u'lláh:

> I have taught and studied for over thirty years and yet, when students question me, I am obliged to refer to my books. Your accomplished child, on the other hand, is able to give explanations which have never occurred to me.[29]

Nabíl has recorded the following explanation which Bahá'u'lláh gave to this learned man:

> The essence of the Most Great Branch is indicative of the essence of God . . . The Most Great Branch effortlessly comprehends scientific matters and perceives realities which others are incapable of fathoming; even as the Báb, Who, with only a few pages of practice, was able to produce such exquisite handwriting, and although He spent no more than a few days in school, prolific was the divine knowledge which flowed from His heart. In the same way, as soon as some aspect of knowledge comes to the attention of the Most Great Branch, He comprehends it to a degree that no scholar, however competent, can ever match.[30]

While 'Abdu'l-Bahá was in His early teens, Bahá'u'lláh
began to refer to His eldest son as 'the Master' and it was
by this title that He began to be generally referred to
amongst the believers in Baghdád. Even at this early stage
in His life He was beginning to take on the role that was
to occupy Him throughout Bahá'u'lláh's mission, acting as
His deputy and shielding Him from those who came to
request an audience with Bahá'u'lláh merely out of idle
curiosity. Mírzá Maḥmúd-i-Káshání, a believer who served
Bahá'u'lláh in Baghdád and who accompanied Him on His
later exiles, recounted the following incident which took
place in Baghdád:

> The word Áqá (The Master) was a designation given to
> 'Abdu'l-Bahá. I recall that one day when Bahá'u'lláh
> was in the Garden of Vashshásh which was a delightful
> place situated outside Baghdád, which He occasionally
> used to visit, someone referred to certain individuals
> as the Áqá. On hearing this Bahá'u'lláh was heard to
> say with a commanding voice: 'Who is the Áqá? There
> is only one Áqá, and He is the Most Great Branch.'[31]

'Abdu'l-Bahá's relationship to His father was not merely
that of a son who deeply loved His human father. From the
time that He recognized Bahá'u'lláh as His Lord, the One
for whom the Báb had given up life itself, 'Abdu'l-Bahá
manifested, in His attitude and in all His actions, the
utmost humility, respect and submissiveness towards
Bahá'u'lláh.

In these same years, Bahá'u'lláh also bestowed upon
'Abdu'l-Bahá the title 'the Mystery of God'. In describing
'Abdu'l-Bahá's role as Centre of the Bahá'í Covenant, Adib
Taherzadeh writes:

It would be a mistake to consider 'Abdu'l-Bahá as an ordinary human being who persevered in His efforts until He emptied Himself of selfish desire and consequently was appointed by Bahá'u'lláh as His Successor. Such a concept is contrary to the belief of those who have embraced the Faith of Bahá'u'lláh. 'Abdu'l-Bahá was created by God for the sole purpose of becoming the recipient of God's Revelation in this age. We shall never know His real station, because He was the 'Mystery of God', a title conferred upon Him by Bahá'u'lláh. He was the priceless gift of Bahá'u'lláh to mankind.[32]

As He grew to manhood in Baghdád 'Abdu'l-Bahá began to take on the task of supervising the routine work and daily activities of the large household in exile, ensuring that provisions were adequate and that the affairs of Bahá'u'lláh's family functioned smoothly. Bahá'u'lláh had travelled to Baghdád with His two wives and children and with His two faithful brothers, Mírzá Músá and Mírzá Muḥammad Qulí. Mírzá Yaḥyá, his half-brother, had joined them on the journey to Baghdád. During the years in Baghdád Bahá'u'lláh's second wife, Mahd-i-'Ulyá, gave birth to several sons. The eldest of these sons was named Muḥammad-'Alí.

In Baghdád, Bahá'u'lláh married a third wife, Gawhar Khánum. Thus there was by this time a considerable family of exiles, all connected by ties of kinship to the family of which Bahá'u'lláh was the head.

About 1860 Mírzá Mihdí was brought to Baghdád and reunited with his family and great was 'Abdu'l-Bahá's joy at this reunion. Mírzá Mihdí's pure heart was magnetized by the vitalizing breezes of Bahá'u'lláh's writings and he too now devoted every moment of his time to the service of his father and the believers.

When He was 15 or 16, 'Abdu'l-Bahá, at the request of a certain 'Alí Shawkat Páshá, a highly-cultured and well-educated nobleman, wrote a commentary on the well-known Islamic tradition ascribed to the Prophet Muḥammad: 'I was a Hidden Treasure and loved to be known, therefore I created beings to know.' This lucid commentary reveals 'Abdu'l-Bahá's remarkable intellectual powers and His ability to convey profound concepts with beauty and clarity.

In 1862 Bahá'u'lláh revealed the Kitáb-i-Íqán, His foremost theological work, in response to questions raised by one of the Báb's maternal uncles. 'Abdu'l-Bahá transcribed the book and an original manuscript exists in His handwriting. From this time onwards He was often occupied with the transcription of His father's writings.

Though exiles, Bahá'u'lláh and His family were not yet prisoners. 'Abdu'l-Bahá was able to enjoy horse-back riding and to walk outside the city. 'Once, when I lived in Baghdad,' He later recalled,

> I was invited to the house of a poor thorn-picker. In Baghdad the heat is greater even than in Syria, and it was a very hot day. But I walked twelve miles to the thorn-picker's hut. Then his wife made a little cake out of some meal for Me and burnt it in cooking it, so that it was a black, hard lump. Still that was the best reception I ever attended.[33]

5

To the Great City – Constantinople

In late March of 1863, as a result of pressure exerted by those antagonistic to Bahá'u'lláh in Baghdád, Constantinople and Ṭihrán, the Sháh's government, eager for the removal of the exile even further from its borders, persuaded the Ottoman government to invite Bahá'u'lláh to move to Constantinople. So unwilling was the governor of Baghdád, Námiq Páshá, to supervise this removal that he could not bring himself to meet personally with Bahá'u'lláh but sent his deputy to convey the instructions received from the Ottoman capital. 'Abdu'l-Bahá and Mírzá Músá, acting on Bahá'u'lláh's instructions, visited Námiq Páshá and were given a splendid reception. 'Abdu'l-Bahá wrote of those days:

> Such hath been the interposition of God that the joy evinced by them [the adversaries] hath been turned to chagrin and sorrow, so much so that the Persian consul-general in Baghdád regrets exceedingly the plans and plots the schemers had devised.[34]

The news of Bahá'u'lláh's imminent departure from Baghdád provoked consternation and grief amongst His own followers and amongst many in the city. So many people came to His house to pay their respects to Him that His family could not begin the work of packing up their belongings. It was 'Abdu'l-Bahá who arranged for Bahá'u'lláh to move to the Riḍván Garden so that His family would be able to prepare for the journey to Constantinople. 'Abdu'l-Bahá and His brothers were with Bahá'u'lláh in the boat that took them across the Tigris to the Garden of Riḍván. 'Abdu'l-Bahá was present, with a few other believers, when Bahá'u'lláh declared, on His first day in the Riḍván Garden, that He was the One whose coming the Báb had foretold, the Promised One of all religions.

Munírih Khánum, the wife of 'Abdu'l-Bahá, shared with Lady Blomfield in much later years her recollections of what she knew of the Master's early life. Lady Blomfield herself paraphrased these recollections, stating that 'Abdu'l-Bahá:

> . . . well-endowed with a peculiar receptiveness that was inborn, and strengthened by the education given to Him by His Father, saw, as in a radiant vision, the world of the future, when the divine Message, having become known and comprehended by 'men of good-will' would change the heart of the world . . .[35]

This insight imparted to 'Abdu'l-Bahá a fresh measure of joy in the wonder of the new Revelation.

When the exiles left Baghdád 'Abdu'l-Bahá was 19 years old and, in the words of Hasan Balyuzi, was 'handsome, gracious, agile, zealous to serve, firm with the wilful, generous to all'.[36]

On that three-month journey to Constantinople, whenever possible, 'Abdu'l-Bahá rode by the side of His father's howdah. Writing in later years, 'Abdu'l-Bahá described how Jináb-i-Muníb, an ardent and gifted young believer, gave up ease and comfort to accompany the exiles: 'he gladly measured out the desert miles, and he spent his days and nights chanting prayers, communing with God and calling upon Him.'

Recalling the exhilaration of that journey, 'Abdu'l-Bahá continued:

> There were nights when we would walk, one to either side of the howdah of Bahá'u'lláh, and the joy we had defies description. Some of those nights he would sing poems; among them he would chant the odes of Ḥáfiẓ, like the one that begins, *'Come, let us scatter these roses, let us pour out this wine'* . . . [37]

From the time when Bahá'u'lláh's declaration was made at Baghdad, Bahíyyih Khánum recalled that 'Abdu'l-Bahá took on the role of special attendant, servant and body-guard of His father. She relates that on this journey to Constantinople

> He guarded him day and night . . . riding by his wagon and watching near his tent. He thus had little sleep, and, being young, became extremely weary. His horse was Arab and very fine, and so wild and spirited that no other man could mount him, but under my brother's hand as gentle and docile as a lamb. In order to get a little rest, he adopted the plan of riding swiftly a considerable distance ahead of the caravan, when, dismounting and causing his horse to lie down, he would throw himself on the ground and place his head on his horse's neck. So he would sleep until the caval-cade came up, when his horse would awake him by a kick and he would remount. [38]

The hardship and stress of that journey 'Abdu'l-Bahá has also captured for us:

> Often, by day or by night we covered a distance of from twenty-five to thirty miles. No sooner would we reach a caravanserai than from sheer fatigue everyone would lie down and go to sleep: utter exhaustion having

overtaken everybody they would be unable even to move.[39]

He Himself seldom rested for He had taken on the responsibility of ensuring that everyone in the large party had the necessary supplies and that there was fodder and water for the 36 pack animals. This was far from a simple task. Near Márdín, about half-way through the journey, they crossed a famine-stricken region. 'Abdu'l-Bahá relates:

> When we reached a station Mirza Jafar and I would ride from one village to another, from one Arab or Kurdish tent to another trying to get food, straw, barley, etc., for men and animals. Many a time we were out till midnight . . . In brief, everywhere we encountered many difficulties, until we arrived in Karpout. Here, we saw that our animals had become lean, and walked with great difficulty. But we could not get straw and barley for them.[40]

Bahíyyih Khánum recalled the journey as a very hard one for the women and children. Much of the time the weather was bad and many days they went without proper food. 'On one occasion', she relates,

> during a long and cold march, my brother having obtained some bread, rice, and milk, my father made up with his own hands a sort of pudding by boiling these together with a little sugar, which was then distributed to all. The preparation of this food was a reminiscence of my father's two-years' sojourn in the mountains, where he was dependent on what might be given him, and this dish – which he sometimes made for himself – was the only warm food he had.
>
> Such times as these were moments of pleasure; but there was always present a feeling of apprehension – as though a sword were hanging over our heads.[41]

When it was time to move on to another caravanserai, 'Abdu'l-Bahá was always awake and alert to cheer and encourage the weary or faint-hearted. He has given us a delightful account of two of the believers, Áqá Riḍá and Mírzá Maḥmúd-i-Káshání, who acted as cooks and who:

> . . . rested not for a moment. After our arrival they would immediately become engaged in cooking for this party of nearly seventy-two people – and this after their arduous work of guiding all day or all night the horses which carried the palanquin of the Blessed Perfection. When the meal was cooked and made ready all those who had slept would wake, eat and go to sleep again. These two men would then wash all the dishes and pack them up. By this time they would be so tired that they could have slept even on a hard boulder.
>
> During the journey when they became utterly weary they would sleep while walking. Now and again I would see one of them take a bound and leap from one point to another. It would then become apparent that he was asleep and had dreamed that he had reached a wide creek – hence the jump.
>
> In a word, from Bagdad to Samsoun they served with rare faithfulness. Indeed no human being had the fortitude to bear cheerfully all this heavy labour. But, because they were kindled (by the spirit of God) they performed all these services with greatest happiness. I remember how, in the early morning, when we wanted to start for another caravanserai, we often saw these two men fast asleep. We would go and shake them and they would wake with much difficulty. While walking they always chanted communes and supplications.[42]

6

In Constantinople and Adrianople

The exiles reached the Ottoman capital in mid-August of 1863. 'Arrived in Constantinople', Bahíyyih Khánum recalls,

> we found ourselves prisoners. We were put into a small house, the men below and the women above. My father and his family were given two rooms. The weather was very cold and damp, and we had no fires or proper clothing. Because of the crowding the atmosphere was foul. We petitioned for better quarters, and were given another house, which was to some extent an improvement.[43]

Bahá'u'lláh had been courteously invited to transfer His residence from Baghdád to Constantinople. Pressure from Ṭihrán, combined with the intrigues of the Persian ambassador in Constantinople, now ensured that His stay in the Ottoman capital was short. In December of the same year He was peremptorily ordered out of the city. 'They expelled Us,' He later wrote, '. . . with an abasement with which no abasement on earth can compare.'[44]

Bahíyyih Khánum recalled:

> Before we set out a threat was made of separating us – of sending the Blessed Perfection to one place, his family to another, and his followers elsewhere. This overwhelmed us with apprehension, which hung over

us and tormented us during the whole of the journey and long after. The dread of this or of the execution of my father was the greatest of our trials – a horrible fear of unknown danger always menacing us. Such threats were frequently repeated after this time also. Had it not been for them we could have borne our sufferings with greater resignation; but these kept us always in a heart-sickening suspense.[45]

The exiles were ordered to depart at once for Adrianople, 'the place', Bahá'u'lláh wrote of that city, 'which none entereth except such as have rebelled against the authority of the sovereign'.[46] Bahá'u'lláh gave to 'Abdu'l-Bahá and Mírzá Músá the task of receiving the official who delivered the edict of banishment. Hurried preparations were made to leave. Once again, 'Abdu'l-Bahá took on the responsibility of supervising these preparations.

In midwinter the entire party of exiles was forced to undertake a twelve-day journey through snow and ice and bitter winds to the remote city of Adrianople, known today by its ancient name, Edirne. Inadequately clothed, fed and sheltered along the way, in a winter of unusual severity, all suffered greatly.

'The journey to Adrianople,' Bahíyyih Khánum remembered, 'although occupying but nine days, was the most terrible experience of travel we had thus far had . . . We arrived at Adrianople all sick – even the young and strong. My brother again had his feet frozen on this journey.'[47]

Arriving in Adrianople, the entire party was at first crowded into a miserable caravanserai. Then, Bahíyyih Khánum relates:

> Our family, numbering eleven persons, was lodged in a house of three rooms just outside the city . . . It was like a prison; without comforts and surrounded by a guard of soldiers. Our only food was the prison fare

allowed us, which was unsuitable for the children and the sick.

That winter was a period of intense suffering, due to cold, hunger and, above all, to the torments of vermin, with which the house was swarming. These made even the days horrible, and the nights still more so. When they were so intolerable that it was impossible to sleep, my brother would light a lamp (which somewhat intimidated the vermin) and by singing and laughing seek to restore the spirits of the family.

In the spring, on the appeal of the Blessed Perfection to the Governor, we were removed to somewhat more comfortable quarters within the city.[48]

Through all those months of travel, upheaval and discomfort 'Abdu'l-Bahá served indefatigably. Increasingly He shouldered the burden of all domestic cares for Bahá'u'lláh's household and also saw to the welfare of the other exiles.

In Adrianople the festering jealousy of Mírzá Yaḥyá, fuelled by the obsessive ambitions of Siyyid Muḥammad, came to a head. Mírzá Yaḥyá decided to murder Bahá'u'lláh. He also poisoned the well from which Bahá'u'lláh and His family took their water. Though he succeeded in making them all sick, there were no fatalities. Next he invited his half-brother to drink tea with him and gave Him tea in a poisoned teacup. Bahá'u'lláh fell desperately ill and was near death. He remained seriously ill for an entire month. The effects of that attempt on His life remained with Him for the rest of His days. 'Abdu'l-Bahá, so close to His Father and ready to give His own life to protect Him from harm, could only watch and endure.

Thwarted a second time, Mírzá Yaḥyá now ingratiated himself with the barber of the party, Ustád Muḥammad-'Alíy-i-Salmání, and then hinted to the barber that he might put an end to Bahá'u'lláh's life during one of His

regular visits to the bath house. Ustád Muḥammad, appalled by this suggestion, went straight to 'Abdu'l-Bahá
with his tale. 'Abdu'l-Bahá strongly urged him to remain
silent but Ustád Muḥammad was much too distraught to
heed this advice. Soon all the exiles knew. A tremendous
commotion began. When challenged, Mírzá Yaḥyá dis-
claimed any intention of harming Bahá'u'lláh and accused
Ustád Muḥammad of himself harbouring these murderous
intentions. When challenged by Bahá'u'lláh to acknowledge
Him as the One foretold by the Báb, Mírzá Yaḥyá responded with his own claim.

These events caused Bahá'u'lláh overwhelming anguish.
He lamented: 'He who for months and years I reared with
the hand of loving-kindness hath risen to take My life.'[49]

Bahá'u'lláh knew that the exiles must choose between
Himself and Mírzá Yaḥyá. He knew that the continuation
of such internal dissension would destroy the infant Faith
and bring to naught all for which the Báb and His companions had given their lives. He therefore secluded Himself
in His own house advising His grieving companions to
avoid all contention and to pray and trust in God.

Unhindered, Siyyid Muḥammad and Mírzá Yaḥyá
widened the scope of their intrigues against Bahá'u'lláh,
spreading ever more damaging fabrications far and wide.
They were aided in these schemes by a newly-recruited
accomplice, Áqá Ján Big-i-Kaj-Kuláh, a former Turkish
artillery officer. Amongst many discreditable ventures,
these three wrote slanderous letters to the recently-
appointed governor of Adrianople, Khurshíd Páshá.

This action quickly rebounded on them for the governor, although new to the city, was already well acquainted
with Bahá'u'lláh's character and reputation. Confused and
puzzled by the letters, he sought clarification from Bahá'u-
'lláh Himself.

Bahá'u'lláh understood that things could no longer continue in this manner. He therefore took the drastic step of totally disassociating Himself from His own half-brother and asked all His faithful followers to do likewise.

It is hard for many of us today to appreciate just how drastic a step this was. In 19th-century Persian society, the bonds of family loyalty took precedence over all other ties. In a society where poverty and want were widespread and where justice was very scarce, the large extended Persian families provided not only a person's very identity but a network of essential material support based on mutual trust and loyalty, often referred to as 'the bond of bread and salt'. If this was so in Persia itself, it would apply even more strongly to a noble Persian family in exile, strangers in an alien land.

Mírzá Yaḥyá was not the only relative of Bahá'u'lláh creating confusion and disunity amongst the believers. His son, Muḥammad-'Alí, 'Abdu'l-Bahá's young half-brother, added to His father's anguish. Adib Taherzadeh tells us that:

> In Muḥammad-'Alí's childhood Bahá'u'lláh conferred upon him the power of utterance, and this became obvious as he grew up. But instead of utilizing this gift to promote the Cause of God, he embarked on a career which hastened his downfall. When he was in his early teens in Adrianople, he composed a series of passages in Arabic and without Bahá'u'lláh's permission disseminated them among some of the Persian Bahá'ís, introducing them as verses of God which, he claimed, were revealed to him. He intimated to the believers that he was a partner with Bahá'u'lláh in divine Revelation. Several believers in Qazvín were influenced by him and drawn to him. This created a great controversy in Qazvín, and resulted in disunity among some of the believers there. The city of Qazvín was already notori-

ous for its different factions among the Bábís, and there were some followers of Mírzá Yaḥyá actively disseminating false propaganda against the followers of Bahá'u'lláh.

Now, in the midst of these conflicting groups, Mírzá Muḥammad-'Alí's claim to be the revealer of the verses of God brought about an added confusion . . .

Such preposterous claims, such a display of personal ambition, evoked the wrath of Bahá'u'lláh, who rebuked him vehemently and chastised him with His own hands . . .[50]

7

'This Branch of Holiness'

While the poisonous boil of jealousy and treachery was being so agonizingly lanced within His own family, 'Abdu'l-Bahá continued to act in the public gaze as Bahá'u'lláh's deputy. On one occasion Khurshíd Páshá was present at an assembly of the city's most distinguished divines when 'Abdu'l-Bahá, in the words of Shoghi Effendi 'briefly and amazingly, resolved the intricacies of a problem that had baffled the minds of the assembled company'.[51] There and then the governor made a glowing public tribute to the youthful 'Abdu'l-Bahá. So deeply affected was the Páshá, Shoghi Effendi relates, 'that from that time onwards he could hardly reconcile himself to that Youth's absence from such gatherings'.[52]

It was also during the years in Adrianople that Shaykh Aḥmad-i-Rúḥí, a follower of Mírzá Yaḥyá whom Bahá'u'lláh referred to as a 'foreboder of evil' on account of his fierce and constant opposition to the Bahá'í Faith, announced from the pulpit that had Bahá'u'lláh no other proof to substantiate His exceptional powers, the fact that He had raised such a son as 'Abdu'l-Bahá would be sufficient.

In addition to the other duties that He had taken on in order to lighten Bahá'u'lláh's burden, 'Abdu'l-Bahá now assisted pilgrims arriving from Persia intent on seeking admission to Bahá'u'lláh's presence.

In the last years spent in Adrianople, after the Most Great Separation occurred, Bahá'u'lláh revealed a veritable torrent of majestic and soul-stirring Tablets proclaiming His mission to the kings, rulers and peoples of the world and defining its tenets for His followers.

'I swear by God! In those days the equivalent of all that hath been sent down aforetime unto the Prophets hath been revealed,' Bahá'u'lláh Himself has stated with regard to this copious outpouring.[53]

One of those present has recorded,

Day and night the Divine verses were raining down in such number that it was impossible to record them. Mírzá Áqá Ján wrote them as they were dictated, while the Most Great Branch was continually occupied in transcribing them. There was not a moment to spare.[54]

In one of these Tablets, the Súriy-i-Ghusn, the Tablet of the Branch, addressed to Mírzá 'Alí-Riḍá, the Vizier of Khurásán, a well-respected official and a believer in the new revelation, Bahá'u'lláh thus alludes to 'Abdu'l-Bahá and to the unique station His eldest son was destined to assume.

There hath branched from the Sadratu'l-Muntahá this sacred and glorious Being, this Branch of Holiness; well is it with him that hath sought His shelter and abideth beneath His shadow. Verily the Limb of the Law of God hath sprung forth from this Root which God hath firmly implanted in the Ground of His Will, and Whose Branch hath been so uplifted as to encompass the whole of creation. Magnified be He, therefore, for this sublime, this blessed, this mighty, this exalted Handiwork! . . . A Word hath, as a token of Our grace, gone forth from the Most Great Tablet – a Word which God hath adorned with the ornament of His own Self, and made it sovereign over the earth and all that is therein, and a sign of His greatness and power among its people . . . Render thanks unto God, O people, for

His appearance; for verily He is the most great Favour unto you, the most perfect bounty upon you; and through Him every mouldering bone is quickened. Whoso turneth towards Him hath turned towards God, and whoso turneth away from Him hath turned away from My Beauty, hath repudiated My Proof, and transgressed against Me. He is the Trust of God amongst you, His charge within you, His manifestation unto you and His appearance among His favoured servants . . . We have sent Him down in the form of a human temple. Blest and sanctified be God Who createth whatsoever He willeth through His inviolable, His infallible decree. They who deprive themselves of the shadow of the Branch, are lost in the wilderness of error, are consumed by the heat of worldly desires, and are of those who will assuredly perish.[55]

Section II
1868–92

*Akka's
sea gate*

8

The Journey to 'Akká

In early 1868 Bahá'u'lláh's opponents, alarmed by the rising prestige of the exiles, redoubled their efforts to have Bahá'u'lláh removed from the city. He was now a revered and highly-respected figure in Adrianople. 'Abdu'l-Bahá, acting as His deputy, was frequently invited to the governor's mansion. Pilgrims were arriving in increasing numbers. Fu'ád Páshá, the Turkish Foreign Minister, after a tour of the city, sent to Constantinople a report which contained an exaggerated account of the size and influence of the exiled community.

The authorities in Constantinople were deeply disturbed. This banishment was not working out as they had planned. Letters sent by the Azalís, the followers of Mírzá Yahyá, slandering Bahá'u'lláh and accusing Him of plotting with foreign powers, now fell on fertile ground.

In late July the two Ottoman ministers, 'Alí Páshá and Fu'ád Páshá, at the insistent prompting of Hájí Mírzá Husayn Khán, the Persian ambassador, obtained the Sultán's consent for a further removal. Bahá'u'lláh was to be banished to the remote penal colony of 'Akká and condemned to perpetual imprisonment within its walls. Five others were to go with Him: His two faithful brothers, one other believer and the arch-accomplices of Mírzá Yahyá, Siyyid Muhammad and Áqá Ján Big.

The imperial edict was sent to Khurshíd Páshá instructing the governor to make its terms known to Bahá'u'lláh at once. Deeply distressed, <u>Kh</u>ur<u>sh</u>íd Pá<u>sh</u>á sought an audience with Bahá'u'lláh and there expressed his abhorrence at these instructions. All the efforts he had made to prevent a further banishment had failed. Embarrassed by this failure and feeling unequal to the task imposed on him, he took a leave of absence from his post and assigned the task of supervising the exiles' departure to his deputy, the registrar.

Bahíyyih <u>Kh</u>ánum relates that this new peril broke upon them with the abruptness of a tornado.

> We were sitting one day in our house, when we heard discordant music, loud, insistent! We wondered what could be causing this uproar. Looking from the windows we found that we were surrounded by many soldiers.[56]

The Bahá'ís who had opened shops or businesses in the city were rounded up and taken to the *Seraye* (the government office). There they were interrogated, informed that all their possessions would be auctioned off on the following day and notified that they must prepare for immediate departure. Bahá'u'lláh was told that He and His family, together with twelve of His companions, must leave the city immediately.

Bahá'u'lláh refused to leave at such short notice. His steward had substantial debts in the town and these could not be paid until His followers who had been imprisoned in Constantinople were released. Only then would they be able to sell several valuable horses which had been given to Bahá'u'lláh. Only when all His debts were paid, He stated, would He be prepared to leave.

The first night Bahá'u'lláh and His family were unable to obtain food. The soldiers remained on duty day and night for eight days. Each day officers came to meet with

'Abdu'l-Bahá in the outer apartments. Several consuls of foreign powers also came offering to intercede with the Ottoman authorities. Bahá'u'lláh refused their offers but they continued to come and to meet with 'Abdu'l-Bahá, despite the presence of the soldiers.

Bahá'u'lláh counselled several pilgrims who had recently arrived in the city to stay apart from the exiles so that they too would not also have to leave for some unknown destination. The turmoil and confusion of those days and the distress of the believers is graphically described by Ḥusayn-i-Áshchí, who served as cook in Bahá'u'lláh's household:

> Among those whom Bahá'u'lláh counselled to stay away were two brothers, Ḥájí Ja'far-i-Tabrízí and Karbilá'í Taqí . . . who had come to Adrianople to attain the presence of Bahá'u'lláh. They were men of courage, tall in stature, enthusiastic and full of excitement . . . Ḥájí Ja'far privately decided that he preferred to die than to live away from His Lord. He took a razor with him to the outer apartment of the house which was crowded with military officers and government officials, put his head out of a window which opened onto the street and cut his own throat.[57]

Ḥájí Ja'far had not managed to sever the carotid artery but his terrifying shout alerted those in the room. He was hauled back in through the window and as Ḥusayn-i-Áshchí relates:

> Immediately they called 'Abdu'l-Bahá. Everyone was appalled at the sight. At that moment I arrived in the outer apartment to count the number of people so that I could bring supper for everybody. The Greatest Holy Leaf was in the kitchen waiting for me to tell her the number. But when I saw Ḥájí Ja'far in that state staggering all over the place with blood pouring out I was

riveted to the scene . . . The soldiers were telling Ḥájí Ja'far that a surgeon would be coming to attend to his wounds, but although he could not speak, he made it clear to them by sign language that even if the surgeon was able to stitch his wounds he could cut his throat again . . .

As I did not return to the kitchen the Greatest Holy Leaf sent the widow of Mírzá Muṣṭafá to come and fetch me at once. But when she saw Ḥájí Ja'far in that frightful state she fainted and fell unconscious on the ground. Then from the kitchen they sent another person – a Christian maid – to come and see what was the cause of delay. She also fainted and dropped beside the widow of Mírzá Muṣṭafá!

In the meantime 'Abdu'l-Bahá sent me into the inner apartments of the house to bring some of His own clothes so that He could change Ḥájí Ja'far's clothes . . .

As to Ḥájí Ja'far, 'Abdu'l-Bahá urged him to co-operate with the surgeon when he came and promised him that he would be allowed to join Bahá'u'lláh.[58]

Bahá'u'lláh's request for a delay in departure was agreed to and provision made for the outstanding debts to be paid. Ḥusayn-i-Áshchí has also left us a vivid portrait of the exiles' departure from Adrianople:

Then preparations began for the journey and the standard of bereavement was hoisted in the city. The souls of many people burnt in the fire of separation from their Beloved and their hearts cried out in their remoteness from Him . . . All the furniture was auctioned at a very low price. It took eight days before everything was ready. Then they brought fifty carriages for all of us. Many people, Muslims, Christians and Jews crowded around the carriages, sobbing and grief-stricken . . . The scenes of lamentation were more heart-rending than those of a few years before at the time of Bahá'u'lláh's departure from Baghdád . . .

Baháʼuʼlláh spoke words of comfort to all and bade them farewell . . . At Gallipoli we housed all our belongings in a caravanserai while we stayed in a house. Baháʼuʼlláh, the holy family and the females among the party stayed upstairs and the rest of us downstairs.[59]

At Gallipoli all were kept in suspense for three days. The fear of imminent separation and dispersal caused acute distress. Then their worst fears were realized. They heard that they were indeed to be separated. Baháʼuʼlláh and His faithful brothers were to proceed to ʿAkká, Mírzá Yaḥyá to Cyprus and the rest of the party to Constantinople. Baháʼuʼlláh insisted they remain together. With the help of the Ottoman officer accompanying them and through the efforts of ʿAbduʼl-Bahá, the terms of this edict were changed. Bahíyyih Khánum later recalled:

Finally my brother, by his eloquence in argument and power of will, succeeded in gaining for the second time from the Constantinople government the concession that we should remain together.[60]

They all embarked on a crowded Austrian-Lloyd steamer bound for Alexandria. Bahíyyih Khánum relates:

In the hurry, distress, and uncertainty of the moment, we neglected to provide food for the voyage, but to one old servant, on his way to the ship, the thought occurred that he had not seen any provisions prepared, and he bought a box of bread. This, with the ship's prisoners' rations, which were almost inedible, was the only food we had for five days . . .[61]

One of the party, Jináb-i-Muníb, the believer who had walked with ʿAbduʼl-Bahá by the side of Baháʼuʼlláh's howdah on the journey from Baghdád, had fallen ill in

Adrianople. Jináb-i-Muníb, 'Abdu'l-Bahá tells us, 'was a fine youth, handsome, full of charm and grace . . . wise and perceptive; staunch in the Faith of God; a flame of God's love'; 'steadfast, modest and grave; and there was no one like him for faith and certitude'.[62] But stricken by a severe illness, he was pitifully weak.

'Still,' 'Abdu'l-Bahá relates,

> he would not agree to remaining behind in Adrianople where he could receive treatment . . . We journeyed along till we reached the sea. He was now so feeble that it took three men to lift him and carry him onto the ship. Once he was on board, his condition grew so much worse that the captain insisted we put him off the ship, but because of our repeated pleas he waited till we reached Smyrna.
>
> . . . We carried Jináb-i-Muníb to the hospital, but the functionaries allowed us not more than one hour's time. We laid him down on the bed; we laid his fair head on the pillow; we held him and kissed him many times. Then they forced us away. It is clear how we felt.[63]

Heartsore, they returned to the boat. At Alexandria the entire party was transferred to another, smaller vessel bound for Haifa via Port Said and Jaffa. Bahíyyih Khánum relates:

> Here the rumour that we were to be separated was renewed; and all were so terrified by it that no one was willing to leave the ship to buy provisions lest he be prevented from returning. We were able to procure only some grapes and mineral water.
>
> The little bread we had was now spoiled; and, what with hunger, fright, and grief, we were almost bereft of reason.[64]

In this small boat we, seventy-two persons, were crowded together in unspeakable conditions, for eleven days of horror. Ten soldiers and two officers were our escort.

There was an appalling smell in the boat, and most of us were very ill indeed.[65]

There was no place in which we could lie down in that vessel . . .

Our lack of food had reduced us to a seriously weak state of health.[66]

In the early morning of 31 August 1868, their vessel dropped anchor at Haifa. The rumours and the fear of separation had been with them all the way. Now the moment had come.

'Abdu'l-Ghaffár, a believer from Iṣfahán, was one of the four loyal followers of Bahá'u'lláh condemned to accompany Mírzá Yaḥyá to Cyprus. He was, 'Abdu'l-Bahá tells us,

a highly perceptive individual who, on commercial business, had travelled about Asia Minor for many years . . .

On the journey from 'Iráq to the Great City, Constantinople, 'Abdu'l-Ghaffár was a close and agreeable companion. He served as interpreter for the entire company, for he spoke excellent Turkish, a language in which none of the friends was proficient . . . in the Great City, he continued on, as a companion and friend. The same was true in Adrianople and also when, as one of the prisoners, he accompanied us to the city of Haifa.

Here the oppressors determined to send him to Cyprus. He was terrified and shouted for help, for he longed to be with us in the Most Great Prison. When they held him back by force, from high up on the ship he threw himself into the sea.[67]

It was just at the moment that Bahá'u'lláh stepped into the boat that was to carry Him to the landing-stage that 'Abdu'l-Ghaffár hurled himself into the ocean shouting 'Yá Bahá'u'l-Abhá'. The guards dragged him from the water. He was resuscitated with difficulty and comforted by Bahá'u'lláh. Bahíyyih Khánum later remembered how Bahá'u'lláh and 'Abdu'l-Bahá cheered all the exiles.

'Why did you jump into the sea?' Bahá'u'lláh gently asked 'Abdu'l-Ghaffár. 'Did you wish to give a banquet to the fishes?'[68]

The soldiers then held 'Abdu'l-Ghaffár a prisoner on the ship, 'cruelly restraining him, and carrying him away by force to Cyprus'.[69]

So weak were the women of the party by this time that they had to be carried to the Haifa shore in chairs. Then they were all kept waiting for several hours at the dockside before embarking on the last stage of the journey.

'The heat of that month of July was overpowering,' Bahíyyih Khánum remembered.

> We were put into a sailing boat. There being no wind, and no shelter from the burning rays of the sun, we spent eight hours of positive misery, and at last we had reached 'Akká, the end of our journey.[70]

There was no landing-stage at 'Akká and no landing facilities of any kind. The men were obliged to wade ashore. The authorities had intended that the women of the party be unceremoniously bundled ashore on the backs of the men. But, as Bahíyyih Khánum relates:

> My brother was not willing that this should be done, and protested against it. He was one of the first to land, and procured a chair, in which, with the help of one of the believers, he carried the women ashore.[71]

9

In the Desolate City

Once inside the prison city, the exhausted exiles were greeted by jeers and curses. The authorities had taken good care to spread a number of rumours amongst the townspeople. These Persian prisoners, they said, were dangerous, the vilest criminals, despicable traitors. Worst of all, they were heretics, destroyers of Islam, deserving only hatred and contempt.

'When we had entered the barracks,' Bahíyyih <u>Kh</u>ánum recalls,

> the massive door was closed upon us and the great iron bolts thrown home. I cannot find words to describe the filth and stench of that vile place. We were nearly up to our ankles in mud in the room into which we were led. The damp, close air and the excretions of the soldiers combined to produce horrible odours.[72]

On that first evening the prisoners were given no food or water. In the sultry summer heat, in those airless quarters, they all suffered acute thirst. The older children were screaming from thirst and hunger and could neither sleep nor be soothed and the women breast-feeding their babies, on account of their own hunger and thirst, could not feed their infants.

'Abdu'l-Bahá made several appeals on behalf of the
children to the guards and at about midnight He succeeded in getting a message to the governor of the city.

'We were then sent a little water', Bahíyyih Khánum
relates,

> and some cooked rice; but the latter was so full of grit
> and smelled so badly that only the strongest stomach
> could retain it . . . Later on, some of our people in
> unpacking their goods found some pieces of the bread
> which had been brought from Gallipoli, and a little
> sugar. With these a dish was prepared for the Blessed
> Perfection, who was very ill. When it was taken to him,
> he said: 'I command you to take this to the children.'
> So it was given to them, and they were somewhat qui-
> eted.
>
> The next morning conditions were no better . . .[73]

'Abdu'l-Bahá was allocated a room on the ground floor of
the prison which had previously served as the prison
morgue. Its moist air affected His health and He was to
feel the effects of that unhealthy confinement for the rest
of His life.

Three days after their arrival in 'Akká the Sultán's edict
condemning Bahá'u'lláh to life imprisonment was read
aloud in the mosque. The exiles were pronounced criminals guilty of corrupting the morals of the people. They
were, the Sultán's order stated, confined to the prison and
forbidden to associate with anyone.

Just a few days after their arrival in 'Akká the governor
came through the prison on a tour of inspection. 'Abdu'l-
Bahá and a few of the believers obtained an interview with
him. The governor spoke curtly and dismissively, threatening to cut off the Bahá'ís' meagre bread supply if anyone
tried to escape. The young Husayn-i-Áshchí could not
bear to be spoken to so rudely. He retorted with some

impolite remarks of his own. In front of the governor 'Abdu'l-Bahá slapped Ḥusayn-i-Áshchí hard on the face and ordered him to return to his room. It was then that the governor began to take note that there was a leader amongst the group and that these were, perhaps, no ordinary prisoners. Not long after this the authorities stopped issuing the standard prison ration of black bread to the exiles. Instead, they allocated them a small sum of money and allowed a few of them to go out each day, under strict guard, into the town to purchase supplies for the whole party.

Adib Ṭaherzadeh relates that 'Abdu'l-Bahá was summoned by the governor

> to hear the contents of the edict. When it was read out to Him that they were to remain in prison for ever, 'Abdu'l-Bahá responded by saying that the contents of the edict were meaningless and without foundation. Upon hearing this remark, the Governor became angry and retorted that the edict was from the Sulṭán, and he wanted to know how it could be described as meaningless. 'Abdu'l-Bahá reiterated His comment and explained that it made no sense to describe their imprisonment as lasting for ever, for man lives in this world only for a short period, and that sooner or later the captives would leave this prison either dead or alive. The Governor and his officers were impressed by the vision of 'Abdu'l-Bahá and felt easier in His presence.[74]

The guards in the barracks were callous and greedy, their sensitivities blunted by the conditions under which they had to work. One of their tasks was to put newly-arrived prisoners in chains. While in America decades later, 'Abdu'l-Bahá recounted how they put Him in chains and locked circlets of steel around His ankles and knees. While they were doing this, He laughed and sang. The guards were astonished and said to Him,

> 'How is this? You are laughing and singing. When prisoners are ironed in this way, they usually cry out, weep and lament.' 'Abdu'l-Bahá replied, 'I rejoice because you are doing me a great kindness; you are making me very happy. For a long time I have wished to know the feelings of a prisoner in irons, to experience what other men have been subjected to. I have heard of this; now you have taught me what it is. You have given me this opportunity. Therefore I sing and am very happy. I am very thankful to you.'[75]

'Akká was indeed a wretched place, 'the most desolate of the cities of the world', Bahá'u'lláh has written of it, 'the most unsightly of them in appearance, the most detestable in climate, and the foulest in water'.[76]

There was no source of water within the city walls. Sanitary facilities were non-existent and disease was rampant. The honeycomb of winding, narrow alleyways where sunlight never penetrated was filthy, damp and vermin-infested. The majority of 'Akká's people were grossly ignorant and steeped in prejudice. They were ill-fed, ill-housed and sick much of their lives. There was an almost entire absence of grass, plants and growing things. 'There were a few trees inside the walls,' 'Abdu'l-Bahá later recalled, 'and on their branches, as well as up on the battlements, the owls cried all night long.'[77]

Autumn, a time of especially virulent fevers in 'Akká, was now upon them. The appalling conditions the prisoners had to endure, huddled together on the damp earth floor of the barracks, the filth, the absence of good food and adequate hygiene, the lack of fresh air and exercise, now took their toll. Almost all the exiles fell ill with various fevers, malaria and dysentery. 'Abdu'l-Bahá, Mírzá Músá and one other believer named Áqá Riḍáy-i-Qannád managed to nurse their companions, fed them, washed them and kept watch with them. Nine of their ten guards also fell sick. No doctor was allowed into the prison and they were unable to obtain any medicine.

'Abdu'l-Bahá monitored very carefully the provisions brought in from the town. When those who had made the daily purchases returned to the citadel, He inspected all they had bought and even asked to see the contents of their pockets. Anything that He regarded as harmful to their health He threw away. A simple broth and a little boiled rice was their daily diet over a period of four months.

Despite these precautions, three of the exiles died, two of them on the same night, brothers, locked in each other's arms. Then, when the rest had recovered, Áqá Riḍá and 'Abdu'l-Bahá both fell sick. Bahíyyih Khánum remembered how exhausted 'Abdu'l-Bahá was:

> He took no rest. When at length he had brought the rest of us . . . through the crisis and we were out of danger, he was utterly exhausted and fell sick himself, as did also my mother and the three others who had theretofore been well. The others soon recovered, but 'Abbás Effendi was taken with dysentery, and long remained in a dangerous condition. By his heroic exertions he had won the regard of one of the officers, and when this man saw my brother in this state he went to the governor and pleaded that 'Abbás Effendi might have a physician. This was permitted, and under the care of the physician my brother recovered.[78]

Through those agonizing first months in 'Akká 'Abdu'l-Bahá had never once wavered. In the words of Hasan Balyuzi, He 'tended the sick, shielded His Father, faced the scorn and the fury of the inhabitants of 'Akká, held His ground with callous gaolers and brutal guards and hostile officials. He never wavered.'[79]

Bahíyyih <u>Kh</u>ánum later recalled that on arriving in 'Akká, Bahá'u'lláh gave to 'Abdu'l-Bahá a special charge, that of shielding Him from the outside world. Bahíyyih <u>Kh</u>ánum recollected her father's instructions to 'Abdu'l-Bahá.

> Now I concentrate on My work of writing commands and counsels for the world of the future, to thee I leave the province of talking with and ministering to the people. Servitude is the essence of worship. I have finished with the outer world, henceforth I meet only the disciples.[80]

The exiles' isolation during that first winter was almost total. Yet, despite this imposed isolation, 'Abdu'l-Bahá became known in the city. One day He and a few of the other exiled Bahá'ís went out to buy the daily provisions. While waiting to be served in a butcher's shop, the Master listened, along with the other customers, to a lively discussion between a Christian and a Muslim. Each was holding forth on the merits of his Faith. The Christian appeared to be winning the discussion. Courteously, with simplicity and eloquence, 'Abdu'l-Bahá joined in the conversation and, to the entire satisfaction of the Christian, He proved the validity of Islam. News of this incident spread quickly through the city. The hearts of many were attracted.

However, there was one citizen of 'Akká whose heart burned with fierce hatred of the exiles. His name was <u>Sh</u>ay<u>kh</u> Maḥmúd and he was born into a family of devout Muslims. Adib Taherzadeh relates:

> When he [<u>Sh</u>ay<u>kh</u> Maḥmúd] was about ten years of age, an old <u>Sh</u>ay<u>kh</u>, a religious man revered by Maḥmúd's

father, had a vision of the coming of the Person of the 'Promised One' to 'Akká. He intimated this to Maḥmúd in the presence of his father and told him that his father and himself were old men and would not live to see that day. But he assured Maḥmúd that he would then be a grown-up person and bade him watch out for the coming of the Lord.[81]

At the time of Bahá'u'lláh's arrival in 'Akká, Shaykh Maḥmúd was a highly respected religious leader in the city. He was an extremely devout Muslim, learned and pious. When he heard the Sulṭán's edict, the condemnation of the Bahá'ís and the order for their perpetual incarceration in 'Akká read aloud in the mosque, his heart boiled with rage. He seethed with resentment that the presence of such infidels should be allowed to pollute the air of his city. His agitation increased when he one day encountered 'Abdu'l-Bahá at the mosque. Adib Taherzadeh relates:

> He is reported to have grabbed 'Abdu'l-Bahá by the hand and exclaimed, 'Are you the son of God?' The Master with His characteristic charm pointed out that it was he who was saying it, and not 'Abdu'l-Bahá. He then reminded him of the injunction of Islám as stated in one of the Traditions: 'Be charitable toward the guest even though he be an infidel.'[82]

These words and the loving-kindness of the Master touched the heart of Shaykh Maḥmúd. His aggression towards 'Abdu'l-Bahá vanished. 'But being a religious leader,' Adib Taherzadeh continues,

> he could not remain indifferent to the presence of the group of exiles whom he considered ungodly. He therefore decided to put an end to all this by himself. One day he hid a weapon under his cloak and went

straight to the barracks with the intention of assassinating Bahá'u'lláh. He informed the guards at the prison gate that he wished to see Bahá'u'lláh. Since he was an influential personality in 'Akká, the guards complied with his request and went to inform Bahá'u'lláh of the identity of the visitor. 'Tell him', Bahá'u'lláh is reported to have said, 'to cast away the weapon and then he may come in.' On hearing this Shaykh Maḥmúd was astounded, for he was sure that no one had seen the weapon under his cloak. In a state of utter confusion he returned home, but his agitated mind could not be at rest. He continued in this state for some time until he decided to go to the barracks again, but without any weapons this time. Being a strong man he knew he could take Bahá'u'lláh's life by the mere strength of his hands.

So he went again to the prison gate and made the same request to visit Bahá'u'lláh. On being informed of Shaykh Maḥmúd's desire to meet Him, Bahá'u'lláh is reported to have said: 'Tell him to purify his heart first and then he may come in.' Perplexed and confused at these utterances, Shaykh Maḥmúd could not bring himself to visit Bahá'u'lláh that day. Later he had a dream in which his father and the old Shaykh appeared to him and reminded him of their vision regarding the coming of the Lord. After this dream Shaykh Maḥmúd went to the barracks again and attained the presence of 'Abdu'l-Bahá. The words of the Master penetrated his heart and he was ushered into the presence of Bahá'u'lláh. The majesty and glory of His countenance overwhelmed the Shaykh and he witnessed the fulfilment of the prophecy of the coming of the Lord to 'Akká. He prostrated himself at His feet and became an ardent believer.

After recognizing the station of Bahá'u'lláh, he arose to serve Him and His Cause.[83]

There was just one Bahá'í, named Mírzá 'Abdu'l-Aḥad, living in the city when the exiles arrived. Bahá'u'lláh had instructed him to move there while the exiles were all still in Adrianople. He had done as instructed, opened a small store in the city and lived there very quietly, revealing to no one his identity and allegiance. It was March of 1869 before the prisoners were able to contact him. So close a watch did the guards keep on those who went out to buy the daily supplies that all through the autumn and winter months such a contact was impossible.

Through those lonely, difficult months, 'Abdu'l-Bahá remained the most cheerful of companions to all the exiles. At the end of each day, however difficult it had been, they would gather together and recount to each other the most fantastic and funny occurrences they could remember and laugh over them.

10

In Supreme Joy

The exiles' difficulties and trials were not confined to the barracks. Áqá Ján Big and Siyyid Muḥammad had settled in their quarters over the inner gate of the city and there kept watch, day and night, for any Bahá'í pilgrims attempting to enter 'Akká. 'Whenever they saw anyone arriving,' 'Abdu'l-Bahá relates,

> they immediately reported to the government that the person newly arrived had brought letters with him and would take letters back. The authorities would then arrest the friend who had come, confiscate his papers, throw him into gaol, and finally expel him. This procedure became the rule and the government followed it for a long time.[84]

'Abdu'l-Bahá was still in chains but after a time, as He Himself later explained,

> . . . the men who had been appointed to keep guard over me became as loving brothers and companions. They strove to lighten my imprisonment by acts of kindness. They said, 'In order that you may not be subjected to the jeers of the people when you walk upon the streets we will arrange your clothing so these chains are not visible.' They took the chains which were upon my limbs, gathered the ends together and wrapped them as a girdle around my waist, then arranged my clothing so no chains were visible. One day I wished to

go the hammam (public bath). The guards said, 'It will
not be possible for you to go to the bath unless these
chains are removed; and furthermore it will attract
notice from the people in the streets.'[85]

But 'Abdu'l-Bahá said He would go, so the guards gathered
the dangling chains carefully around His waist, covered
them with His clothing, and off they set. As they walked
along the street, in full view of the passers-by, 'Abdu'l-Bahá
took the chains from around His waist and flung their
dangling ends over his shoulders. This drew a crowd and
He was followed all the way to the hammam by people
jeering and hooting at Him. The guards were most distressed but 'Abdu'l-Bahá was in supreme joy because of this
opportunity to walk in the freedom of the 'Pathway of
God.'[86]

It was not only the guards who were impressed by
'Abdu'l-Bahá's behaviour. The higher officials, those in
charge of the prison, already aware of the striking qualities
of Bahá'u'lláh, noted the loving disposition of His son.
Attracted by His virtues and qualities, they sought Him out
and gained from His counsel.

As a result of this contact, the exiles' strict confinement
was gradually relaxed. Once this began to happen, 'Abdu'l-
Bahá was able to hire an Egyptian mat-maker to come into
the prison and teach the exiles how to make rush mats. He
Himself was skilled in the craft of basket-weaving. He often
said that everyone should acquire a skill in some kind of
craft.

The chief religious leader of 'Akká, the Muftí, a man of
strongly orthodox views, whose name was Shaykh 'Alí-i-
Mírí, one day asked 'Abdu'l-Bahá if he could meet with
Bahá'u'lláh. At that time Bahá'u'lláh granted few interviews. The Ottoman government had sentenced Him to
solitary and perpetual confinement and Bahá'u'lláh did not

wish to upset the authorities by disregarding this edict. But 'Abdu'l-Bahá pleaded on the Mufti's behalf and Bahá'u'lláh gave His permission for the Muftí to enter the barracks. Ḥusayn-i-Áshchí was working in the kitchen on that day and has left us the following account:

> He [the Muftí] was shown to his seat while 'Abdu'l-Bahá stood by the door. The kitchen in which I was working happened to be opposite the room of Bahá'u'lláh. I could see and hear Him. The Muftí asked some questions and then the Tongue of Grandeur began to speak. At one stage when the utterances of Bahá'u'lláh were still continuing, the Muftí was moved to say something. 'Abdu'l-Bahá gave him an emphatic and commanding signal with his hand that he should not interrupt the words of Bahá'u'lláh. He complied but his pride was hurt.[87]

Although the Master accompanied him to the prison gate when he left, the Muftí was annoyed at the incident. Everyone in 'Akká showed him marked respect and deference. At that time the Muftí had no idea of the greatness of the Cause. 'But', Adib Ṭáherzádeh continues,

> it did not take very long before he realized that in the presence of 'Abdu'l-Bahá he was as utter nothingness. He used to visit the Master and partake of His knowledge and wisdom. He therefore changed his attitude. In the streets and bazaars, whenever he accompanied 'Abdu'l-Bahá he always walked a few steps behind Him and was never found to be walking in front . . . 'Abdu'l-Bahá always showered his favours upon the Muftí . . .[88]

One of the fruits of the relaxation of the exiles' strict confinement was that the authorities allowed 'Abdu'l-Bahá the use of a small room at the mosque where He could pray and meditate alone. It was at the mosque, in the summer of 1869, that Badí', who, dressed as a humble water-carrier, had slipped into the city under the very noses of the Azalís, recognized 'Abdu'l-Bahá amongst the group of Persians and managed to pass Him a note. That very night 'Abdu'l-Bahá arranged for Badí' to enter the citadel and attain the presence of Bahá'u'lláh. As other pilgrims arrived, 'Abdu'l-Bahá lent some of them very small sums of money with which they were able to support themselves as pedlars or itinerant traders.

Shaykh Maḥmúd played a significant role in helping the pilgrims to enter 'Akká. Sometimes he left the city and returned at night accompanied by one of the believers posing as his servant and carrying a lantern in front of him. Sometimes he arranged for ropes to be lowered over the walls so that the Bahá'í pilgrims could enter the city without risking discovery at the land gate. He would then shelter these visitors until they could enter the presence of Bahá'u'lláh and then he would enable them to leave the city safely.

In June of 1870, towards the end of the exiles' second year of confinement in the barracks, tragedy engulfed Bahá'u'lláh's family. 'Abdu'l-Bahá's younger brother, Mírzá Mihdí, the Purest Branch, fell through a skylight while walking and praying on the roof of the barracks. He was fatally injured. 'Abdu'l-Bahá, grief-stricken, entered Bahá'u'lláh's presence and begged His father to heal Mírzá Mihdí.

'O my Greatest Branch,' Bahá'u'lláh is reported to have said, 'leave him in the hands of his God.'[89]

Bahá'u'lláh then dismissed all members of the family and remained alone with His son. Mírzá Mihdí's dying wish was that the believers would be able to enter Bahá'u'lláh's presence.

'And so it shall be,' Bahá'u'lláh assured him. 'God will grant your wish.'[90]

Áqá Ḥusayn-i-Áshchí recalled hearing Bahá'u'lláh lamenting aloud: 'Mihdí! O Mihdí!'[91]

'Abdu'l-Bahá made all the arrangements for His brother's burial. Ḥusayn-i-Áshchí has left us an account of that grievous day:

> When the Purest Branch passed away, Shaykh Maḥmúd begged the Master to allow him to have the honour of washing the body and not to let anyone from the city of 'Akká perform this service. The Master gave permission. A tent was pitched in the middle of the barracks. We placed his blessed body upon a table in the middle of the tent and Shaykh Maḥmúd began the task of washing it. The loved ones of God were wailing and lamenting with tearful eyes and, like unto moths, were circling around that candle which the hands of God had lighted. I brought water in and was involved in washing the body. The Master was pacing up and down outside the tent. His face betrayed signs of deep sorrow . . .
>
> . . . The casket was carried high on the shoulders of men out of the barracks with utmost serenity and majesty. It was laid to rest outside 'Akká in the graveyard of Nabí Ṣáliḥ . . . At the time of returning to the barracks an earth tremor shook the area . . .[92]

In October of 1870 the barracks were needed for troops. The exiles were moved out and were allowed to rent a small house in the city. Within the next year Bahá'u'lláh and His family were obliged to move three times, as accommodation was so hard to obtain. Eventually, they moved into the house of 'Údí Khammár near the sea wall. This house was far too small for their needs.

Their companions had been moved from the barracks to the main caravanserai of the town, the Khán-i-'Avámíd.

This building was not fit for permanent habitation. It was damp, filthy and vermin-ridden. 'Abdu'l-Bahá occupied a room here while the rest of His family lived in the house of 'Údí Khammár. The roof of His room dripped with a steady leak whenever it rained, its wall ran with damp and the floor was thick with dust. 'Abdu'l-Bahá sat and slept on a mat in that small room. His bedcover was a sheepskin. In the dust of that room there lived a multitude of fleas and, as Adib Taherzadeh relates:

> . . . when He slept under the sheepskin, fleas gathered and began biting. 'Abdu'l-Bahá had worked out a tactic of defeating the fleas by turning over his sheepskin at intervals. He would sleep for a while before the fleas found their way again to the inner side. He would then turn the sheepskin over again. Every night He had to resort to this tactic eight to ten times.[93]

It was in this room that pilgrims now arriving from Persia were welcomed by 'Abdu'l-Bahá. There He made sure that they were ready to attain the presence of Bahá'u'lláh and, when He could, provided them with clean clothes so that they could change from their travel-stained garments. The pilgrims were fed at the khán. The food was meagre – soup, rice and sometimes, as a real treat, a little pilau.

'Abdu'l-Bahá sold a gift which He had been given in Baghdád and with the proceeds of the sale began to repair the rooms of the caravanserai which were occupied by the exiles. He left the repair of His own room to the last but the money ran out before any improvements could be made to it.

The exiles continued to live very simply. Food was often scarce and of poor quality. They were not able to buy supplies of fuel inside the city for the merchants were still so hostile that no one would sell them any. Hasan Balyuzi relates, in his biography of 'Abdu'l-Bahá, an incident from those days:

There was a Christian merchant in 'Akká who, like many of his fellow-citizens, held the Bahá'ís in scant respect. It happened that he came upon a load of charcoal which some of the Bahá'ís had been permitted to buy outside 'Akká. The merchant, noticing that the fuel was of a fine grade, took it for his own use. For him Bahá'ís were beyond the pale, and so their goods could be impounded. When 'Abdu'l-Bahá heard of the incident, He went to the place where the merchant transacted his business to ask for the return of the charcoal. There were many people about in that office, bent on their trade, and they took no notice of 'Abdu'l-Bahá. He sat and waited. Three hours passed before the merchant turned to Him and said: 'Are you one of the prisoners in this town?' 'Abdu'l-Bahá said that He was, and the merchant then enquired: 'What was the crime for which you were imprisoned?' 'Abdu'l-Bahá replied: 'The same crime for which Christ was indicted.' The merchant was taken aback. He was a Christian, and here was a man speaking of similarity between His action and the action of Christ. 'What could you know of Christ?' was his retort. 'Abdu'l-Bahá calmly proceeded to tell him. The arrogance of the merchant was confronted by the patience of 'Abdu'l-Bahá. When 'Abdu'l-Bahá rose to go, the merchant also rose and walked with Him into the street, betokening his respect for this Man – one of the detested prisoners. From then on, he was a friend, even more, a stout supporter.[94]

11

In Darkest Days

As the authorities gradually began to relax the rules of strict confinement, Siyyid Muḥammad and Áqá Ján, alarmed at the rising prestige of the Bahá'ís, stepped up their campaign of harassment. Unceasingly they attempted to poison the minds of the officials and leading citizens of 'Akká against the exiles and to blacken the reputation of Bahá'u'lláh and 'Abdu'l-Bahá. But the more these same officials and notables came into contact with 'Abdu'l-Bahá, the more their respect for Him grew. Each time that this happened, the Azalís became ever more frantic with envy and resorted to ever more extreme measures.

A believer named Mírzá Riḍá-Qulí, a brother-in-law of Mírzá Yaḥyá, who had openly behaved in so disgraceful a manner that Bahá'u'lláh had expelled him from the community, now threw in his lot with Siyyid Muḥammad and Áqá Ján. Together these three won the confidence of a local man who worked as Persian consul in 'Akká. He agreed to work with them in return for promises of money and honours. 'Abdu'l-Bahá tried hard to prevent him from taking this course but without success. With their numbers thus increased, the Azalís began an intense campaign of slander and vilification.

Thus just as the authorities were beginning to realize the true qualities of their prisoners, doubts were again sown in their minds. The campaign of lies quickly had an effect on the townspeople. Warned against the exiles once, when they had first arrived in the city, the citizens of 'Akká were an easy prey for the lies and slander of the Azalís. Some became openly hostile to the Bahá'ís and in their frenzy of rage and jealousy, the Azalís threatened to kill Bahá'u'lláh. 'Abdu'l-Bahá left His room at the Khán-i-'Avámíd and moved back into the house of 'Údí Khammár to be near His Father.

Bahá'u'lláh decided, as He had once before, in Adrianople, to see no one. The Azalís then took advantage of Bahá'u'lláh's seclusion. They began to mingle with some of Bahá'u'lláh's faithful followers, poisoning their minds and working to undermine their loyalty. Mírzá Riḍá Qulí collected some of Bahá'u'lláh's writings, made alterations to them so that they sounded provocative and heretical and then circulated them to the public. He then announced that he and his sister, Badrí-Ján, an estranged wife of Mírzá Yaḥyá, had renounced the new Faith and were now Muslims. Siyyid Muḥammad and Áqá Ján did the same. Siyyid Muḥammad wrote letters to the believers in Persia stating that Bahá'u'lláh had dissociated Himself from His followers.

So disruptive was all this to the life of the exiles that a group of the believers sought Bahá'u'lláh's permission to deal with the Azalís in their own way. Bahá'u'lláh condemned any idea of retaliation and counselled them to patience and forbearance. When a believer came from Beirut, intent on silencing Siyyid Muḥammad and his allies once and for all, Bahá'u'lláh promptly ordered him home.

But on 22 January 1872, seven of Bahá'u'lláh's faithful followers, the headstrong young Ḥusayn-i-Áshchí amongst them, burst into the house where Siyyid Muḥammad, Áqá Ján and Mírzá Riḍá-Qulí were lodging and slew all three of them. Then the city rose up as one against the exiles. Armed with whatever weapons they could find, reinforced by the governor and his troops, a mob encircled the house of 'Údí Khammár. Bahá'u'lláh, 'Abdu'l-Bahá and several of the believers were apprehended and taken to the *Seraye*, the government headquarters. Other believers living in the city were rounded up and arrested.

'Abdu'l-Bahá was put in chains and kept in prison overnight and was then kept in custody with Bahá'u'lláh. After three days they were both released but the damage done was severe. The restrictions which had been relaxed were once again strictly imposed on the exiles. They were openly cursed on the streets and their children, whenever they ventured onto the streets, met with stones and verbal abuse. Ilyás 'Abbúd, a relative and immediate neighbour of 'Údí Khammár, was so terrified by what had happened that he reinforced the wall between his house and the house of 'Údí Khammár. The governor was now implacably hostile to the Bahá'ís. A man of mediocre capacity, his mind, in the words of Shoghi Effendi, 'had been hopelessly poisoned against the Faith and its followers'.[95] Pilgrims were forbidden to enter 'Akká.

For a considerable time, while accusations made by the surviving Azalís against Bahá'u'lláh and 'Abdu'l-Bahá were investigated, the entire family remained under suspicion. It was months before these accusations were shown to be baseless, months which Bahíyyih Khánum remembered as a time of terrible suspense and anxiety. In those dark days, it was 'Abdu'l-Bahá who represented Bahá'u'lláh and who met with the government officials investigating the murders and it was 'Abdu'l-Bahá who bore the brunt of the fury generated in 'Akká by those murders. Hasan Balyuzi writes:

> What 'Abdu'l-Bahá had to achieve, in this hour of humiliation, was no less than a miracle. Qualities that He now brought forth amply and visibly demonstrated that He was indeed what His Father had affirmed of

Him – the 'Mystery of God'. He was immeasurably,
tirelessly patient. He was undeviatingly, unshakably
firm. He was magnanimous. He was uncompromising.
He was kindness personified. He was stern. He walked
in the ways of humility. He spoke in tones unmistakably
authoritative. He was meek. He was the archetype of
majesty. Divine paradoxes were revealed in His being,
His actions, His words.[96]

Once Bahá'u'lláh and 'Abdu'l-Bahá were cleared of any
possible involvement in the murder of the Azalís, 'Abdu'l-
Bahá was able to resume the work that He had already
begun in 'Akká. Whatever small amounts of money were
at His disposal He shared with the poor, the hungry and
the sick. He wore clothes made of the cheapest material.
He spent many hours of each day visiting, cheering and
providing for the needs of the sick and needy. Through
His daily actions, the spirit of the Bahá'í teachings shone
in the darkness of that prison city. Now even Ilyás 'Abbúd,
the exiles' suspicious neighbour, became a friend of the
Master and dismantled the barrier which he had so hur-
riedly and fearfully put up in order to protect himself from
his dangerous neighbours.

In early 1873, while the restrictions re-imposed on the
exiled community were still strictly enforced, Bahá'u'lláh
began to reveal the Kitáb-i-Aqdas, His Book of Laws, which
He Himself described as the 'Mother Book' of His dispensation. There are just two sentences in the Kitáb-i-Aqdas
which touch on the question of Bahá'u'lláh's successorship:

> When the ocean of My presence hath ebbed and the
> Book of My Revelation is ended, turn your faces toward
> Him Whom God hath purposed, Who hath branched
> from this Ancient Root.[97]

and:

O people of the world! When the Mystic Dove will have winged its flight from its Sanctuary of Praise and sought its far-off goal, its hidden habitation, refer ye whatsoever ye understand not in the Book to Him Who hath branched from this mighty Stock.[98]

There is no mention of a specific name, only the certainty that Bahá'u'lláh's successor would be a member of His family.

In the spring of that same year, at a time when Bahá'í pilgrims were still forbidden to enter the prison city, a young woman from Iṣfahán, Fáṭimih Khánum, known to us as Munírih Khánum, the name given to her by Bahá'u'lláh, reached 'Akká.

Munírih Khánum was the daughter of two of the early followers of the Báb. Her father's name was Mírzá Muḥammad-'Alíy-i-Nahrí and he was a member of a prominent family of Iṣfahán. When the Báb was exiled from His home in Shíráz and sent to Iṣfahán, the governor of Iṣfahán requested the Imám-Jum'ih, the chief religious dignitary of the city, to act as host to the Báb. As Hasan Balyuzi relates:

> One night, a number of people were invited to dine with the Báb, and Mírzá Muḥammad-'Alíy-i-Nahrí was one of the guests. The Báb asked him if he had any children, and on hearing that although married twice he had remained childless, the Báb offered a spoonful of His own sweet to Mírzá Muḥammad-'Alí, who ate some and kept the rest for his wife. Not long after, she found herself with child.[99]

The daughter who was born to them was Munírih Khánum. When she was nine years old her father travelled to Baghdád in order to attain the presence of Bahá'u'lláh.

Munírih <u>Kh</u>ánum herself developed a keen interest in religion.

'When I was a young girl,' she told Lady Blomfield, 'I loved to think over the lives of the Holy Ones, the Lord Christ, Muḥammad, and the other prophets of God. I used to weep and lament that I had not lived in their time.'[100]

As a girl Munírih <u>Kh</u>ánum accepted the new teachings and became a firm believer in the new Revelation. She told Lady Blomfield:

> I remember when I was a girl the news came to Isfahán [*sic*] from Nabíl that Jamál-i-Mubárak was imprisoned in the fortress town of 'Akká, shut in behind iron doors, never going out!
>
> As I thought of Him in that poisonous climate – He Who loved the seas, the hills, and the plains, gardens, flowers, and quick movement in the open air – my heart seemed broken, and I shut myself into my room alone, that I might weep rivers of tears.[101]

Not long after the murder of the Azalís, Bahá'u'lláh sent <u>Sh</u>ay<u>kh</u> Salmán, His courier, to Iṣfahán, with instructions to escort Munírih <u>Kh</u>ánum and her brother, Siyyid Yaḥyá, to 'Akká.

'I was beside myself with joy,' Munírih <u>Kh</u>ánum later recalled,

> that I should, whilst I lived, see my Lord! Even though the journey should be full of difficulty and danger, of suffering indescribable, of risks uncountable, none of these considerations weighed anything in the balance against the gladness of starting on a pilgrimage, with my face steadfastly set towards the presence of the Holy One.[102]

The journey was a slow one for Bahá'u'lláh had instructed them first to go on pilgrimage to Mecca. This they did, in the company of 20 other believers. They kept their destination a close secret and only when these 20 companions had all returned to their homes, and after waiting some time in Jiddah, did they start for 'Akká. At Alexandria a telegram reached them which stated: 'Do not land until fetched.'[103]

They waited and waited as the ship stood off the shore at 'Akká but nobody came.

'We thought that our boat would depart with us still on board,' Munírih Khánum related.

> At the last moment we saw a small boat coming swiftly towards us. 'Shaykh Salmán, Shaykh Salmán!' We heard the cry; our joyful hearts were singing glad songs as we climbed down into the tiny skiff.
> And we had arrived at 'Akká.[104]

Munírih Khánum and Siyyid Yaḥyá were allowed into 'Akká as guests of Ilyás 'Abbúd who himself waited that night by the shore with Mírzá Músá to welcome the new arrivals. When Munírih Khánum first attained the presence of Bahá'u'lláh, His first words to her were:

> We brought you into the prison-city, at a time when the prison-gates were closed in the face of all, to make clear and evident to all the power of God.[105]

After a few days at a caravanserai, Munírih Khánum and Siyyid Yaḥyá went to stay at the house of Mírzá Músá. Munírih Khánum has told her own story of those days:

> My brother and I used to stand at a window and watch 'Abbás Effendi swimming; such a strong and graceful swimmer. Every afternoon about five o'clock the wife of Mírzá Músá would go with me to Bahá'u'lláh. I

cannot describe the wonder and gladness and happiness of being in His presence . . .

Many beautiful daughters were offered from time to time by parents anxious that their child should have the honour of becoming the wife of the Master. He refused to consider any of them, until I arrived; we met each other once, and our marriage was arranged.

There was a delay because there was no room available in the 'little house'.

Now 'Abbúd, the landlord of the 'little house', and of the larger one next to it, had become devoted to the Master . . .

One day he asked to be received by Bahá'u'lláh, to Whom he said:

'Wherefore the delay in the marriage?'

Being told the reason, he exclaimed:

'I can arrange about the room. I pray Thee, let me have the honour of preparing a place for the Master and his bride.'

He hastened to have the door opened through into an extra room, which he furnished simply and comfortably.[106]

The wedding took place on the following day. Bahá'u'lláh had asked 'Abdu'l-Bahá to return in good time that day from His errands of mercy in the city. Ásíyih Khánum had made a dainty white dress for the bride. In this new dress and adorned with a fresh white headdress, Munírih Khánum was led into the presence of Bahá'u'lláh that evening. The guests were few, the ceremony very simple. Bahá'u'lláh spoke these words to Munírih Khánum:

O My Leaf and My Handmaiden, verily We chose thee and accepted thee to serve My Most Great Branch, and this is by My grace which is not equalled by all the treasures of Earth and Heaven. Many maidens, in Baghdád, in Adirnih, in this Most Great Prison, hoped for this bounty, but it was not given to them. You must render thanks unto God for this great bounty, and this exalted bestowal given unto you. May God be with you.[107]

Bahá'u'lláh Himself chanted the prayers and Munírih Khánum chanted a Tablet which Bahá'u'lláh had revealed especially for the occasion.

'At the wedding there was no cake,' Munírih Khánum relates, 'only cups of tea; there were no decorations, and no choir, but the blessing of Jamál-i-Mubárak; the glory and beauty of love and happiness were beyond and above all luxury and ceremony and circumstance.'[108]

12

Through the City Gate

Not long after the murders of the Azalís, a wise and humane man named Aḥmad Big Tawfíq was appointed to the governorship of 'Akká. On his arrival, Badrí-Ján, sister of the murdered Mírzá Riḍá-Qulí, took to him some of Bahá'u'lláh's writings. She hoped to use them to convince the new governor of Bahá'u'lláh's complicity in the murder of her brother and his companions.

Aḥmad Big Tawfíq read these Tablets. So impressed was he by their contents that he sought out 'Abdu'l-Bahá. They met, for the first time, on the sea-shore, where 'Abdu'l-Bahá had just been swimming. There, by the sea, the Master and the new governor sat and spoke at length. All the governor's doubts were dispelled. From that time on, out of reverence for 'Abdu'l-Bahá, Aḥmad Big Tawfíq would remove his shoes whenever he entered the Master's presence. Soon he sent his own son to receive instruction from 'Abdu'l-Bahá. He himself regularly turned to the Master, seeking His counsel on matters relating to the governing of 'Akká.

In 1875 'Abdu'l-Bahá rented a small area of land, an island called Na'mayn on either side of which flowed a small stream, just a short distance from 'Akká. Here he began to create a garden. It was to take Him six to seven years to transform this small island into a flourishing garden. To this spot were taken the plants which pilgrims lovingly brought all the way from Persia. Bahá'u'lláh named this garden the Garden of Riḍván, the Garden of Paradise, but He did not yet visit it.

Through letters brought to 'Akká from Persia once a year by <u>Sh</u>ay<u>kh</u> Salmán, Bahá'u'lláh's trusted courier, the exiles were kept informed of events in their homeland. From these letters, and from the accounts of visiting pilgrims, news came of the harassment and persecution of the believers and of the terrible famine of 1871 which killed a third of the country's population.

Although 'Abdu'l-Bahá took upon Himself the routine work of managing Bahá'u'lláh's household affairs, although He saw to the needs of the local believers and the pilgrims, He never wrote a single letter to any of the believers without the sanction and blessing of Bahá'u'lláh. Many of the believers wrote letters to 'Abdu'l-Bahá during the ministry of Bahá'u'lláh but 'Abdu'l-Bahá did not respond to any of them. He did, however, write regularly to Mi<u>sh</u>kín-Qalam, a loyal follower of Bahá'u'lláh who had been banished to Cyprus with Mírzá Yaḥyá. It was these letters from the Master which nourished the faith of this stalwart believer.

In 1875 'Abdu'l-Bahá wrote *The Secret of Divine Civilization*, a brief treatise addressed to the rulers of His native land. Paying tribute to the <u>Sh</u>áh's apparent resolve to advance the welfare of his people, the security and prosperity of his realm, 'Abdu'l-Bahá states the He 'felt it necessary to put down, for the sake of God alone and as a tribute to this high endeavour, a brief statement on certain urgent questions'.[109]

This book was first published in Persian in Bombay in 1882, not under 'Abdu'l-Bahá's name but as written by an eminent Persian philosopher. It contains a succinct and penetrating analysis of the issues confronting the rulers and peoples of Persia, lays down the necessary prerequisites of just and effective representative government, outlines the principles of international collective security and firmly establishes the primary importance of religion and spirituality in the development of civilization. It demonstrates 'Abdu'l-Bahá's wide-ranging knowledge of the history, laws and culture of both Europe and Asia and foreshadows, in extraordinarily prescient passages, the steps necessary for the establishment of a just and lasting global peace. This treatise has been consistently ignored by the rulers of Persia.

In 1876 Sultán 'Abdu'l-'Azíz, the Ottoman ruler who had banished the Bahá'ís to perpetual imprisonment in 'Akká, was deposed from power on the grounds of incapacity and extravagance. Four days later he died. It is not certain if he was assassinated or, as testified to by 19 physicians, he killed himself.

In 'Akká the governorship of Aḥmad Big Tawfíq lasted only two years. At his departure, 'Abdu'l-Bahá, who had sought no special favours from Aḥmad Big Tawfíq during his governorship, with Bahá'u'lláh's blessing, hosted a splendid farewell feast for him. A tent was set up near the shore where the governor could receive those bidding him farewell.

The next governor, 'Abdu'r-Raḥmán Páshá, while outwardly friendly and respectful towards 'Abdu'l-Bahá, quickly fell in league with the Azalís. He sent reports to his superiors in Damascus which resulted in the arrival of fresh orders forbidding the Bahá'í prisoners to keep shops or engage in other business.

It was the month of Ramaḍán, the Muslim month of fasting, and 'Abdu'r-Raḥmán intended to put these orders into effect during the time of the fast. He planned to walk into the bazaar with his officials and publicly order the Bahá'ís to close up their shops. 'Abdu'l-Bahá, however, learnt of this plan and shared what He had learnt with

Bahá'u'lláh. Bahá'u'lláh told the Bahá'ís not to open their shops at all on the day in question.

That morning the governor made a great show of entering the bazaar with a group of officials and some of the Azalís in attendance. He found all the Bahá'í-owned shops closed but waited for a couple of hours in the house of a sentry, confident that the exiles would soon arrive. It was the Muftí of 'Akká who arrived, however, bringing a cable from Damascus announcing the dismissal of 'Abdu'r-Raḥmán Páshá.

Succeeding governors showed great respect towards Bahá'u'lláh and 'Abdu'l-Bahá, one of them going so far as to indicate that Bahá'u'lláh could leave the prison-city and establish His residence outside it any time that He chose.

'Abdu'l-Bahá has left us, in His own words, an account of Bahá'u'lláh's departure from 'Akká.

Bahá'u'lláh loved the beauty and verdure of the country. One day He passed the remark: 'I have not gazed on verdure for nine years. The country is the world of the soul: the city is the world of bodies.' When I heard indirectly of this saying I realized that He was longing for the country, and I was sure that whatever I could do towards the carrying out of His wish would be successful. There was in 'Akká at that time a man called Muḥammad Páshá Ṣafwat, who was very much opposed to us. He had a palace called Mazra'ih, about four miles north of the city, a lovely place, surrounded by gardens and with a stream of running water. I went and called on this Páshá at his home. I said: 'Páshá, you have left the palace empty, and are living in 'Akká.' He replied: 'I am an invalid and cannot leave the city. If I go there it is lonely and I am cut off from my friends.' I said: 'While you are not living there and the place is empty, let it to us.' He was amazed at the proposal, but soon consented. I got the house at a very low rent, about five pounds per annum, paid him for five years and made a contract. I sent labourers to repair the place and put the garden in order and had a bath built. I also had a carriage prepared for the use of the Blessed Beauty. One day I determined to go and see the place for myself. Notwithstanding the repeated injunctions given in successive firmans that we were on no account to pass the limits of the city walls, I walked out through the city gate. Gendarmes were on guard, but they made no objection, so I proceeded straight to the palace. The next day I again went out, with some friends and officials, unmolested and unopposed, although the guards and sentinels stood on both sides of the City Gates. Another day I arranged a banquet, spread a table under the pine trees of Bahjí, and gathered round it the notables and officials of the town. In the evening we all returned to the town together.

One day I went to the Holy Presence of the Blessed Beauty and said: 'The palace at Mazra'ih is ready for you, and a carriage to drive you there.' (At that time there were no carriages in 'Akká or Haifa.) He refused to go, saying: 'I am a prisoner.' Later I requested Him again, but got the same answer. I went so far as to ask Him a third time, but He still said 'No!' and I did not dare to insist further. There was, however, in 'Akká a certain Muḥammadan Shaykh, a well-known man with considerable influence, who loved Bahá'u'lláh and was greatly favoured by Him. I called this Shaykh and explained the position to him. I said, 'You are daring. Go tonight to His Holy Presence, fall on your knees before Him, take hold of His hands and do not let go until He promises to leave the city!' He was an Arab . . . He went directly to Bahá'u'lláh and sat down close to His knees. He took hold of the hands of the Blessed Beauty and kissed them and asked: 'Why do you not leave the city?' He said: 'I am a prisoner.' The Shaykh replied: 'God forbid! Who has the power to make you a prisoner? You have kept yourself in prison. It was your own will to be imprisoned, and now I beg you to come out and go to the palace. It is beautiful and ver-

dant. The trees are lovely, and the oranges like balls
of fire!' As often as the Blessed Beauty said: 'I am a
prisoner, it cannot be,' the <u>Sh</u>ay<u>kh</u> took His hands and
kissed them. For a whole hour he kept on pleading. At
last Bahá'u'lláh said, '<u>Kh</u>aylí <u>kh</u>úb (very good)' and the
<u>Sh</u>ay<u>kh</u>'s patience and persistence were rewarded . . .
In spite of the strict firman of 'Abdu'l-'Azíz which pro-
hibited my meeting or having any intercourse with the
Blessed Perfection, I took the carriage the next day and
drove with Him to the palace. No one made any objection. I left Him there and returned myself to the city.[110]

13

'He Has Made Himself Our Shield'

For the next 15 years 'Abdu'l-Bahá lived in 'Akká while Bahá'u'lláh lived at Mazra'ih and later at Bahjí. This separation was painful to both Bahá'u'lláh and 'Abdu'l-Bahá. It was, however, necessary for two reasons. First, by living in 'Akká 'Abdu'l-Bahá could best serve as a shield to His Father, bearing the burden of meeting with government officials and others, thus assuring that Bahá'u'lláh had the time needed to reveal His writings and meet with the pilgrims.

Some years later, Ḥájí Mírzá Ḥaydar-'Alí recorded, in these words, Bahá'u'lláh's own reflections on the services rendered to Him by 'Abdu'l-Bahá:

> In the days when We lived in Baghdád We used to go to a coffeehouse where We would meet friends, strangers, and all sorts of people. This was the means by which the Word of God could be heard, and many souls were led into the Cause. But in Adrianople, and here in 'Akká, it is the Master who performs these services. He must face the same hardships which We faced previously. In Baghdád We were not imprisoned, and the fame of the Cause was not even a hundredth part of what it is today. Also, the enemies of the Cause were not as many or as powerful as they are now. In Adrianople We met many people, but in the Most Great Prison, We seldom receive visitors who are not believers. The burden of all these affairs has fallen upon the

shoulders of the Master. To provide Us with some
peace and comfort, He has made Himself Our shield,
and thus He sees to Our affairs both with the government and with the people. He first prepared for Us the
house at Mazra'ih, and then He procured this Mansion
in Bahjí. He is so devoted to His services and so in-
tensely occupied that sometimes weeks pass by and He
cannot come here to visit Us. While We consort with the
friends and reveal Tablets, He is immersed in the toils
and troubles of the world.[111]

The second, far more painful reason for this separation, was that 'Abdu'l-Bahá's half-brothers, in particular,
Muḥammad-'Alí, had grown jealous of 'Abdu'l-Bahá. They
resented the reputation He had gained and were envious
of the great love which Bahá'u'lláh felt for His eldest son.
Remaining in 'Akká was one means of moderating this
jealousy.

'Abdu'l-Bahá and Munírih Khánum continued to live in
the house of 'Údí Khammár, 'the little house' immediately
behind the house of 'Abbúd. In that house nine children
were born to them, two sons and seven daughters. One son
and two daughters died in infancy. A daughter died at 15
and in 1888, another son, Ḥusayn, died when only four
years old. This small boy, an eager and active child, was
greatly loved by Bahá'u'lláh. He spent long intervals at
Bahjí, where Bahá'u'lláh delighted in taking him for short
walks. Marzieh Gail relates:

We read in *Maḥmúd's Diary* that one day the Master
said: 'I had a little son. When he was three or four, and
I would be asleep, he would come and very gently, very
softly, slip into bed beside me. It was an indescribable
joy.' A year or so later, the little boy was gone.[112]

In later years, Munírih Khánum related to Lady Blomfield:

When my darling little son Ḥusayn passed away, Bahá'u'lláh wrote the following:

> 'The knowledge of the reason why your sweet baby has been called back is in the mind of God, and will be manifested in His own good time. To the prophets of God the present and the future are as one.'[113]

The four surviving daughters were named Ḍíyá'iyyih, Túbá, Rúḥá and Munavvar.

In later years, Túbá Khánum described for Lady Blomfield a typical day spent by her father in 'Akká during those years:

> He would rise very early, take tea, then go forth to His self-imposed labours of love. Often He would return very late in the evening, having had no rest and no food.
>
> He would go first to the Bírúní, a large reception room which had been hired, on the opposite side of the street to our house. We often used to watch from our windows, the people crowding there to ask for help from the Master.
>
> A man who wished to take a shop must ask advice from Him. Another would request a letter of introduction, or recommendation for some government post. Again, it would be a poor woman whose husband had been falsely accused, or had been taken for a soldier, whilst she and the children were left to starve. One would tell Him of children who were ill-treated, or of a woman beaten by husband or brother.
>
> 'Abbás Effendi would send a competent person with these poor people to state the case to the judge at the Court House, so that they might have justice.
>
> The Bírúní also received other guests; it came to be looked upon as a centre of interest.

The Muftí, the Governor, Shaykhs, and officials of the Court came singly or in groups to call on the Master at the Bírúní. Here they would be offered a specially delicious make of 'qahviyi-khánigí (coffee). Sipping this, they would talk over all the news, appealing for explanations, advice or comment, to the Master, Whom they grew to look upon as learned, wise, full of compassion, practical help, and counsel for all.

When the Court rose the judge invariably came to the Bírúní, where he would speak of any complicated case, sure that 'Abbás Effendi would solve the problem, however difficult. In this way He was often able to steer the course of law, preventing the triumph of the tyrant, and bringing comfort to the oppressed.

Some days He hardly saw His own family, so hard pressed was He by those who crowded to the Bírúní for some kind of help.

The many sick people, Bahá'í and others, were His constant care; whenever they wished to see Him, He went . . .

Never did He neglect anything but His own rest, His own food; the poor were always His first care.

. . . The Arabs called Him the 'Lord of Generosity'.

. . . As there was no hospital in 'Akká, the Master paid a doctor, Nicolaki Bey, a regular salary to look after the very poor. This doctor was asked not to say who was responsible for this . . .

It would be impossible to write even a small part of the many compassionate acts of love and charity wrought by the Master . . .[114]

The Muftí and the Valí of the city both visited 'Abdu'l-Bahá regularly at the Bírúní where they shared with him the news they had heard of the world beyond 'Akká. On His weekly visits to Bahá'u'lláh, 'Abdu'l-Bahá would share with His father the news they had brought Him.

'Azíz Páshá, who had met with Bahá'u'lláh and 'Abdu'l-Bahá in Adrianople, was now Valí in Beirut. Twice he came to 'Akká for the specific purpose of gaining an audience with Bahá'u'lláh and to renew his friendship with 'Abdu'l-Bahá. Then sometime in 1878 or 1879, while Bahá'u'lláh resided at Mazra'ih, Midḥat Páshá, a leading liberal reformer and gifted statesman, invited 'Abdu'l-Bahá, still officially a prisoner of the Sulṭán, to visit Beirut. On this occasion Bahá'u'lláh revealed the following significant words:

> Praise be to Him Who hath honoured the Land of Bá (Beirut) through the presence of Him round Whom all names revolve. All the atoms of the earth have announced unto all created things that from behind the gate of the Prison-city there hath appeared and above its horizon there hath shone forth the Orb of the beauty of the great, the Most Mighty Branch of God – His ancient and immutable Mystery – proceeding on its way to another land . . . Blessed, doubly blessed, is the ground which His footsteps have trodden, the eye that hath been cheered by the beauty of His countenance, the ear that hath been honoured by hearkening to His call, the heart that hath tasted the sweetness of His love, the breast that hath dilated through His remembrance, the pen that hath voiced His praise, the scroll that hath borne the testimony of His writings.[115]

Shaykh Yúsuf, the Muftí of Nazareth, invited 'Abdu'l-Bahá to visit that town, hallowed as the home town of Jesus Christ. As 'Abdu'l-Bahá approached Nazareth, He was met a long distance out of the town by a party of officials and dignitaries, a mark of respect reserved for visitors of the highest rank.

The house at Mazra'ih was proving too small to accommodate Bahá'u'lláh's family and provide space enough for Bahá'u'lláh to meet with increasing numbers of pilgrims.

'Abdu'l-Bahá now arranged to rent the mansion of Bahjí and in 1879, after only two years at Mazra'ih, Bahá'u'lláh moved there and lived there for the remainder of His earthly years. Bahjí was nearer to 'Akká than Mazra'ih and 'Abdu'l-Bahá always walked there on His weekly visits to His father. When in sight of the mansion, He would prostrate Himself, bending His forehead to the earth in humility. Bahá'u'lláh always knew when 'Abdu'l-Bahá was approaching and would send members of His family to meet and welcome Him.

'Abdu'l-Bahá, His wife, Munírih Khánum, His sister, Bahíyyih Khánum, His mother, Navváb and 'Abdu'l-Bahá's own children continued to live in the larger of the two 'Akká houses, the house of 'Abbúd, near the sea wall to which Bahá'u'lláh had moved on being released from confinement in the barracks. In the 1880s, a new governor named Muḥammad-Yúsuf was appointed to govern 'Akká. There was no official residence for him, for the governor's house had been sold and demolished. Muḥammad-Yúsuf, who had a reputation for avarice and fanaticism, fell under the influence of a group of people who were hostile to Bahá'u'lláh.

At their urging, Muḥammad-Yúsuf began to demand for his own use the house of 'Abbúd, in which 'Abdu'l-Bahá and His family were living. 'Abdu'l-Bahá's mother, Navváb, was terminally ill but 'Abdu'l-Bahá responded to the governor's request courteously. As soon as He could find another house, He told the governor, He would move. The gentle and saintly Navváb passed away. In spite of this circumstance, the governor continued to demand the house. 'Abdu'l-Bahá, with His entire family, vacated it as soon as He could, without once uttering a single word of complaint. In the following year, 1886, Mírzá Músá, Bahá'u'lláh's faithful brother and closest companion, passed away. This too was a grievous loss for 'Abdu'l-Bahá.

Within a short while Muḥammad-Yúsuf himself left 'Akká in disgrace. He was charged with embezzlement of government funds and was dismissed from his post.

14

'May God Protect Him . . .'

In the spring of 1890 Edward Granville Browne, a Cambridge orientalist, visited the Holy Land for the express purpose of gaining an interview with Bahá'u'lláh. During his visit he was the guest of 'Abdu'l-Bahá. He has left us this description of the Master:

> Seldom have I seen one whose appearance impressed me more. A tall strongly-built man holding himself straight as an arrow, with white turban and raiment, long black locks reaching almost to the shoulder, broad powerful forehead indicating a strong intellect combined with an unswerving will, eyes keen as a hawk's, and strongly-marked but pleasing features – such was my first impression of 'Abbás Effendí, 'the master' (Áká) as he *par excellence* is called by the Bábís. Subsequent conversation with him served only to heighten the respect with which his appearance had from the first inspired me. One more eloquent of speech, more ready of argument, more apt of illustration, more intimately acquainted with the sacred books of the Jews, the Christians, and the Muhammadans, could, I should think, scarcely be found even amongst the eloquent, ready, and subtle race to which he belongs. These qualities, combined with a bearing at once majestic and genial, made me cease to wonder at the influence and esteem which he enjoyed even beyond the circle of his father's followers. About the greatness of this man and his

power no one who had seen him could entertain a doubt.[116]

Mírzá Maḥmúd-i-Káshání has written eloquently of the great love and delight which Bahá'u'lláh expressed in the company of 'Abdu'l-Bahá:

Many a time I was in the presence of Bahá'u'lláh when the Master was also present. Because of His presence Bahá'u'lláh would be filled with the utmost joy and gladness. One could see His blessed countenance beaming with delight and exultation so lovingly that no words can adequately describe it. Repeatedly He would laud and glorify the Master, and the mere mention of His name would suffice to evoke an indescribable feeling of ecstasy in the Person of the Blessed Beauty. No pen is capable of fully describing this.[117]

Some years later Mírzá 'Alí-Muḥammad Varqá, the distinguished poet, an Apostle of Bahá'u'lláh who would later attain the station of martyrdom in His Cause, asked Bahá'u'lláh which member of His family would be the successor to whom He had alluded in the Kitáb-i-Aqdas. Adib Taherzadeh relates that:

In a Tablet addressed to Varqá, Bahá'u'lláh indicated that the intended person was the Most Great Branch, and after Him the Greater Branch. But this disclosure was not shared with the Bahá'í community.[118]

Ḥájí Mírzá Ḥaydar-'Alí, another follower of Bahá'u'lláh who suffered very greatly for his beliefs, presented to Bahá'u'lláh a commentary he had written, citing certain Islamic traditions which he understood to relate to 'Abdu'l-Bahá. Bahá'u'lláh praised this compilation, assuring Ḥájí

Mírzá Ḥaydar-'Alí that he was correct in his reasoning. He added, as the Ḥájí recalled:

> The force of the utterance of the Most Great Branch and His powers are not as yet fully revealed. In the future it will be seen how He, alone and unaided, shall raise the banner of the Most Great Name in the midmost heart of the world, with power and authority and Divine effulgence. It will be seen how He shall gather together the peoples of the earth under the tent of peace and concord.[119]

Hasan Balyuzi relates an incident from the pilgrim's notes of Ṭarázu'lláh Samandarí when:

> . . . Bahá'u'lláh administered to him a gentle, kindly, but highly significant admonition. For several days he had not been called to the presence of Bahá'u'lláh and, encountering a small child of the household, he asked her to be the bearer of a petition for him to Bahá'u'lláh, after ascertaining that He was alone. His petition was for the bounty of admission to His presence. When he attained it, Bahá'u'lláh asked him: Do you not meet the Master every day? Samandarí's answer was affirmative. And Bahá'u'lláh said: Then why do you speak of not having been here in My presence for several days, you who meet the Master every day and receive the honour of His company? He equated meeting 'Abdu'l-Bahá with meeting Himself.[120]

Another believer who made the pilgrimage in 1891 was Ḥájí Mírzá Ḥabíbu'lláh-i-Afnán. Adib Taherzadeh has summarized and translated the following extract from his memoirs in which he describes a visit by Bahá'u'lláh and a number of pilgrims to the Junaynih garden near 'Akká:

His Blessed Person was extremely happy that day and each one of the friends received his share of the bounties from His presence. We had lunch in the garden, then we assembled together and attained His presence.

It was at that time that 'Abdu'l-Bahá arrived from 'Akká. The Blessed Beauty said, 'The Master is coming, hasten to attend Him' . . . On those days Bahá'u'lláh used to sow the seeds of loyalty and servitude toward 'Him Whom God hath purposed' ['Abdu'l-Bahá] in the hearts of the believers and explained the lofty station and hidden reality of the Master to all.

Attended by everyone, 'Abdu'l-Bahá came with great humility into the presence of the Blessed Beauty. Then the Tongue of Grandeur uttered words to this effect, 'From morning until now this garden was not pleasant, but now with the presence of the Master it has become truly most delightful.' Then, turning to the Master, He remarked, 'You should have come in the morning.' 'Abdu'l-Bahá responded, 'The Governor of 'Akká and some residents had requested to meet with Me. Therefore I had to receive and entertain them.' Bahá'u'lláh, with a smiling face, said, 'The Master is our shield. Everybody here lives in the utmost comfort and peace. Association with the outside people such as these is very, very difficult. It is the Master who stands up to everything, and prepares the means of comfort for all the friends. May God protect Him from the evil of the envious and the hostile.'[121]

Bahá'u'lláh was well aware that grievous tests and trials lay ahead for His successor. On another occasion He revealed these words:

By God, O people! Mine eye weepeth, and the eye of 'Alí (the Báb) weepeth amongst the Concourse on high, and Mine heart crieth out, and the heart of Muḥammad crieth out within the Most Glorious Tabernacle, and My soul shouteth and the souls of the Prophets shout before them that are endued with understanding . . . My sorrow is not for Myself, but for Him Who shall come after Me, in the shadow of My Cause, with manifest and undoubted sovereignty, inasmuch as they will not welcome His appearance, will repudiate His signs, will dispute His sovereignty, will contend with Him, and will betray His Cause . . .[122]

Section III
1892–1902

Lua Getsinger

15

'This Calamitous Day'

Bahá'u'lláh was well aware that the end of His earthly existence was now approaching. We do not know exactly when He revealed the Kitáb-i-'Ahd (the Book of the Covenant) in which He appoints His successor but we know that it was probably written by 1891. In that year He revealed His last major work, *The Epistle to the Son of the Wolf*, and in this work He refers to the Kitáb-i-'Ahd as the 'Crimson Book'. He did not share the contents of this book, His Will and Testament, with anyone and He kept the document in His own possession until His last illness, when He entrusted the locked box in which He had kept it to 'Abdu'l-Bahá.

In 1891, during His last visit to Haifa, Bahá'u'lláh charged 'Abdu'l-Bahá with a special mandate. Standing on the slope of Mount Carmel, in the shade of some cypress trees which still grow there today, Bahá'u'lláh pointed out the exact spot where the mutilated remains of the Báb should be buried. He instructed 'Abdu'l-Bahá to build on that spot a beautiful edifice to honour the martyred Báb. At that time those sacred remains were still hidden in Persia.

In September of 1891 Bahá'u'lláh intimated to 'Abdu'l-Bahá His desire to depart from this world. On 8 May 1892 He fell ill. Shoghi Effendi describes Bahá'u'lláh's final illness in these words:

. . . He contracted a slight fever which, though it mounted the following day, soon after subsided. He continued to grant interviews to certain of the friends and pilgrims, but it soon became evident that He was not well. His fever returned in a more acute form than before, His general condition grew steadily worse, complications ensued . . .[123]

Túbá Khánum, 'Abdu'l-Bahá's daughter, relates that:

On this day of sadness a servant rode in from Bahjí with a tablet for the Master from Bahá'u'lláh: 'I am not well, come to Me and bring Khánum.'

The servant, having brought horses for them, my Father and my aunt set off immediately for Bahjí; we children stayed at home with my mother, full of anxiety. Each day the news came that our adored Bahá'u-'lláh's fever had not abated. He had a kind of malaria.

After five days we all went to Bahjí; we were very distressed that the illness had become serious.[124]

'Abdu'l-Bahá has Himself written an account of those grievous days. It is called the Lawḥ-i-Hizár Baytí (Tablet of One Thousand Verses). Adib Taherzadeh summarizes one part of this Tablet in these words:

. . . during the days of Bahá'u'lláh's illness, He, 'Abdu'l-Bahá, was in attendance on His blessed Person by day and by night, most of the time in a state of deep sorrow and depression. One day as He lay in His sick-bed, Bahá'u'lláh ordered 'Abdu'l-Bahá to gather all those of His papers which were in the room and place them in two special cases. It was Bahá'u'lláh's practice that whenever He left the Mansion for 'Akká or elsewhere, He used to put all His papers in these large cases. Aware of the implications of this command, 'Abdu'l-Bahá was shaken to the very depths of his being. As He hesitated to comply, Bahá'u'lláh reiterated His orders. With trembling hands and tearful eyes, 'Abdu'l-Bahá was beginning to gather the papers when Majdu'd-Dín entered the room.

Majdu'd-Dín was a son of Bahá'u'lláh's faithful brother Áqáy-i-Kalím, but he was utterly different from his father. The most treacherous among the family, he was the most formidable enemy of 'Abdu'l-Bahá. Indeed . . . he was the backbone, if not the principal instigator, of Mírzá Muhammad-'Alí, the archbreaker of the Covenant of Bahá'u'lláh.

In this Tablet, 'Abdu'l-Bahá further describes the agony of His heart as He forced Himself to gather Bahá'u'lláh's papers. Seeing Majdu'd-Dín, 'Abdu'l-Bahá asked for his assistance, so that this task, so extremely painful to Him, might be soon finished. When all the papers, the seals and other items had been locked into the cases, Bahá'u'lláh said to 'Abdu'l-Bahá, 'These two now belong to you.' These words, implying the approach of the final hours of Bahá'u'lláh's earthly life, pierced 'Abdu'l-Bahá's heart like an arrow.[125]

Túbá Khánum's account continues:

Bahá'u'lláh asked for us, the ladies and children, to go to Him. He told us that He had left in His will directions for our future guidance; that the Greatest Branch, 'Abbás Effendi, would arrange everything for the family, the friends, and the Cause.[126]

At dawn on 29 May Bahá'u'lláh's spirit left its mortal frame. 'Abdu'l-Bahá at once sent a cable to Sultán 'Abdu'l-Hamíd, which read: 'The Sun of Bahá has set.' In that same cable, 'Abdu'l-Bahá proposed to bury His Father near the Mansion of Bahjí. The Sultán consented to this plan.

'Abdu'l-Bahá was in a state of intense shock and grief. A few hours after the passing of Bahá'u'lláh, in the first light of morning, He, along with His brother Mírzá

Muḥammad-'Alí, began to prepare the body of Bahá'u'lláh
for burial. Adib Taherzadeh gives us a detailed account of
what then happened.

> When they were about to wash Bahá'u'lláh's blessed
> body, Mírzá Muḥammad-'Alí suggested to 'Abdu'l-Bahá
> that since the floor of the room would become wet, it
> would be better to take the two cases out of the room
> into Badí'u'lláh's room. 'Abdu'l-Bahá was at that point
> in such a state of shock and grief that He was almost
> unconscious of His surroundings. He never thought
> that behind this suggestion could be a treacherous plot
> designed to rob Him of that precious trust.
>
> He agreed, and the two cases were taken out and
> that was the last He saw of them.[127]

On the evening of the same day Bahá'u'lláh's sacred remains were interred within a small room of a house adja-
cent to the mansion.

As soon as news of Bahá'u'lláh's passing spread, a great
number of people flocked to Bahjí to pay their final respects and to grieve with His family. Túbá Khánum relates
that 'People from all the villages of the country-side
crowded to Bahjí to show their respect and to join in the
mourning.' She adds:

> Many of the guests encamped under the trees round
> the Palace of Bahjí, where more than five hundred were
> entertained for nine days.
>
> This hospitality entailed much trouble on the Mas-
> ter, Who made all the arrangements and superintended
> every detail; money also was given by Him on each of
> the nine days to the poor.[128]

All this 'Abdu'l-Bahá had to take care of when His own
heart was breaking. For three consecutive days and nights,

He Himself later related, He could not rest for even a single moment. Though He wept for hours at a time, He could not find relief. His was also the task of communicating the news of Bahá'u'lláh's passing to the Bahá'ís in Persia and other lands. Ḥájí Mírzá Ḥaydar-'Alí who was in Yazd when the grievous news came, later wrote:

> I was so stunned that I could not even cry . . . The news of His ascension spread everywhere and, though the population of Persia was at that time in the grip of a merciless attack of cholera, the people made merry and rejoiced and ridiculed the Bahá'ís.[129]

On the fourth night after Bahá'u'lláh's passing, 'Abdu'l-Bahá relates in the Tablet of One Thousand Verses, He rose from His bed near midnight. He began to walk a little in His room, hoping that this activity would calm His agonized heart. In these words Adib Taherzadeh has summarized what the Master then saw.

> As He began to pace the room, He saw through the window a scene His eyes could scarcely believe. His unfaithful brothers had opened the cases [which had been removed from Bahá'u'lláh's room] and were looking through Bahá'u'lláh's papers, those papers which had been entrusted to Him!
> 'Abdu'l-Bahá was deeply disturbed by the treachery of His brothers so soon after the ascension of their Father. This act of unfaithfulness committed so dishonourably against the most sacred trust of God, inflicted further pain and suffering upon His sorrow-laden heart. He returned to His bed immediately after this incident, for He did not wish His brothers to know He had seen them interfering with the contents of the cases . . .[130]

16

'An Excellent and Priceless Heritage'

Immediately after the passing of Bahá'u'lláh, 'Abdu'l-Bahá had sent to 'Akká for the locked box in which the Kitáb-i-'Ahd (the Will and Testament of Bahá'u'lláh) had been kept since Bahá'u'lláh revealed it. On the ninth day after the ascension of Bahá'u'lláh, the seal which Bahá'u'lláh had Himself placed upon the document was broken. The Kitáb-i-'Ahd was then read aloud by Áqá Riḍáy-i-Qannád, a believer from Shíráz who had been a companion in exile with Bahá'u'lláh since the days in Baghdád. He read the document in the presence of nine witnesses chosen from Bahá'u'lláh's family and companions. One of those chosen as a witness was Mírzá Muḥammad-'Alí.

The Kitáb-i-'Ahd opens with these words:

> Although the Realm of Glory hath none of the vanities of the world, yet within the treasury of trust and resignation We have bequeathed to Our heirs an excellent and priceless heritage. Earthly treasures We have not bequeathed, nor have We added such cares as they entail.[131]

Towards the end of this brief Tablet Bahá'u'lláh clearly designates His successor in these words:

> The Will of the divine Testator is this: It is incumbent upon the Aghṣán, the Afnán and My kindred to turn, one and all, their faces towards the Most Mighty

Branch. Consider that which We have revealed in Our Most Holy Book: 'When the ocean of My presence hath ebbed and the Book of My Revelation is ended, turn your faces toward Him Whom God hath purposed, Who hath branched from this Ancient Root.' The object of this sacred verse is none other except the Most Mighty Branch ['Abdu'l-Bahá]. Thus have We graciously revealed unto you our potent Will, and I am verily the Gracious, the All-Powerful. Verily God hath ordained the station of the Greater Branch [Muḥammad-'Alí] to be beneath that of the Most Great Branch ['Abdu'l-Bahá]. He is in truth the Ordainer, the All-Wise. We have chosen 'the Greater' after 'the Most Great', as decreed by Him Who is the All-Knowing, the All-Informed.[132]

Bahá'u'lláh concludes His Will and Testament with these words:

That which is conducive to the regeneration of the world and the salvation of the peoples and kindreds of the earth hath been sent down from the heaven of the utterance of Him Who is the Desire of the world. Give ye a hearing ear to the counsels of the Pen of Glory. Better is this for you than all that is on the earth. Unto this beareth witness My glorious and wondrous Book.[133]

On the same day a large group of the believers gathered in the Shrine of Bahá'u'lláh. There the Kitáb-i-'Ahd was read again, this time by Majdu'd-Dín. 'Abdu'l-Bahá then met with the women and servants of the household and Majdu'd-Dín again read the Tablet aloud to those assembled. Túbá Khánum relates that Mahd-i-'Ulyá, the mother of Muḥammad-'Alí, expressed pleasure, at that time, at the appointment of 'Abdu'l-Bahá as the Centre of the Covenant.

'Abdu'l-Bahá arranged for copies of the Kitáb-i-'Ahd to be sent to the friends in Persia. Ḥájí Mírzá Ḥaydar-'Alí relates that the copy sent to Yazd arrived there just one week after the news of the passing of Bahá'u'lláh:

> Emphatically and explicitly, He had appointed the beloved Master as the sole Interpreter of His Word. When the friends received this great news, they were calmed, and, with hearts full of hope, they arose to raise the banner of servitude and uphold it with their utmost strength.[134]

Soon after the Kitáb-i-'Ahd was shared with the friends one of the believers asked 'Abdu'l-Bahá if He would seal a Tablet written by Bahá'u'lláh for his brother with one of Bahá'u'lláh's own seals. These seals 'Abdu'l-Bahá had placed in one of the two large cases which Bahá'u'lláh had instructed Him to pack in the last days of His life. 'Abdu'l-Bahá asked His two half-brothers to give Him the seals. Their reply was that they did not know what He was asking for as they knew nothing at all about any cases. 'Abdu'l-Bahá later related that His whole being began to tremble when He heard such a response for it meant that terrible tests and trials lay ahead.

Túbá Khánum relates the following:

> Whilst we were all at Bahjí there was a serious outbreak of cholera in the town of 'Akká. Now it was the custom that members of the family should remain in the house of the departed one for a period of forty days. But the mother of Muḥammad-'Alí, and her other sons, showed us by many discourtesies that they did not wish us to remain.
>
> Accordingly, in spite of the raging cholera, we all, Sarkár-i-Áqá ['Abdu'l-Bahá], Khánum, my mother, my

sisters, and I, left Bahjí and returned to our house at 'Akká, trusting in the protection of God.

We were almost the only family left in 'Akká. Most of the people had fled in fear of the terror; others had died in great numbers.[135]

Many years later 'Abdu'l-Bahá recounted that most of the people who fled the epidemic entrusted the care of their homes to the Bahá'ís. 'Abdu'l-Bahá appointed watchmen to guard the houses.

Túbá Khánum continues her account of those stressful days:

We children were much frightened, the sight of the poor dead people being carried out for burial appalled us.

. . . After bringing us back to 'Akká, the Master went back to the shrine at Bahjí, returning to us next day very sad; the two younger half-brothers were with Him. My mother asked them to stay and help Sarkár-i-Áqá with the numberless matters needing to be done. They refused, saying that they were too busy. There was no man of the family to assist our beloved Father in all the work of that difficult time.[136]

Once the Kitáb-i-'Ahd had been read and heard by all, 'Abdu'l-Bahá wrote a Tablet to the believers in Persia and other lands:

He Is the All-Glorious

The world's great Light, once resplendent upon all mankind has set, to shine everlastingly from the Abhá Horizon, His Kingdom of fadeless glory, shedding splendour upon His loved ones from on high, and breathing into their hearts and souls the breath of eternal life.

O ye beloved of the Lord! Beware, beware lest ye hesitate and waver. Let not fear fall upon you, neither be troubled nor dismayed. Take ye good heed lest this calamitous day slacken the flames of your ardour, and quench your tender hopes. To-day is the day for steadfastness and constancy. Blessed are they that stand firm and immovable as the rock, and brave the storm and stress of this tempestuous hour. They, verily, shall be the recipients of God's grace, shall receive His divine assistance, and shall be truly victorious.

The Sun of Truth, that most great Light, has set upon the horizon of the world to rise with deathless splendour over the Realm of the Limitless. In His *Most Holy Book* He calleth the firm and steadfast of His friends: 'O peoples of the world! Should the radiance of My beauty be veiled, and the temple of My body be hidden, feel not perturbed, nay arise and bestir yourselves, that My Cause may triumph, and My Word be heard by all mankind.'[137]

17

'Alone and Unaided'

This first Tablet of 'Abdu'l-Bahá was read with joy by the believers in Persia and other lands in the Near East, in India and in Egypt. It inspired the steadfast followers of Bahá'u'lláh to arise and teach His Word with new enthusiasm. Ḥájí Mírzá Ḥaydar-'Alí, travelling through Persia at that time, later wrote of those early days of 'Abdu'l-Bahá's ministry:

> The ministry of 'Abdu'l-Bahá began so vigorously that Bahá'í communities everywhere were overwhelmed. Letters from the Master poured into every village, town and country like the drops of the rains of spring. The friends were cheered and enamoured by His life-giving words. Whoever received a Tablet would make many copies and send them as precious gifts to friends throughout the length and breadth of the East. This opened a new field of activity, that of regular and informative correspondence amongst all the believers.[138]

It was not only to Persia that 'Abdu'l-Bahá wrote, but to Egypt, Iraq, India and Burma; to wherever the Faith had spread, 'Abdu'l-Bahá sent His guidance. But Mírzá Muḥammad-'Alí, prompted by the ambition of his cousin, Majdu'd-Dín, was already working to oppose 'Abdu'l-Bahá's appointment as Centre of the Covenant of Bahá'u'lláh.

During the lifetime of Bahá'u'lláh, Mírzá Muḥammad-'Alí had made contact with several influential Bahá'ís in Persia who wished to increase their own prestige and standing in the ranks of the believers. Two believers in particular, Muḥammad-Javád-i-Qazvíní and Jamál-i-Burújirdí, had greatly inflated opinions of their own importance. They convinced Mírzá Muḥammad-'Alí that the entire community of believers in Persia looked to them for leadership and that they could persuade all the Bahá'ís to turn to Mírzá Muḥammad-'Alí, rather than 'Abdu'l-Bahá, as the Centre of the Covenant of Bahá'u'lláh.

Mírzá Muḥammad-'Alí began his campaign of disaffection very quietly. First he won over all those of Bahá'u'lláh's family who were living at Bahjí by poisoning their hearts and minds against 'Abdu'l-Bahá. Then he began to spread his intrigues to the other believers who were resident in the Holy Land.

'Abdu'l-Bahá knew very well what was going on. He forbade the friends in other lands to open any envelope which did not bear His own seal and He privately counselled his half-brothers and others of His relatives against actions which would damage the Cause of their father. But as Ḥájí Mírzá Ḥaydar-'Alí recounts, all these counsels fell on deaf ears.

In that first summer of His ministry 'Abdu'l-Bahá was so grieved by the actions of His half-brothers that He spent an entire month in seclusion on Mount Carmel. He rented a small apartment in a stone building near the lower cave of Elijah and there spent many hours in prayer and supplication.

In a Tablet written in later years to Mírzá Muḥammad-Báqir Khán, 'Abdu'l-Bahá relates how the treachery of His own brothers on the passing of Bahá'u'lláh affected Him:

The centre of violation purloined, in its entirety, the Divine trust which specifically appertained to this servant. He took everything and returned nothing. To this day the usurper unjustly remains in possession. Although each single item is more precious for 'Abdu'l-Bahá than the dominion of earth and heaven, till now I have kept silent and have not breathed a word, lest it bring us into disrepute amongst strangers. This was a severe blow to me. I suffered, I sorrowed, I wept, but I spoke not.[139]

Even as 'Abdu'l-Bahá attempted to hold in check the dissension within the family of Bahá'u'lláh, He continued to supply those of His relatives living at Bahjí with all they demanded from Him. They demanded far more than they needed in a deliberate attempt to impoverish Him and they interpreted His sorrow at their disaffection as a sign of weakness. Those of Bahá'u'lláh's family living at Bahjí enjoyed a life of leisure and luxury while 'Abdu'l-Bahá and His own family lived a life of simple austerity in 'Akká.

At the same time, 'Abdu'l-Bahá never slackened in His charitable work in the mean streets of 'Akká. Myron Phelps relates that 'Abdu'l-Bahá had, since His arrival in 'Akká 24 years earlier, frequently given help to a certain Afghan. He recounts:

When the Master came to 'Akká there lived there a certain man from Afghanistan, an austere and rigid Mussulman. To him the Master was a heretic. He felt and nourished a great enmity towards the Master, and roused up others against him. When opportunity offered in gatherings of the people, as in the Mosque, he denounced him with bitter words.

. . . And when he passed the Master on the street he was careful to hold his robe before his face that his sight might not be defiled.

Thus did the Afghan. The Master, however, did thus: The Afghan was poor and lived in a mosque; he was frequently in need of food and clothing. The Master sent him both. These he accepted, but without thanks. He fell sick. The Master took him a physician, food, medicine, money. These, also, he accepted; but as he held out one hand that the physician might take his pulse, with the other he held his cloak before his face that he might not look upon the Master. *For twenty-four years* the Master continued his kindnesses and the Afghan persisted in his enmity. Then at last one day the Afghan came to the Master's door, and fell down, penitent and weeping, at his feet.

'Forgive me, sir!' he cried. 'For twenty-four years I have done evil to you, for twenty-four years you have done good to me. Now I know that I have been in the wrong.'

The Master bade him rise, and they became friends.[140]

Even before Bahá'u'lláh's passing 'Abdu'l-Bahá had suffered the loss of the constant support of His mother, the saintly Navváb, who had spent her later years in His home in 'Akká. His own sons had all died in infancy. His beloved uncle, Mírzá Músá, Bahá'u'lláh's strongest supporter and most loyal follower, had passed away in 1887. His other paternal uncle, Mírzá Muḥammad-Qulí, was now elderly and, though loyal, was unable to help Him in many duties. Mírzá Muḥammad-Qulí and his family had settled on lands in the Jordan valley on the Eastern shore of the Sea of Galilee.

On His return from the month spent on Mount Carmel, 'Abdu'l-Bahá moved into His mother's room in the House of 'Abbúd. The room next to it, which Bahá'u'lláh had occupied, was kept as it had been during Bahá'u'lláh's lifetime. 'Abdu'l-Bahá's wife, His unmarried sister, Bahíyyih <u>Kh</u>ánum, and four daughters longed to be able to help Him bear the burdens which His appointment as the Centre of Bahá'u'lláh's Covenant laid upon Him but, as Túbá <u>Kh</u>ánum relates:

> The ladies of the family were helpless, as according to the Muslim law, they were unable to speak to any man, even on business affairs; so that it was only within the house that we were able to do anything at all to lighten the burden of our beloved Master.[141]

There was, indeed, no one who could lighten 'Abdu'l-Bahá's burden. However, Bahá'u'lláh had conferred upon Him special powers which enabled Him to carry that heavy burden and to fulfil all the responsibilities which Bahá'u-'lláh had given Him. As Adib Taherzadeh explains:

> Unlike a human being whose mind can only deal with one subject at a time, 'Abdu'l-Bahá, who had all the powers of Bahá'u'lláh conferred upon Him, was free from this limitation. Usually a person becomes over-whelmed when afflicted by sufferings or faced with insurmountable obstacles. Under such circumstances even men of outstanding ability show their weakness and reveal their human frailty. They try to cope with one problem at a time, and they often seek the help of experts and advisors to help them make a decision.
>
> Not so with 'Abdu'l-Bahá. In the first place He acted independently, for no individual was qualified to advise or assist Him in His manifold activities. His soul was not bound by the limitations of the world of humanity, and His mind was not overwhelmed when faced with a host of problems simultaneously. In the midst of calamities, when the ablest of men would have suc-cumbed to pressure, He remained detached, while directing His attention to whatever He desired.[142]

Thus, despite His grief at the passing of His beloved father and the anguish caused by the disloyalty of His half-brothers and many of His close relatives, 'Abdu'l-Bahá was not deflected from His course. He was in touch with the believers who were in distant places, such as Jamál Effendi, who had been travelling throughout India and as far afield as Tibet, Thailand, Indonesia and Sri Lanka. He was in communication with Mírzá Abu'l-Faḍl, the most distinguished Bahá'í scholar of the day who had been on a teaching trip to Samarqand and Bukhara when the news of Bahá'u'lláh's passing reached him.

In 1894 'Abdu'l-Bahá invited Mírzá Abu'l-Faḍl to the Holy Land. There the scholar found comfort in his great grief and fresh inspiration in the Master's presence. After ten months 'Abdu'l-Bahá sent him to teach the Faith in Cairo, advising him to take an indirect approach which would give him access to the leading intellectual circles of the city.

When the loyal believers in the Holy Land grew dispirited and downcast because of the apparently endless machinations of the Covenant-breakers, 'Abdu'l-Bahá cheered their spirits, strengthened their faith and gave them a vision of the greatness and the potency of the Cause. And, as His faithless relatives persisted in their efforts to injure the Cause, 'Abdu'l-Bahá prayed for yet more suffering.

But the activities of the Covenant-breakers took a very heavy toll. Túbá Khánum relates that:

> The time passed on until about three years after the passing of Bahá'u'lláh, when the conditions of our lives, owing to the ceaseless action of the enemy (cunningly devised false representations and accusations), became much more difficult.

Suddenly the Master went to Tiberias to spend some time in retreat. He was accompanied by one servant only.

We, the ladies of the family, were in much despair; we had no man to do anything for us; none that we could trust; our veiling kept us, of necessity, almost prisoners.[143]

'Abdu'l-Bahá's wife, sister and daughters wrote to 'Abdu'l-Bahá asking Him to give permission for His eldest daughter, Ḍíyá'iyyih Khánum, to marry a young relative of the Báb, Áqá Mírzá Hádí, of whom Bahá'u'lláh had expressed approval. In a Tablet giving His permission for this marriage, 'Abdu'l-Bahá includes these words:

The calamities of my family are beyond endurance, and the troubles of those sorrowful leaves (sister, wife, daughters) are without end.

From all directions the arrows of hardship are being showered upon them, like rain-drops in spring, and the spears of the unfaithful are being hurled upon them without ceasing . . .

Hearts are sore wounded. With hidden wounds are they smitten. Lamentations rend the soul, and the shaft of grief, piercing through all our hearts, joins them together . . .

Verily the table of disaster is spread with every imaginable food!

Oh, family of this sorrowful one, all is sacrifice.

No pleasure is desired by you.

I know your sorrows.

The Mufti may be asked to chant the Marriage Chant at the Holy Shrine on Sunday.[144]

The marriage took place at Bahjí. Bahíyyih Khánum invited the family of Mírzá Muḥammad-'Alí to join them in the evening. Túbá Khánum relates that they did indeed come:

> They came and jeered at the simplicity of the wedding with great ridicule. . .
>
> We were all full of sorrow because of the Master's sufferings for the good of the Cause of God.
>
> There was no ordinary marriage happiness. A sense of difficulty and danger oppressed us. We seemed to be under a dark cloud of grief and sorrow, but we all welcomed Áqá Mírzá Hádí as a great help and comfort in our distress.[145]

The dissension within the family of Bahá'u'lláh affected 'Abdu'l-Bahá so deeply that it aged Him prematurely. His features bore traces of that great sorrow to the end of His days.

'I swear by the Ancient Beauty!' 'Abdu'l-Bahá wrote at that time. 'So great is My sorrow and regret that My pen is paralyzed between My fingers.'[146]

But even as the darkness of this bitter disloyalty deepened and grew ever more intense, the light of Bahá'u'lláh's teaching reached out to a distant continent.

18

'So Momentous a Development'

In 1888 a Syrian Christian named Ibráhím Khayru'lláh began to investigate the Bahá'í teachings. One of the early graduates of the Syrian Protestant College, he had moved to Egypt on completing his education, for jobs in his homeland were very scarce. There, in 1890, he met 'Abdu'l-Karím-i-Ṭihrání, a Bahá'í businessman who had moved from Ṭihrán a decade or more earlier.

Ibráhím Khayru'lláh could not speak or read Persian and his knowledge of Arabic was very limited but he visited 'Abdu'l-Karím every day over a period of two years in order to learn more about Bahá'u'lláh's claim. His interest in the fulfilment of biblical prophecy was very strong and in 1890 he became a Bahá'í. Apart from his enthusiasm for biblical prophecy and his conviction that Bahá'u'lláh was indeed a Manifestation of God, the One foretold in Jewish and Christian scripture, Khayru'lláh's knowledge of the Bahá'í teachings was extremely scanty. He was, however, honoured to receive a Tablet from Bahá'u'lláh. He was also inspired by the first-hand accounts related to him by Bahá'ís who had visited the Holy Land and attained the presence of Bahá'u'lláh.

'Abdu'l-Karím encouraged Khayru'lláh in his desire to travel to the West. Khayru'lláh had told his closest friend, a fellow Syrian named Anton Haddad, about the Bahá'í teachings and Haddad was eager to learn more. 'Abdu'l-Karím helped Khayru'lláh persuade Haddad to go with him to Europe and the United States and probably provided some financial backing. As the time for them to leave Egypt drew near, Haddad accepted the new Faith.

While they were making final preparations for their journey, the news of Bahá'u'lláh's passing reached Cairo. With 'hearts heavy with grief' they sailed from Alexandria in late June of 1892. Anton Haddad arrived in New York during the summer. Khayru'lláh went first to St Petersburg in Russia and in December joined Haddad in New York in order to help him in a joint business venture which was proving difficult.

About a year later, in September of 1893, an unprecedented meeting took place in Chicago. The Parliament of Religions was one of hundreds of conferences held that year in conjunction with the Columbian Exposition celebrating the fourth centenary of Columbus's arrival in North America. During this Parliament a paper entitled 'The Religious Mission of the English Speaking Nations' written by Rev. Henry H. Jessup, a Doctor of Divinity and Director of Presbyterian Missionary Operations in North Syria, was presented. It was read to the Parliament by Rev. George A. Ford, also a missionary in Syria. The paper closed with these words:

> In the Palace of Bahjí, or Delight, just outside the Fortress of 'Akká, on the Syrian coast, there died a few months since, a famous Persian sage, the Bábí Saint, named Bahá'u'lláh – the 'Glory of God' – the head of that vast reform party of Persian Muslims, who accept the New Testament as the Word of God and Christ as the Deliverer of men, who regard all nations as one, and all men as brothers. Three years ago he was visited by a Cambridge scholar and gave utterance to sentiments so noble, so Christlike, that we repeat them as our closing words:

'That all nations should become one in faith and all men as brothers; that the bonds of affection and unity between the sons of men should be strengthened; that diversity of religions should cease and differences of race be annulled. What harm is there in this? Yet so it shall be. These fruitless strifes, these ruinous wars shall pass away, and "the Most Great Peace" shall come. Do not you in Europe need this also? Let not a man glory in this, that he loves his country; let him rather glory in this, that he loves his kind.'[147]

Though described as a Parliament of the World's Religions, the overwhelming majority of those who attended were Christian. One hundred of the speakers were Protestants and most of those were ministers. It is a matter of some irony that this first reference to the new Revelation made on North American soil was delivered at the end of a paper which presented a case for the superiority of the Anglo-Saxon race and its mandate to Christianize humanity. Its author, the Reverend Jessup, was not well disposed to the new Faith, yet his mention of Bahá'u'lláh lingered in the hearts of a few who heard him.

Five months later, in February 1894, Ibráhím Khayru'lláh settled in the Chicago area. That same year he began to share his understanding of the new teachings with a number of seekers. He also wrote to 'Abdu'l-Bahá informing Him of these teaching activities and received His approval.

At the start he had just four pupils, one of whom was an insurance salesman named Thornton Chase. Thornton Chase had begun to undertake an investigation of the Bahá'í Faith on his own for he was a most earnest seeker after truth. In June of 1894 Thornton Chase declared his belief in Bahá'u'lláh.

By 1896 Khayru'lláh was giving a regular series of lessons and by May of the following year there were about 60 believers in the Chicago area. These new Bahá'ís wrote to 'Abdu'l-Bahá when they became believers but they did not receive individual replies. For the time being all correspondence had to go through Khayru'lláh, for there was no one in 'Akká who could translate from English into Arabic or Persian.

The establishment of the Bahá'í Faith on the North American continent, amongst a people accustomed to regard Christianity as greatly superior to all other religions, and at a time when 'Abdu'l-Bahá had only just taken up the burden of leadership Bahá'u'lláh had laid upon Him and when He was in the grip of the most grievous crisis He was ever to confront, was indeed a remarkable development.

19

The Covenant-Breakers
Announce Themselves

In 1896, as the numbers of seekers attending <u>Kh</u>ayru'lláh's classes in the Chicago area began to increase rapidly, in the Holy Land the unfaithful members of Bahá'u'lláh's family brought into the open their opposition to the Centre of the Covenant.

For four distressful years 'Abdu'l-Bahá had done everything in His power to guide and enlighten His misguided relatives. The believers in the Holy Land were aware of the grievances nursed by Mírzá Muḥammad 'Alí but the believers in Persia and the other lands where the Faith was established were unaware of his disloyalty. Adib Taherzadeh relates that:

> . . . after four years of strengthening their position, Mírzá Muḥammad-'Alí and his party felt that it was time to unmask themselves. They did this by printing letters loaded with falsehoods, misleading statements, and calumnies against the Centre of the Covenant, posing themselves as the voice of truth trying to purify the Cause which they shamelessly claimed to have been polluted by those who were faithful to 'Abdu'l-Bahá. In his propaganda, Mírzá Muḥammad-'Alí did not contest the authenticity of the *Kitáb-i-'Ahd*, rather he expressed his grievance that he had been barred from partnership with 'Abdu'l-Bahá in directing the affairs of the Cause.

He wanted to share with Him the station of the Centre of the Covenant.[148]

Dr Yúnis Khán-i-Afrúkhtih, a secretary to 'Abdu'l-Bahá, remembered 'Abdu'l-Bahá's words to His half-brother Mírzá Díyá'u'lláh when He learnt that these letters had just been dispatched:

> I swear by the Righteousness of God, a day shall come when Mírzá Muḥammad-'Alí would wish that his fingers had been cut off so that he could not have taken the pen to announce his breaking of the Covenant. For four years I have concealed this matter so that the beloved of God might not learn of your unfaithfulness to the Covenant. It is now beyond my power to conceal it any longer. You have announced yourselves to the believers.[149]

In several Tablets revealed during these years, 'Abdu'l-Bahá makes it very clear that, though appointed by Bahá'u'lláh as the Centre of His Covenant and the sole Interpreter of His words, His station was, above all else, the station of servitude:

> This is my firm, my unshakable conviction the essence of my unconcealed and explicit belief – a conviction and belief which the denizens of the Abhá Kingdom fully share: The Blessed Beauty is the Sun of Truth, and His light the light of truth. The Báb is likewise the Sun of Truth, and His light the light of truth . . . My station is the station of servitude – a servitude which is complete, pure and real, firmly established, enduring, obvious, explicitly revealed and subject to no interpretation whatever . . . I am the Interpreter of the Word of God; such is my interpretation.[150]

The Master and His family were, at this time, still living in the House of 'Abbúd. The house was too small to accommodate the family, now that His daughters were grown and married. In October of 1896 'Abdu'l-Bahá rented the main building of the former governorate of 'Abdu'lláh Páshá. This house is situated in the Mujádalih Quarter in the north-west corner of 'Akká. It now became the Master's home and a home also for His daughters, their husbands and families. It was in this house, in March of 1897, that 'Abdu'l-Bahá eldest grandchild, Shoghi Effendi, was born.

In 1897 Mírzá Áqá Ján, the former amanuensis of Bahá'u'lláh and the first to recognize the station of Bahá'u'lláh in the years before He declared His mission, leagued himself with the Covenant-breakers. Mírzá Áqá Ján had served Bahá'u'lláh for nearly 40 years as secretary, servant and close companion. But near the end of His life Bahá'u'lláh dismissed Mírzá Áqá Ján from His service.

Mírzá Áqá Ján had become proud that he was so close to Bahá'u'lláh and had begun to act in ways that caused Bahá'u'lláh extreme displeasure. Mírzá Áqá Ján had a weakness for material possessions and had begged Bahá'u'lláh to give him a number of the precious gifts sent to Him by the believers. In addition, he had, with the help of 'Abdu'l-Bahá's half-brothers, acquired a number of properties in the 'Akká area. Soon after Bahá'u'lláh's passing, these same half-brothers plotted to kill Mírzá Áqá Ján, in order to obtain these gifts and properties themselves.

Mírzá Áqá Ján fled to 'Abdu'l-Bahá's presence where he begged forgiveness for his past conduct and implored shelter in 'Abdu'l-Bahá's house. 'Abdu'l-Bahá granted both requests. But soon the Covenant-breakers regretted their former persecution of Mírzá Áqá Ján. They now planned to persuade him to join them at Bahjí so that they could make use of him for their own purposes. They wrote a

letter which purported to be addressed to Mírzá Áqá Ján
from the Bahá'ís of Persia, encouraging him to take a
leadership role in the community and suggesting that he
speak out amongst the believers who would be gathered
at Bahjí for the fifth anniversary of the passing of Bahá'u-
'lláh.

Once the Covenant-breakers had come out into the
open, they expanded the scope of their activities by attempting to blacken 'Abdu'l-Bahá's reputation amongst
local government officials, accusing Him of exalting His
own station and of being a fomenter of discord and strife.
On this occasion of the fifth anniversary of Bahá'u'lláh's
passing, they arranged for a high-ranking government
official to be present at Bahjí. They invited him to remain
out of sight but to keep a close watch on what was happen-
ing. Their hope was that Mírzá Áqá Ján's actions would
incite violence amongst the believers and provide a pretext
for a report to be sent to Constantinople which would lead
to the arrest and detention of 'Abdu'l-Bahá Himself.

These plans went sadly awry. Mírzá Áqá Ján did attempt
to speak out and an uproar began but as soon as 'Abdu'l-
Bahá arrived on the scene, Mírzá Áqá Ján fled, shouting
abuse, into the shrine of Bahá'u'lláh. 'Abdu'l-Bahá's dignified presence calmed all those present but after this
episode Mírzá Áqá Ján openly declared his support for the
Covenant-breakers.

Once the Covenant-breakers became openly hostile to
'Abdu'l-Bahá, they would no longer allow Him the use of
a room on the ground floor of the mansion of Bahjí where
He rested, along with other believers who had walked from
'Akká, before entering the shrine. 'Abdu'l-Bahá then began
to use another small house near the shrine for this purpose
and this is today the Pilgrim House at Bahjí.

A year or two later the Covenant-breakers allowed Mírzá Áqá Ján to take up residence in the very building where Bahá'u'lláh was buried. When this happened, 'Abdu'l-Bahá forbade any of the believers to enter the shrine and He did not enter it Himself. This situation continued until Mírzá Áqá Ján's passing in 1901.

Shortly after Mírzá Áqá Ján joined Mírzá Muḥammad-'Alí and his followers, Mírzá Muḥammad-'Alí and his brothers bribed the chief of police in 'Akká and had an official indictment against 'Abdu'l-Bahá drawn up. They then took their case to a court in 'Akká with a list of preposterous accusations, the first of which was that Bahá'u'lláh was not a prophet of God but only a holy man who spent a life of seclusion in prayer and meditation. 'Abdu'l-Bahá, on the other hand, they claimed, had exalted the station of Bahá'u'lláh for political reasons.

'Abdu'l-Bahá appeared in the court and there read aloud the Kitáb-i-'Ahd, Bahá'u'lláh's Will and Testament, in which 'Abdu'l-Bahá is unequivocally appointed as the Centre of the Covenant. He explained clearly that the Covenant-breakers had, through their own actions, severed themselves entirely from the Bahá'í community. He refuted the other charges brought against Him with equal forcefulness. The case was dismissed.

Though the Covenant-breakers failed in this attempt, they continued to do all that they could to damage the reputation of 'Abdu'l-Bahá, to humiliate Him and to cause Him intense pain. Over the years since the passing of Bahá'u'lláh they had built up a considerable network of correspondents but throughout this severe crisis the believers in Persia, with the exception of a very few individuals who had leagued themselves with Mírzá Muḥammad-'Alí, remained completely loyal to 'Abdu'l-Bahá.

'Abdu'l-Bahá continued to keep in close touch with his homeland where the believers were experiencing many difficulties in these years. When Mírzá Maḥmúd-i-Furúghí, an outstanding teacher of the Faith, was on pilgrimage, 'Abdu'l-Bahá indicated to him that the Sháh would be assassinated and told him to warn the believers to be on their guard.

In 1896 Náṣiri'd-Dín Sháh was indeed struck down by an assassin on the very eve of his jubilee celebrations. The Bahá'ís had nothing whatever to do with this deed but memories of the assassination attempt made by three deranged Bábís in 1852 were still powerful. In its report the London *Times* supposed that the murderer was a 'Bábí'. Only gradually was it realized that the Bahá'ís were not responsible.

The immediate reaction of the populace was to blame those they still called Bábís. It was as a direct consequence of this assassination that the famed Bahá'í poet Varqá and his twelve-year old son Rúḥu'lláh, already held in prison in Ṭihrán, were brutally put to death. Atrocities were committed against the Bahá'ís in several other localities.

As the movement in support of a constitutional government in Persia grew, political reactionaries denounced the Bahá'ís, labelling them as inspirers and supporters of this movement. The Azalís, on the other hand, spread false rumours to the effect that the Bahá'ís were supporters of the Sháh. It was during these years that 'Abdu'l-Bahá counselled the believers against joining any political parties or factions.

In these years the Covenant-breakers gave up demanding that the Master pay for their upkeep but at the same time two attempts were made by them to kill 'Abdu'l-Bahá. Poison was twice placed by one individual in a jug of drinking water used by Him but on both occasions it was discovered in time. Another individual concealed a dagger under his clothes with the intention of using it to kill 'Abdu'l-Bahá but the attempt was not successful. Dr Yúnis Khán relates that both men later regretted their actions and that 'Abdu'l-Bahá forgave one and turned a blind eye to the other.

While 'the ever-moving pen' of 'Abdu'l-Bahá counselled, cheered and inspired the believers, He had also to plan for the safe removal of the bodily remains of the Báb from Persia to the Holy Land and for their entombment on the slopes of Mount Carmel. 'Abdu'l-Bahá had already taken steps to purchase the ground which Bahá'u'lláh had designated as the spot on which the Shrine of the Báb was to be built. It would have been a simple transaction, had it not been for the Covenant-breakers.

'Abdu'l-Bahá had asked a German businessman who was living in Haifa to negotiate with the owner of the land on His behalf. But Mírzá Muḥammad-'Alí raised so many obstacles in the path of a successful negotiation that this man was obliged to put the deal back in 'Abdu'l-Bahá's hands. When the owner of the land did, finally, agree to sell the land for a reasonable sum, the Covenant-breakers incited several individuals to lay petitions before the authorities, claiming ownership of the land. It took six more months to prove the falsity of these claims. Only then was 'Abdu'l-Bahá able to purchase the land.

20

'Heaven is There . . .'

In 1897 Anton Haddad travelled from the United States to the Middle East. Ibrahim Khayru'lláh urged him to visit 'Akká and meet with 'Abdu'l-Bahá before returning to the States. He did so and shortly after returning to New York in December of that year, he wrote these words to Khayru'lláh:

> O my dear brother heaven is there & the paridise [sic] of God. Every body would desire to be a servant in that place . . . The appearance of glory & besides these attributes the signs of kindness & generosity, love & happiness for the human race. On account of this he ['Abdu'l-Bahá] cannot sleep nights, people not leaving him a minute. Every body goes to him for help & he never rejects them. His time is spent enlightening all – rich as well as poor, it makes no difference to him. His knowledge, understanding & high attributes are his characteristics . . .[151]

Anton Haddad's description of 'Abdu'l-Bahá fired the early believers with enthusiasm to visit Him themselves.

Amongst the newly-formed Bahá'í community in California were a number of wealthy individuals, the most well-known of them Mrs Phoebe Hearst, widow of the late Senator George Hearst. Mrs Hearst was widely renowned for her philanthropic activities. She had already planned a visit to Egypt for the autumn of 1898 and now decided to visit 'Akká also. She invited Edward and Lua Getsinger, through whom she had heard of the Bahá'í teachings, to accompany her. She sent another invitation to Ibráhím Khayru'lláh and his wife. It was promptly accepted. Khayru'lláh was writing a book on what he knew of the Bahá'í teachings and was eager to gain 'Abdu'l-Bahá's approval of this project. Phoebe Hearst included in the party a number of her own relatives and employees who had become believers, including her butler, Robert Turner, the first black American to accept the new teachings.

The entire party sailed from New York to Cherbourg in late September and proceeded to Paris. Khayru'lláh then went on ahead to Egypt, where he had relatives to visit, while his wife went to England to visit an aunt who had become a Bahá'í. Mrs Hearst had an apartment in Paris and in it were staying two of her nieces and a young woman named May Ellis Bolles. Within a short time May Ellis Bolles and Mrs Hearst's nieces accepted the Bahá'í teachings and joined the pilgrimage party.

After spending three weeks in Egypt, Khayru'lláh reached 'Akká on 11 November 1898. 'Abdu'l-Bahá commemorated his arrival by ending the six and a half years of mourning for Bahá'u'lláh and, for the very first time, opened the room directly above Bahá'u'lláh's tomb to the pilgrims. He also bestowed on Khayru'lláh the unique privilege of assisting Him in breaking ground on the spot on Mount Carmel where He had been instructed by Bahá'u'lláh to lay to rest the mortal remains of the Báb.

Khayru'lláh had carried to 'Akká a number of letters from the American believers. To these 'Abdu'l-Bahá replied. Though His replies would not arrive in the United States until February 1899, direct correspondence between Him and the American believers had now begun.

The other pilgrims from the West had to wait in Egypt until hearing from 'Abdu'l-Bahá that they could proceed to 'Akká. Because of the suspicions which Mírzá Muḥammad-'Alí and his accomplices had aroused in official circles, the entire party of nine could not travel to 'Akká together. Edward and Lua Getsinger were invited to 'Akká first and they arrived on 10 December 1898, the first North American believers to attain the presence of 'Abdu'l-Bahá.

In Akká there was only one believer, besides Ibrahim Khayru'lláh, who spoke English. Thus communication in words was difficult but Lua Getsinger soon wrote to Thornton Chase that:

> The atmosphere of the place is wondrous, knowledge and understanding seem to float in the air . . . I feel that there are no words in which to describe it [the household], that one must see for himself to *know*. Not that the house is so grand or its surroundings – *not at all* for everything – even their manner of dress – is simplicity itself – but there is a dignity and grandeur in *this simplicity* that is quite beyond description. The Face of the Master – is gloriously beautiful – His eyes read one's very soul – still they are full of divine love – and fairly melt one's heart! His hair and beard are white, but soft and fine like silk. His features are finely chiselled and very classical – His forehead high and full – and His mouth supremely beautiful, while His hands are small and white like a woman's. Now I have tried to describe Him – but you see it is a feeble attempt, and I assure you it is inadequate in the extreme![152]

The Getsingers were loath to leave 'Akká and 'Abdu'l-Bahá allowed them to remain in the city in order that they might learn Persian and study the Faith more deeply. Khayru'lláh also was permitted to remain but the other Western pilgrims were allowed to stay only a few days in 'Akká lest the authorities became suspicious at the presence of so many foreigners.

Around 20 December, Mrs Hearst and a few others arrived, amongst them Mrs Thornburgh-Cropper, from Britain, who described their arrival in these words:

> We then took a small, miserable boat to Haifa . . . we were beaten about unmercifully in our all too inadequate steamer. Upon arrival we went to an hotel, where we remained until nightfall as it was too dangerous for us, and for 'Abdu'l-Bahá . . . for strangers to be seen entering the city of sorrow.[153]

They travelled by night along the hard sands from Haifa to the gates of the prison city where their trusted driver arranged for them to enter. The narrative continues:

> Once inside we found the friends who were awaiting us, and we started up the uneven stairs that led to Him. Someone went before us with a small piece of candle, which cast strange shadows on the walls of this silent place.
>
> Suddenly the light caught a form that at first seemed a vision of mist and light. It was the Master which the candle-light had revealed to us. His white robe, and silver, flowing hair, and shining blue eyes gave the impression of a spirit, rather than of a human being. We tried to tell Him how deeply grateful we were at His receiving us. 'No,' He answered, 'you are kind to come . . .'
>
> Then He smiled, and we recognized the Light which He possessed in the radiance which moved over His fine and noble face. It was an amazing experience. We four visitors from the Western world felt that our voyage, with all its accompanying inconvenience, was a

small price to pay for such treasure as we received from the spirit and words of the Master . . .[154]

The pilgrims were able to stay only for a few days but, as Mrs Hearst wrote to a friend a year later:

> . . . I assure you those three days were the most memorable days of my life, still I feel incapable of describing them in the slightest degree.
>   . . . The Master I will not attempt to describe: I will only state that I believe with all my heart that He is the Master and my greatest blessing in this world is that I have been privileged to be in His presence . . .[155]

In another letter written in the same year she wrote:

> Tho [sic] He does not seek to impress one at all, strength, power, purity, love and holiness are radiated from His majestic, yet humble, personality, and the spiritual atmosphere which surrounds Him and most powerfully affects all those who are blest by being near Him, is indescribable . . .[156]

In mid-February a third small party of pilgrims arrived. May Ellis Bolles has recounted their arrival in these words:

> . . . we continued on our journey, sitting quietly on deck until the twilight fell about us, the shadows deepened, and with the gathering darkness the stars shone out one by one, large and effulgent in that clear atmosphere. We arose and went forward and saw looming up through the darkness, dimly at first, but growing ever more distinct and grand, the noble outline of Mount Carmel . . .
>   There were two Russian pilgrims on board who for hours had been standing motionless at the ship's rail facing the east, and now their steadfast gaze was on

'Akká, and thus we all stood in prayer and worship as the ship slowly entered the bay of Haifa and cast anchor.[157]

The next morning, May Ellis Bolles attained the presence of the Master, for He was in Haifa, where He had rented a house for the use of the pilgrims:

> . . . I stood on the threshold and dimly saw a room full of people sitting quietly about the walls, and then I beheld my Beloved. I found myself at His feet, and He gently raised me and seated me beside Him, all the while saying some loving words in Persian in a voice that shook my heart. Of that first meeting I can remember neither joy nor pain nor anything that I can name. I had been carried suddenly to too great a height; my soul had come in contact with the Divine Spirit; and this force so pure, so holy, so mighty, had overwhelmed me. He spoke to each one of us in turn of ourselves and our lives and those whom we loved, and although His Words were so few and so simple they breathed the Spirit of Life to our souls . . .
>
> The Russian Jews who had been on the boat the night before now arrived, their faces shining with a great light as they entered His Presence. We could not remove our eyes from His glorious face: we heard all He said; we drank tea with Him at His bidding; but existence seemed suspended, and when He arose and suddenly left us we came back with a start to life: but never again, thank God, to the same life on this earth! We had 'beheld the King in His beauty. We had seen the land which is very far off.'[158]

The next day May fell ill. 'Abdu'l-Bahá had arranged to meet the pilgrims on Mount Carmel on the following day, a Sunday, but after visiting May in the early morning and finding her still weak and unwell, He announced:

There will be no meeting on Mount Carmel to-day. We shall meet elsewhere, Insha'alláh, in a few days, but we could not go and leave one of the beloved of God alone and sick. We could none of us be happy unless all the beloved were happy.[159]

All were astonished, not least May herself:

That anything so important as this meeting in that blessed spot should be cancelled because one person was ill and could not go seemed incredible . . . The Master's words had opened wide the door of God's Kingdom and given us a vision of that infinite world whose only law is love. This was but one of many times that we saw 'Abdu'l-Bahá place above every other consideration the love and kindness, the sympathy and compassion due to every soul.[160]

From Haifa, May and her companions were taken by carriage along the shore to 'Akká:

. . . Our hearts were too full for words and in reverent silence we gazed upon the walled city as it lay white and clear and beautiful in the still morning light with the deep blue Mediterranean at its feet and the dome of the luminous sky above. We crossed two streams . . . the horses wading up to their sides, and reached at last the stone gates of 'Akká, drove through the narrow, pictur-esque streets where the early-rising oriental world was up and stirring, and arrived at the house of 'Abdu'l-Bahá.[161]

21

'Unfading, Eternal Days'

There, standing beside the window of a small room, overlooking the azure sea, we found our Beloved. We came to His feet and poured out our overwhelming love and thankfulness, while He laid His hands on our heads and spoke low and tenderly to His poor servants. The Greatest Holy Leaf now entered, with the Holy Mother and her daughters, and they welcomed us with love and tears of joy as though we had been parted for awhile but had returned at last to our heavenly home, as indeed we had! They took us to our rooms which, alas!, they had vacated for our sakes . . .[162]

A few days later May wrote:

How wonderful to be able to see our beloved Master at any hour, to hear His divine voice, to lie down beneath the same roof which sheltered His blessed person! . . . When, in the twilight, all in the household had gathered together, and spoke in quiet tones of the Blessed Perfection and our Master, suddenly the glorious light of His presence would shine upon us, and all would rise to meet Him as He entered; then He would sit silently in our midst, while His daughter Rúhá chanted a Tablet, and there would be about Him such heavenly beauty, from His Blessed Being would emanate such supreme mildness, gentleness, and humility as wrung our hearts with shame and sorrow for our sins, yet lifted them on mighty wings of hope and aspiration. He always bade us all good-night, telling us to rest well in

our Father's home and to dream beautiful dreams; and
in the morning He would greet us early and enquire
of each one concerning their spiritual health and happiness, showing the most loving solicitude for those
who were not well.[163]

At mealtimes 'Abdu'l-Bahá gently taught His guests more
of His Father's teachings and shared with them stories of
Bahá'u'lláh's life.

'. . . I have never seen', May writes, 'such happiness nor
heard such laughter as at 'Akká. The Master seems to
sound all the chords of our human nature and set them
vibrating to heavenly music.'[164]

Kindness to animals was a virtue which the Master
particularly stressed. At one mealtime, May relates:

'Abdu'l-Bahá said we should always be kind and merci-
ful to every creature; that cruelty was sin and that the
human race should never injure any of God's creatures,
but ought to be always careful to do nothing to dimin-
ish or exterminate any order of living thing; that human beings ought to use the animals, fishes and birds
when necessary for food, or any just service, but never
for pleasure or vanity and that it was most wrong and
cruel to hunt.[165]

On the last day of this pilgrimage 'Abdu'l-Bahá arranged
for His guests to visit the Garden of Riḍván, which Bahá'u-
'lláh had often visited, and then met them at Bahjí. May
Ellis Bolles relates:

When we alighted we found a group of more than one
hundred oriental believers waiting for us. Knowing that
we were among the first American pilgrims to that Holy
Spot they had come from all directions to behold our
faces, and their own shone with a love and joy that
amazed us and which we can never forget.[166]

Entering the tea-house, they came into the presence of the
Master. May continues:

> He arose to welcome us, and greeting us with infinite
> love, He bade us be seated and to partake of some tea
> . . . Then with a word of excuse He left us. He stepped
> out on to the terrace and with His hands clasped be-
> hind Him and gazing upward He walked to and fro. As
> not the least action or word of the Master's is without
> a purpose and a meaning, we soon saw that He was
> walking on the terrace so that all His servants might
> behold Him; and we saw our oriental brothers standing
> in a group on the grass below, perfectly motionless and
> silent . . .
>   By and by He came to the door of the tea-room, and
> the lightning of His glance fell on us and He said in a
> quiet, low tone: 'We are now going to visit the Holy
> Tomb' . . . He then bade us follow Him and descended
> the steps, followed by the American pilgrims, then all
> the other believers in a body behind us, and in this
> order, the Master walking a few yards in advance, we
> proceeded slowly toward the Tomb of Bahá'u'lláh.
> When we reached the outer door 'Abdu'l-Bahá removed
> His shoes and motioned us to do likewise. We followed
> him through a passage-way into a square court with a
> glass roof, and in the centre a plot of earth where
> flowering bushes and mandarin trees were growing. As
> we entered, a door in the opposite corner opened and
> the ladies of the holy family arrived, thickly veiled; they
> came forward and greeted us tenderly. At the further
> end of the court is a door at one side, and within is the
> Holy Tomb. As we gazed upon this veiled door our
> souls stirred within us as though seeking release . . .
> The blessed Master was calm and radiant and led us to
> the open space at the end of the court beside the Tomb,
> where, in the mellow light of a stained glass window,
> we all stood in silence until He bade one of our group

to sing *The Holy City*. No pen could describe the solemn beauty of that moment, as, in a broken voice, this young girl sang the praise and glory of God, while all were immersed in the ocean of the Divine Presence. The tears of the pilgrims flowed and strong men wept aloud. Then 'Abdu'l-Bahá led us to the door of the Tomb where we knelt for a moment, then He opened the door and led us in. Those who have passed that threshold have been for a brief moment in the presence of God, their Creator, and no thoughts can follow them. The Tablet of the Holy Tomb was chanted by a young Persian, and when we left that blessed spot the oriental pilgrims entered slowly, until all had been within; then our Beloved closed the door, and after singing *Nearer, my God, to Thee* at His request, we quietly withdrew . . .

From that time a great peace descended upon us, and in the heavenly calm and beauty of that last night in 'Akká, we were girded with strength for the future.[167]

The next morning the pilgrims left for Haifa where they were to board their ship the same afternoon. 'Abdu'l-Bahá called them to His presence early in the morning. Some of the believers wept bitterly at the thought of parting from Him. May relates that:

He asked them for His sake not to weep, nor would He talk to us or teach us until all tears were banished and we were quite calm. Then He said:

'Pray that your hearts may be cut from yourselves and from the world, that you may be confirmed by the Holy Spirit and filled with the fire of the love of God . . . nothing shall be impossible to you if you have faith. And now I give you a commandment which shall be for a covenant between you and Me – that ye have faith; that your faith be steadfast as a rock that no storms can move, that nothing can disturb, and that it endure through all things even to the end . . . As ye have faith so shall your powers and blessings be. This is the balance – this is the balance – this is the balance.'[168]

'Abdu'l-Bahá then took them into another room so that they might see the portraits of the Báb and Bahá'u'lláh. May continues:

> . . . I could not keep my eyes from the eyes of Bahá'u-'lláh, until 'Abdu'l-Bahá turned suddenly to us, and raising His voice in a tone so poignant that it pierced every heart, He stretched His hands above us and said:
>
> 'Now the time has come when we must part, but the separation is only of our bodies, in spirit we are united. Ye are the lights which shall be diffused; ye are the waves of that sea which shall spread and overflow the world. Each wave is precious to Me . . .
>
> 'Another commandment I give unto you, that ye love one another even as I love you . . . Look at Me and be as I am; ye must die to yourselves and to the world, so shall ye be born again and enter the Kingdom of Heaven. Behold a candle how it gives its light. It weeps its life away drop by drop in order to give forth its flame of light.'
>
> When He had finished speaking we were led gently away by the members of the Holy Family, and for a moment it seemed that we were dying; but our Master never removed His compassionate gaze from our faces, until we could see Him no longer, for our tears. Then we were clasped one after the other in the arms of the Holy Family, and the hearts were wrung, and it seemed as if all the cords of life were breaking; until, as we drove away from the home of our Heavenly Father, suddenly His spirit came to us, a great strength and tranquillity filled our souls, the grief of the bodily separation was turned into the joy of spiritual union.[169]

As May recorded earlier in this diary of pilgrimage:

. . . every hour spent in His presence has no place in time and no part in the life of this world. Those days are unfading, eternal. They were the goal for which all life before was but a preparation, and the source from which all life since has flowed.[170]

22

Souls Arise as Promised

In 1899 a young Persian pilgrim of noble descent who spoke and wrote fluent English arrived in 'Akká. His name was Ali Kuli Khan. He had endured many hardships on his way to the Holy Land and, in consequence of a vow he had made, had slept on the floor for two years, vowing not to sleep in a bed until he had attained his goal of pilgrimage. When Khan entered the presence of the Master, in 'Abdu'l-Bahá's own room, he collapsed in a heap on the floor. 'Abdu'l-Bahá lifted him up, put His arms around him and kissed him on both cheeks. When Khan had rested and drunk some tea, 'Abdu'l-Bahá welcomed him warmly and said:

> The Blessed Perfection, Bahá'u'lláh, has promised to raise up souls who would hasten to the service of the Covenant, and would assist me in spreading His Faith. His Cause has now reached America and many in the Western world are being attracted to His Teachings. You, with your knowledge of English, are one of those souls promised me by Bahá'u'lláh. You have come to assist me by translating His Sacred Writings as well as my letters to the friends in America and elsewhere in the West.[171]

At the end of a short conversation 'Abdu'l-Bahá stated that He had taken a house in the German colony. Pointing to

His bed in the corner of the room, He said to Khan, 'This is your bed. Sleep in it.'[172]

But it was only after sleeping on the floor for several more nights that Ali Kuli Khan plucked up the courage to obey the Master and sleep in His bed.

In 1899 the Bahá'ís of 'Ishqábád wrote to'Abdu'l-Bahá asking His permission to start building a Bahá'í House of Worship. This town in Russian Transcaspia, over the border from Khurásán province of Persia, had become a place of refuge for Bahá'ís fleeing persecution in their home country. Bahá'u'lláh had indicated that a House of Worship would be built there and 'Abdu'l-Bahá now gave His approval to the project. He wrote to Ḥájí Mírzá Muḥammad-Taqí, a first cousin of the Báb who was living in Yazd and who already owned property in 'Ishqábád, to supervise the work. Ḥájí Mírzá Muḥammad-Taqí speedily wound up his affairs in Yazd in preparation for his move to 'Ishqábád.

In May 1899, Ibráhím Khayru'lláh returned from his travels to the United States. While in the Holy Land he had established contact with Mírzá Muḥammad-'Alí. A few weeks later the Getsingers returned after a five-month stay in 'Akká. Khayru'lláh was hoping for some sort of official appointment as head of the American Bahá'í community. When it became obvious to him that this was not possible, he began to express doubts about 'Abdu'l-Bahá's leadership. Dissension developed in the American community and in April 1900 'Abdu'l-Bahá despatched 'Abdu'l-Karím-i-Ṭihrání to investigate the situation. He was given the tasks of helping Khayru'lláh understand the station of the Master and of deepening the community in the teachings of Bahá'u'lláh. The latter task he carried out well but by the end of June all communication between Khayru'lláh and the Bahá'í community had ceased. K͟hayru'lláh refused to accept the authority of 'Abdu'l-Bahá.

In 1899 'Abdu'l-Bahá instructed the Bahá'ís of Ṭihrán to elect a Spiritual Assembly. This embryonic institution was composed of nine members, one of whom was of Jewish and another of Zoroastrian background. In the same year the Bahá'ís of Rangoon, Burma, sent to the Holy Land a marble sarcophagus to hold the precious remains of the Báb. These remains were kept in 'Abdu'l-Bahá's house until the time when they could be laid to rest on Mount Carmel.

More pilgrims came from the West, amongst them Sarah Farmer, who had founded a conference centre in Eliot, Maine. While on pilgrimage, she offered the facilities of this centre, Green Acre, to 'Abdu'l-Bahá. In 1900 Laura Clifford Barney, another American pilgrim, was asked by 'Abdu'l-Bahá to accompany Mírzá Abu'l-Faḍl from Egypt to the United States. This she did and in the following year, 1901, 'Abdu'l-Bahá sent Ali Kuli Khan to assist Mírzá Abu'l-Faḍl in deepening the American believers.

'Abdu'l-Bahá now focused His attention on building a shrine on Mount Carmel for the precious remains of the Báb. He had already purchased the actual site needed but access to it was difficult and another piece of property, to the south, was required for the building of an access road. Mírzá Muḥammad-'Alí and his accomplices now intervened to cause fresh trouble. They encouraged the owner of the land to demand an exorbitant price, assuring him that they would pay twice as much as 'Abdu'l-Bahá would pay. 'Abdu'l-Bahá then offered to pay a very large sum but the owner still refused to sell.

'One night,' 'Abdu'l-Bahá later recounted, 'I was so hemmed in by My anxieties that I had no other recourse than to recite and repeat over and over again a prayer of the Báb which I had in My possession, the recital of which greatly calmed Me. The next morning the owner of the plot himself came to Me, apologized and begged Me to purchase his property.'[173]

As the new century dawned, construction of the shrine began in earnest. 'Abdu'l-Bahá visited Haifa frequently for the sole purpose of supervising the work and spoke about the project with enthusiasm every day. The slope of Mount Carmel was then rocky, inhospitable and uninhabited. The stone building that 'Abdu'l-Bahá was constructing was a very solid but simple, dignified structure consisting of only six rooms. But the Covenant-breakers were incensed that 'Abdu'l-Bahá was able to proceed with this work and were particularly infuriated by the arrival of more pilgrims from the West. Once the building began in earnest, 'Abdu'l-Bahá discouraged pilgrims from visiting the Holy Land because He knew that Mírzá Muḥammad-'Alí would make use of any visitors to stir up more trouble.

By this time Mírzá Muḥammad-'Alí had lost one of his chief accomplices: His brother, Mírzá Ḍiyá'u'lláh had passed away in 1898. Mírzá Áqá Ján's money and possessions had all been used up in bribes given to officials. Even the clothing and personal effects of Bahá'u'lláh had been used for the same purpose. Before his death in 1901, Mírzá Áqá Ján had warned Mírzá Muḥammad-'Alí not to attempt to obstruct the building work on Mount Carmel, for this project was, he said, foretold in Jewish scripture. His advice was not taken.

Mírzá Muḥammad-'Alí now mortgaged the Mansion of Bahjí in order to obtain fresh funds. He then sent Mírzá Majdu'd-Dín to Damascus with a petition for the governor of Syria, Náẓim Páshá. The petition stated that 'Abdu'l-Bahá was building a fortress on Mount Carmel, that He was planning a rebellion against Ottoman rule and that He was receiving military advisors from the West. Mírzá Majdu'd-Dín obtained an interview with the governor and with another high-ranking official. To both he presented expensive gifts. He returned to 'Akká certain that he had been successful in his mission. But the scheme quickly backfired.

23

Confined to 'Akká Once Again

On 20 August 1901 'Abdu'l-Bahá gathered with the believers at Bahjí to celebrate the Anniversary of the Declaration of the Báb according to the lunar calendar. On His return to 'Akká He learnt that both His brothers Mírzá Muḥammad-'Alí and Mírzá Badí'u'lláh had been fetched in from Bahjí under armed escort and that Mírzá Majdu'd-Dín had been brought from his home in Tiberias in the same humiliating manner.

'Abdu'l-Bahá went to the governor's office immediately and there He learnt that Sulṭán 'Abdu'l-Ḥamíd had issued a decree ordering that both He and His brothers were to be confined within the walls of 'Akká and that the same restrictions which had been imposed on Bahá'u'lláh and His followers when they first had come to 'Akká were to be reintroduced. The governor was an admirer of 'Abdu'l-Bahá and was loath to enforce this decree. He had, in fact, delayed its implementation but now he had no choice.

'Abdu'l-Bahá was detained at the government headquarters for several days and was subjected to long sessions of questioning. He asked that His brothers and the local believers be allowed freedom of movement and assured the authorities that He would Himself remain in 'Akká.

In desperation, Mírzá Muḥammad-'Alí wrote two more letters to Náẓim Páshá begging to be allowed to return to his home but neither letter was acknowledged. But such was the reverence in which 'Abdu'l-Bahá was held in the

'Akká area that it was not possible for severe restrictions to be reimposed. Gradually the furore subsided. 'Abdu'l-Bahá's petitions were granted. His brothers went back to Bahjí and the Bahá'ís of 'Akká were able to resume their daily tasks and routines.

'Abdu'l-Bahá remained in 'Akká. His single greatest sorrow was that He could no longer visit Bahjí to pray at the shrine of Bahá'u'lláh. He arranged for a simple wooden cabin to be built on the roof of His house from which He could look towards Bahjí and there He prayed. There is a low hill overlooking Bahjí where, at that time, red flowers grew in abundance. When the believers returned to 'Akká from their visits to the shrine, He would ask, wistfully, 'Were red, red flowers blooming on Buq'atu'l-Ḥamrá?'[174]

The governor of 'Akká, wishing to make amends for 'Abdu'l-Bahá's confinement in 'Akká, now asked Him to take him to visit the shrine. Then he requested another visit and this time took other prominent local officials with him. Mírzá Muḥammad-'Alí and his followers, viewing their arrival from the balcony and seeing the respect shown to 'Abdu'l-Bahá by the officials, were furious that their plans had so misfired. Mírzá Muḥammad-'Alí realized that the incarceration of 'Abdu'l-Bahá would not harm Him. He therefore began a fresh intrigue, this time to secure His deportation or execution. To this end, he made contact with the principal advisor to Sulṭán 'Abdu'l-Ḥamíd, a man named Shaykh Abu'l-Hudá.

In 1902 the cornerstone of the House of Worship in 'Ishqábád was laid. 'Abdu'l-Bahá had outlined the general plan of the building and a Russian architect named Volkov used this plan as a basis for the design. In the same year, Myron H. Phelps, a New York lawyer, and the Countess M.A. de S. Canavarro spent the month of December as guests of 'Abdu'l-Bahá. Myron Phelps has provided us with invaluable glimpses of the Master's life at that time:

> . . . 'Abbás Effendi's life is spent in quiet and unassuming work. His general order for the day is prayers and tea at sunrise, and dictating letters or 'Tablets', receiving visitors, and giving alms to the poor until dinner in the middle of the day. After this meal he takes a half-hour's siesta, spends the afternoon in making visits to the sick and others whom he has occasion to see about the city, and the evening in talking to the believers or in expounding, to any who wish to hear him, the Qur'án, on which, even among Muslims, he is reputed to be one of the highest authorities, learned men of that faith frequently coming from great distances to consult him with regard to its interpretation.
>
> He then returns to his house and works until about one o'clock over his correspondence. This is enormous, and would more than occupy his entire time, did he read and reply to all his letters personally. As he finds it impossible to do this, but is nevertheless determined that they shall all receive careful and impartial attention, he has recourse to the assistance of his daughter Rúḥá, upon whose intelligence and conscientious devotion to the task he can rely. During the day she reads and makes digests of letters received, which she submits to him at night.[175]

It was Ramadan, the Muslim month of fasting, while the visitors were in 'Akká. Phelps notes that 'Abdu'l-Bahá kept the fast Himself and provided a supper every other night for the poorer Muslims of the area. Every week, without fail, He gave alms to the poor. Phelps describes the ragged crowd that gathered outside the Master's house every Friday:

Many of these men are blind; many more are pale, emaciated, or aged. Some are on crutches; some are so feeble that they can barely walk. Most of the women are closely veiled, but enough are uncovered to cause us well to believe that, if the veils were lifted, more pain and misery would be seen. Some of them carry babes with pinched and sallow faces. There are perhaps a hundred in this gathering, and besides, many children. They are of all the races one meets in these streets . . . [176]

Phelps then describes the Master's appearance:

A door opens and a man comes out. He is of middle stature, strongly built. He wears flowing light-coloured robes. On his head is a light buff fez with a white cloth wound about it. He is perhaps sixty years of age. His long grey hair rests on his shoulders. His forehead is broad, full, and high, his nose slightly aquiline, his moustaches and beard, the latter full though not heavy, nearly white. His eyes are grey and blue, large, and both soft and penetrating. His bearing is simple, but there is grace, dignity, and even majesty about his movements. [177]

Phelps describes how 'Abdu'l-Bahá passed through the crowd, greeting all with kindly words, then stationed Himself at a narrow angle of the street and motioned to the people to come towards Him:

They crowd up a little too insistently. He pushes them gently back and lets them pass him one by one. As they come they hold their hands extended. In each open palm he places some small coins. He knows them all. He caresses them with his hand on the face, on the shoulders, on the head . . . He stops a woman with a babe and fondly strokes the child. As they pass, some

kiss his hand. To all he says, 'Marḥabá, marḥabá' –
Well done, well done!'[178]

Phelps was in 'Akká at the beginning of winter and relates
how 'Abdu'l-Bahá provided warm coats for perhaps five or
six hundred of the poorest people in the city:

> Upon many, especially the most infirm or crippled, he
> himself places the garment, adjusts it with his own
> hands, and strokes it approvingly . . .
>   On feast days he visits the poor at their homes. He
> chats with them, inquires into their health and comfort,
> mentions by name those who are absent, and leaves
> gifts for all . . .
>   All the people know him and love him – the rich and
> the poor, the young and the old – even the babe leap-
> ing in its mother's arms. If he hears of any one sick in
> the city – Muslim or Christian, or of any other sect, it
> matters not – he is each day at their bedside, or sends
> a trusty messenger. If a physician is needed, and the
> patient poor, he brings or sends one, and also the
> necessary medicine. If he finds a leaking roof or a
> broken window menacing health, he summons a work-
> man, and waits himself to see the breach repaired. If
> any one is in trouble, – if a son or a brother is thrown
> into prison, or he is threatened at law, or falls into any
> difficulty too heavy for him, – it is to the Master that he
> straightway makes appeal for counsel or for aid. In-
> deed, for counsel all come to him, rich as well as poor.
> He is the kind father of all the people.[179]

Phelps relates that 'Abdu'l-Bahá spent very little on Himself. In this way, He was able to be generous to others:

> His garments are usually of cotton, and the cheapest
> that can be bought. Often his friends in Persia . . . send
> him costly garments. These he wears once, out of re-
> spect for the sender; then he gives them away. A few

months ago, this happened. The wife of the Master was about to depart on a journey. Fearing that her husband would give away his cloak and so be left without one for himself, she left a second cloak with her daughter, charging her not to inform her father of it. Not long after her departure, the Master, suspecting, it would seem, what had been done, said to his daughter, 'Have I another cloak?' The daughter could not deny it, but told her father of her mother's charge. The Master replied, 'How could I be happy having two cloaks, knowing that there are those that have none?' Nor would he be content until he had given the second cloak away.[180]

The Countess de Canavarro spent much of her time talking with Bahíyyih Khánum and then related what she had heard to Myron Phelps. According to the social customs of the day, it would not have been possible for Phelps to obtain these interviews himself.

Bahíyyih Khánum spoke of the happiness and harmony that characterized the Master's marriage. She explained that her sister-in-law had recently felt it necessary to visit Beirut with two of her daughters on account of their health and that this was the first time in the marriage that Munírih Khánum had been away from 'Abdu'l-Bahá for any length of time. Since a short time after her departure, the first question put by 'Abdu'l-Bahá to his daughter Rúḥá every morning had been, 'Rúḥá, when do you think your mother will come back?'[181]

In 1902 'Abdu'l-Bahá began to ask the believers in the Holy Land to offer special prayers for the Bahá'ís in Persia and especially for the Bahá'ís of Yazd. He warned that severe trials lay just ahead for them.

Section IV
1902–12

Mount
Carmel

24

An Intense Agony

Just one year before Bahá'u'lláh's passing, savage persecution of the Bahá'í community in Yazd had resulted in seven martyrdoms. In the very first year of 'Abdu'l-Bahá's ministry, another Bahá'í was murdered in Yazd. Persecutions continued sporadically in other areas. Immediately after the assassination of Náṣiri'd-Dín Sháh, in 1896, five more Bahá'ís died for their beliefs in Turbat-i-Ḥaydarí in Khurásán province. In 1898 a well-known merchant was murdered in Mashhad and his corpse set on fire.

On the death of his father in 1896, Muẓaffari'd-Dín Sháh succeeded to the throne but virtual power was still in the hands of Amínu's-Sulṭán, the reactionary chief minister who had influenced Náṣiri'd-Dín Sháh in the last years of his reign. In those years, Persia was experiencing the stress of contact with the great powers of the West and the new ideas that Westerners had brought with them. There was considerable resentment felt against the foreign powers which exploited the natural resources of the country, in particular the French, British and Russian.

In addition to the nationalist feelings, a movement for constitutional reform began. However, this reform movement in turn called into being a strong reaction from those groups, such as the clergy, whose power was threatened by the very idea of change. In this turbulent atmosphere the Bahá'ís were a most convenient scapegoat against which both sides could vent their fears.

As the movement for reform grew in strength, the reactionaries increasingly accused the Bahá'ís of fomenting and supporting the nationalist and constitutional movements. Economic stress added to the difficulties encountered by the Bahá'ís. Prices of basic commodities rose rapidly. These price rises were keenly resented by the poorer sections of society. The conservative leaders played on the hardships, fears and prejudices of the uneducated masses for their own ends.

In the north of the country, political agitation against the repressive rule of Amínu's-Sultán and the hardships endured by the ordinary people found expression in sporadic attacks on foreigners, Jews and Zoroastrians. Disturbances began in Tabríz and spread to a number of towns. In the south the discontent was stronger and was expressed in direct attacks on the Bahá'ís.

In early May of 1903 disturbances broke out in Rasht but the courage and prompt action of the governor-general of the province prevented them from spreading further. Disturbances began in Isfahán in the same month, instigated by the leading cleric of the city, Shaykh Muhammad-Taqí. This shaykh was addressed by Bahá'u'lláh in His last major work as 'The Son of the Wolf' on account of the ferocity with which he had already attacked the believers. Now a highly respected Bahá'í citizen, aged 80 years old, was brutally murdered. Shaykh Muhammad-Taqí wrote to the leading clerics in the major cities of Persia, urging them to follow his example.

His letter found fertile ground in Yazd. There a newly-appointed Imám-Jum'ih, anxious to consolidate his authority and demonstrate his religious zeal, preached a sermon against the Bahá'ís just one day after his arrival in Yazd. The same day, 13 June, a rabble went on the rampage, attacking and looting Bahá'í homes. So violent was the mob

that the governor of the city could do nothing to protect
the Bahá'ís and on 15 June the first martyrdom occurred.
The next week saw outbreaks of violence in the villages
around Yazd. In the city itself the riot lasted for two weeks.

It was the worst disturbance ever seen in Yazd. On 28
June the clergy of the city declared it to be lawful to seize
the goods of the Bahá'ís. Women and children were appallingly mistreated and left to die of starvation. The governor
only managed to appease the mob by ordering that one
well-known believer be blown from the mouth of a cannon
and the throat of another be slit.

News of the riot was reported in newspapers around the
world. The London *Times* reported that 120 Bahá'ís had
died in Yazd. Certainly the Bahá'ís had not experienced
such persecution since the terrible summer of 1852. Disturbances followed in Ká<u>sh</u>án, Hamadán and Maláyir.

'Abdu'l-Bahá's agony, on hearing of these events, was
intense. For two weeks He was so overwhelmed with grief
that He hardly slept at all. While the persecution raged on,
He sent urgently to Áqá Mírzá Áqá, a nephew of the wife
of the Báb who was living in <u>Sh</u>íráz, requesting him to
restore the House of the Báb. This house had undergone
alterations since the 1840s and there were very few believers other than Áqá Mírzá Áqá who could recall what it had
looked like when the Báb was living there. Áqá Mírzá Áqá
sent to 'Abdu'l-Bahá a plan showing every detail of the
house as it had been in the Báb's lifetime. His plan was
approved and under his close supervision, despite numerous difficulties and considerable danger, the work was
done. Soon after the restoration was complete, Áqá Mírzá
Áqá passed away.

At the very same time, 'Abdu'l-Bahá wrote to the Bahá'ís
of the United States in answer to their petition to construct
their own House of Worship in North America. He encour-

aged them to consult together and challenged the North American believers to achieve deeds that would bring comfort and joy to the hearts of their sorely-oppressed fellow-believers in Persia.

25

Days of Great Trouble

In the Holy Land itself, Mírzá Muḥammad-'Alí and his supporters were still attempting to halt the building work on Mount Carmel. They spared no effort in their attempts to blacken 'Abdu'l-Bahá's name. They had by now contacted the Válí of Beirut, the Muftí of Damascus and the Christian missionaries in Syria and were still seeking to influence the Sulṭán's chief minister, Shaykh Abu'l-Hudá. Yaḥyá Bey, the chief of police in 'Akká, had been influenced by the Covenant-breakers and secret agents were sent by him to Constantinople carrying false reports.

In February of 1903 Mírzá Badí'u'lláh broke with Mírzá Muḥammad-'Alí and declared his loyalty to 'Abdu'l-Bahá. Hearing that the English scholar Edward G. Browne had visited Bahá'u'lláh and learning of Browne's keen interest in the Bahá'í Faith, Mírzá Badí'u'lláh wrote a letter to Browne in 1903. In this letter he states that all accusations made against 'Abdu'l-Bahá were entirely groundless and that Mírzá Muḥammad-'Alí was acting solely out of malice and personal ambition. As it turned out, Mírzá Badí'u'lláh proved unable to stay away from his former associates, the Covenant-breakers, for long.

Some of the believers now urged 'Abdu'l-Bahá to present His own case to the Ottoman authorities and explain the harm being done by the Covenant-breakers. This 'Abdu'l-Bahá refused to do.

In the West, the Bahá'ís in Paris were collecting money and planning to send envoys to Constantinople to secure 'Abdu'l-Bahá's release. As soon as 'Abdu'l-Bahá heard of this plan, He cabled the friends, telling them to drop any such scheme. But news of this plan reached the Covenant-breakers. They were delighted to be handed such a useful weapon. They added their own malicious slant to the story, informing the Válí of Beirut that he would have benefitted financially had 'Abdu'l-Bahá allowed the plan to proceed but that 'Abdu'l-Bahá had called a halt only because He personally disliked the Válí. Naturally, the Válí was angered and his hostility towards 'Abdu'l-Bahá increased.

In 1904, as a direct result of the intrigues of Mírzá Muḥammad-'Alí, the governor of 'Akká, who had shown such respect for 'Abdu'l-Bahá, was removed from his post and a new governor, hostile to the Master, took his place. Once this was achieved, Mírzá Muḥammad-'Alí stirred up fresh ill-feeling amongst certain sections of the city's inhabitants who had expressed hostility towards the Bahá'ís in earlier years. This he did by spreading rumours damaging to 'Abdu'l-Bahá. As a consequence, disturbing articles about the Master were published in certain Egyptian and Syrian newspapers. As a culmination to all of this, Mírzá Muḥammad-'Alí and his accomplices drew up an official indictment against 'Abdu'l-Bahá.

In order to obtain the required signatures for the document, they had to resort to bribery. This indictment, sent to Constantinople, charged that 'Abdu'l-Bahá was inciting a rebellion against Ottoman rule in Palestine and even amongst the Bedouin peoples beyond the Jordan river, that He had accumulated great wealth and had acquired two-thirds of the land in Haifa as a basis for the kingdom He intended to establish. The document also stated that whereas Bahá'u'lláh was no more than a holy man and a

Sunní Muslim, 'Abdu'l-Bahá claimed for Himself the station of prophethood.

Naturally enough, such charges alarmed the Ottoman authorities. They quickly dispatched a Commission of Inquiry to 'Akká to investigate the situation. Spies were set to watch the Master's house and to report on His every movement. Friends and admirers stopped visiting Him.

'Abdu'l-Bahá was extremely concerned for the safety of the believers of 'Akká. By this time there were about a hundred Persian Bahá'ís resident in the prison-city, earning their livelihoods there. 'Abdu'l-Bahá borrowed money from an American believer in Paris and made arrangements for around 70 of these believers to move to Egypt. Those that remained in 'Akká He forbade to gather at His house. He drastically reduced the number of believers invited on pilgrimage and, for a time, He discontinued these visits altogether. He charged His own secretaries to remove all the Bahá'í writings in their possession to a place of safety. His mail He redirected to Egypt and for a while ordered that it all be held there and nothing at all be forwarded to Him in 'Akká.

As His daughter Rúḥá Khánum related to Lua Getsinger in a letter written at this time:

> It is more than three months that our Lord is in great trouble from the government. He is again confined in the City of Acca, one day they say they are going to exile Him to Sudan and the other day they say something else nobody knows what they are going to do, one of the natives who was a believer since our Lord came to Acca, is put in the prison and is severely punished for leaving his own religion and becoming Bahai. Oh dear Lua; it is so difficult for us to see our Lord in such trouble He never had such a difficult time in Acca before even the people of Acca who were friends to Him now getting great enemies, everyone is trying to

hurt Him, and those few who remain friends the governor sent them away from Acca . . .

. . . My mother is still not well she has to be all the
time out of Acca because the climate is not good for
her, and that is not possible for her therefore she is all
the time ill . . .[182]

Munavvar Khánum, another of the Master's daughters,
wrote to Lua that for three entire months nobody came to
see them and nobody spoke to them on the street for fear
of being arrested.

But through all this 'Abdu'l-Bahá continued to direct
the building of the shrine of the Báb on Mount Carmel,
even though He could not Himself visit the site. These
same troubled times saw a steady outpouring of Tablets to
the believers in the East and West. Eyewitnesses have
testified that 'Abdu'l-Bahá often wrote as many as 90
individual letters in one day and that He was frequently
occupied with His vast correspondence throughout the
night, nor did He slacken the pace of His charitable work
amongst the poor and needy of the city.

'Abdu'l-Bahá was summoned to appear before the
Commission. This He did, several times. Each time He
demonstrated to them that the charges were preposterous
fabrications, disposing of each allegation with clear and
logical arguments, delivered with such dignity and eloquence that the falsity of the charges quickly became
evident to all who heard Him. The Commission then
enquired why Americans came to 'Akká. Hasan Balyuzi
gives a stirring account of what followed:

'Abdu'l-Bahá replied that they came to visit the Shrine
of Bahá'u'lláh and to learn of spiritual matters. The
Commission then asked what 'Abdu'l-Bahá had to say
to the charge that He had distributed seditious literature, seen to be in His possession. Such material, He

answered, had not been in His possession and no one could have seen it. The Commission had cajoled, bribed, or forced a number of people to come and give evidence to the contrary. Now these witnesses were mentioned. At that 'Abdu'l-Bahá rose up, majestic and commanding, declared emphatically that no seditious literature could ever have been in His possession, and walked out of the room unhindered. Thereafter the whole enquiry collapsed.[183]

26

A Useful Incarceration

It was also during these troubled times that Laura Clifford Barney, an American believer, began to set down some of the talks that 'Abdu'l-Bahá gave to the pilgrims visiting in His home. These talks grew into the volume *Some Answered Questions* which Laura published with the Master's approval. In her introduction she writes:

> 'I have given to you my tired moments,' were the words of 'Abdu'l-Bahá as He rose from the table after answering one of my questions.
>
> As it was on this day, so it continued; between the hours of work, His fatigue would find relief in renewed activity; occasionally He was able to speak at length; but often, even though the subject might require more time, He would be called away after a few moments; again, days and even weeks would pass, in which He had no opportunity of instructing me. But I could well be patient, for I had always before me the greater lesson – the lesson of His personal life.[184]

The talks given at mealtimes were set down with the help of Dr Yúnis Khán, who acted as a secretary and interpreter for the Master. He has left us this account of one occasion at the Master's table when spiritual nourishment took priority over the food already on the table:

The Master when elucidating the problems used to speak in such a manner that the hearer would be enchanted. One day when He was insisting that I should first eat and then speak, and I was deeply engrossed in the subject under discussion, He asked Laura what was the English for 'mutarjim': she said 'interpreter'. Again he asked what was the word for 'gorosneh'. She said 'hungry'. Thereupon 'Abdu'l-Bahá, pointing at me, exclaimed: 'Hungry interpreter! Hungry interpreter!'

The years of 1905 and 1906 were relatively tranquil for the Master although the Covenant-breakers did not relax their efforts. But in Persia and the Ottoman Empire the movements for reform gained in strength. Ali Kuli Khan came to 'Akká on pilgrimage with his American wife and infant son. They were on their way to Persia where Khan hoped to find employment in the changing conditions of his country. Marzieh Gail, their daughter, published an account of their pilgrimage in *Summon Up Remembrance*.

Marzieh's mother, Bostonian-born Florence Breed, marvelled at 'Abdu'l-Bahá's dazzlingly fresh and crisp appearance, even when He had been out in the town since early morning, visiting the sick and others in need. 'There is ever', Florence wrote,

> His own spiritual radiance and fragrance coming from Him, which one perceives spiritually and which uplifts one's inner being into a heavenly atmosphere of harmony, delight and content . . . His face is astounding, selfless, the stamp of suffering upon it.[185]

Speaking with Khan, who was in great distress at seeing the Master confined to 'Akká, with guards posted outside His house, 'Abdu'l-Bahá said:

This imprisonment is a rest for me. There is no hardship in it . . .

. . . my outside occupations are not even one half what they were. How can I call this a prison? There are roses here, trees, plants, a view of the sea. Besides, it is necessary for a human being to bear hardships, because they train him for higher effectiveness.[186]

On another occasion, He said, to comfort Khan:

For many reasons, this incarceration is useful to me. One reason is that this protects me, for our enemies, finding us imprisoned, will not think of taking other steps to harm us. Besides, after the Blessed Perfection . . . we must delight in being a prisoner, and no other state can do us good and no freedom can give us rest. Our purpose is to serve at the Threshold of the Almighty, whether we be imprisoned or free. If we lived in a King's pleasure dome, surrounded by beatific gardens and meadows, with every means for tranquillity and peace at hand, but news should come that the believers were not on fire with the Faith and were not acting in accord with the laws and the urgent appeals of God – what comfort could all the gilded luxury of such a palace have to offer?[187]

Though 'Abdu'l-Bahá made light of His imprisonment, other entries in Florence's journal reveal the stress of those days. One time:

. . . in one of the little vaulted hallways, Florence met the Master's wife and saw that she was pale and ill . . . Now she wept and said. 'Yes, they send us here to perish, like the flame in the lamp. Our lives go down, down – and all is over.' That evening the Master arranged for His wife to visit a relative in Tiberias, for a change and rest.[188]

Another time Florence awoke during the night to the sound of abysmal groaning. She and Khan occupied the room next to 'Abdu'l-Bahá's own room:

> She listened. The sound was as if it came from one freely abandoning himself to a supposedly unheard sorrow.
>
> 'Never had I listened to such suffering, such grief. What should I do? Should I awaken Khan? Should I send for help?'
>
> Then to her astonishment she recognized the voice of 'Abdu'l-Bahá. She asked herself; 'What superhuman, not-to-be-borne grief was afflicting His radiant spirit? What had hurt Him? Who had failed Him? What were the always-active enemies of the Faith conspiring still further to do?'
>
> He went on sorrowing and grieving, and the wall between their room and His seemed very thin.
>
> 'It came to me, that awed as I was by such massive grief, perhaps I could understand it even so: 'Abdu'l-Bahá's tender heart, lacerated and bowed under, was bearing all the sufferings and sorrows, the sins and disobediences of all humankind.'
>
> After a while the sounds quieted, and she slept.[189]

In the spring of 1907 Corinne True, an American believer, came to the Holy Land as a pilgrim. Writing of her first meeting with the Master, she related:

> I really was not prepared for such a Manifestation of Power. I expected the Love but pictured Abdul Baha as the Christian does the meek humble Nazareen. I found Him to be a powerful Dynamo – A Lion – as well as the Most Majestic Personage I ever hope to see.[190]

In April of the same year Thornton Chase, the first American believer, reached 'Akká as a pilgrim. He has left us a vivid picture of his first meeting with 'Abdu'l-Bahá.

> Some one said, 'The Master!' – and he came into the room with a free, striding step, welcomed us in a clear, ringing voice . . . and embraced us with kisses as would a father his son, or as would brothers after a long absence. It is no wonder that some have thought that the Master loved them more than all others, because he hesitates not to express his love and he truly *loves all humanity in each one* . . .
>
> He bade us be seated on the little divan; he sat on the high, narrow bed at one side of the room, drew up one foot under him, asked after our health, our trip, bade us be happy, and expressed his happiness that we had safely arrived. Then, after a few minutes, he again grasped our hands and abruptly left us . . . our hearts were full of joyful tears, because we were 'at home'. His welcoming spirit banished strangeness, as though we had always known him. It was as if, after long journeyings, weariness, trials and searchings, we had at last reached home.[191]

Of the house of the Master, Thornton Chase wrote:

> The buildings are all of stone, whitewashed and plastered, and it bears the aspect of a prison.
>
> Our windows looked out over the garden and tent of Abdul-Baha on the sea side of the house. That garden is bounded on one side by the house of the Governor, which overlooks it, and on another by the inner wall of fortification. A few feet beyond that is the outer wall upon the sea, and between these two are the guns and soldiers constantly on guard. A sentry house stands at one corner of the wall and garden, from which the sentry can see the grounds and the tent where Abdul-Baha meets transient visitors and the officials who often

call on him. Thus all his acts outside of the house itself are visible to the Governor from his windows and to the men on guard. Perhaps that is one reason why the officials so often become his friends.[192]

27

'In Very Great Danger'

In 1906, amid rising discontent and under pressure from the reformists, Muẓaffari'd-Dín Sháh gave a promise that Persia would have a constitution and an elected national assembly. These events greatly alarmed Sulṭán 'Abdu'l-Ḥamíd, who feared for the loss of his own power. The Covenant-breakers decided to seize this opportunity. They rephrased the charges they had earlier brought against 'Abdu'l-Bahá and forwarded them to Constantinople.

In the winter of 1907 'Abdu'l-Bahá told the Bahá'ís of a dream He had just dreamed. He saw, He related, a ship sailing into the bay of Haifa. Birds resembling sticks of dynamite flew from the ship towards the land, causing panic and terror amongst the people of 'Akká. In His dream 'Abdu'l-Bahá stood among them, without fear, simply watching these birds which circled again and again over the town before flying back to the ship from which they had come. Danger, 'Abdu'l-Bahá said, was imminent but it would pass.

A few days later a new Commission of Inquiry, a party of four led by 'Árif Bey, arrived directly from Constantinople. They had brought with them the documents which the previous Commission had found to be worthless. They chose to stay near Bahjí, at the home of a local notable of 'Akká who was a close associate of the Covenant-breakers, and they made their plans in consort with Mírzá Muḥammad-'Alí and his supporters.

Ignoring the Válí of Damascus, they established a direct link with the Sulṭán's chief ministers in Constantinople. They set spies to watch 'Abdu'l-Bahá's house. They kept a close watch on mail and telegrams going in and out of the city. They put pressure on local people to testify against 'Abdu'l-Bahá. When a local grocer refused to do so, they threw him into gaol. Once again 'Abdu'l-Bahá's friends dared not visit Him. Even the poor were afraid to come near. The town was rife with rumour. 'Abdu'l-Bahá, it was certain, would very soon be exiled to Fízán in Tripolitania, a desert area of the Ottoman Empire, from which He would never return.

All the prominent men in 'Akká paid courtesy calls on the members of the Commission, except 'Abdu'l-Bahá. Many of His admirers urged 'Abdu'l-Bahá to do so. The members of the Commission, they knew, were angry that 'Abdu'l-Bahá had not gone to them. He should visit them, they urged, if only to assure His personal safety. This 'Abdu'l-Bahá categorically refused to do. He had nothing to answer for, He said, and nothing to ask for. If He went and was then acquitted of the charges, it would look as if He had curried favour and obtained an acquittal through bribery.

'During this period', Adib Taherzadeh relates,

the Master remained unperturbed and confident. He continued to write His Tablets to the Bahá'ís of the East and the West, spent some time in planting a few trees in His small garden, and to the astonishment of some notables of 'Akká who considered His banishment to be imminent, was seen to be attending to repairs of His rented house. Their surprise was further intensified when they learned that he had bought and stored fuel for the winter.[193]

<u>Kh</u>alíl Pá<u>sh</u>á, the Válí, furious that his authority had been bypassed by the Commission, now ordered that 'Abdu'l-Bahá be put on trial. The movements of the local Bahá'ís were once again restricted. Some were molested. Visiting Bahá'í merchants from Egypt were not allowed to leave 'Akká. The Spanish Consul, an Italian who lived in Haifa, drove secretly and urgently, at night, to 'Akká to see 'Abdu'l-Bahá. There was an Italian cargo boat anchored in the bay. The Consul offered 'Abdu'l-Bahá a safe passage to anywhere 'Abdu'l-Bahá might wish to go and delayed the ship's departure while he waited for an answer.'Abdu'l-Bahá consulted with a number of the believers as to whether He should accept this offer. They all advised that He leave but 'Abdu'l-Bahá's response was that He would stay. The Báb did not run away, He said, and nor would He.

The members of the Commission were now receiving frequent cables from Sulṭán 'Abdu'l-Ḥamíd. They were very much occupied in taking down evidence gleaned from the very same people who had signed the indictment against 'Abdu'l-Bahá.

It was at some point during these perilous times that 'Abdu'l-Bahá wrote His Will and Testament in which He appointed Shoghi Effendi, His eldest grandchild, then ten years old, as His successor and gave him the title of 'Guardian of the Cause of God'. The Will and Testament was buried secretly, so great was the peril in which 'Abdu'l-Bahá then stood. One paragraph begins:

> O dearly beloved friends! I am now in very great danger and the hope of even an hour's life is lost to me. I am thus constrained to write these lines for the protection of the Cause of God, the preservation of His Law, the safeguarding of His Word and the safety of His Teachings.[194]

In one of the prayers found in the Will and Testament the agony of those days is vividly expressed:

> Lord! My cup of woe runneth over, and from all sides blows are fiercely raging upon me. The darts of afflic-tion have compassed me round and the arrows of distress have rained upon me. Thus tribulation over-whelmed me and my strength, because of the onslaught of the foemen, became weakness within me, while I stood alone and forsaken in the midst of my woes. Lord! Have mercy upon me, lift me up unto Thyself and make me to drink from the Chalice of Martyrdom, for the wide world with all its vastness can no longer contain me.[195]

The perils 'Abdu'l-Bahá faced were not only from the Commission. His half-brothers were conspiring to kill Him. Having stated that He claimed the station of prophethood for Himself, they inferred from this that it would be a worthy deed to put an end to His life, citing as their sup-port the verses written by Bahá'u'lláh which read:

> Whoso layeth claim to a Revelation direct from God, ere the expiration of a full thousand years, such a man is assuredly a lying imposter . . . If, however, he persisteth in his error, God will, assuredly, send down one who will deal mercilessly with him. Terrible, in-deed, is God in punishing.[196]

Adib Taherzadeh relates that:

> In one of His talks the Master is reported to have said that God always assisted the Covenant-breakers during His Ministry and enabled them to make every possible breach in the stronghold of the Cause, so that the Master might stop them all, and thus ensure that others in the future would be unable to do likewise.[197]

In this same period, 'Abdu'l-Bahá sent a Tablet to Ḥájí Mírzá Muḥammad-Taqí, the Vakílu'd-Dawlih, the cousin of the Báb who had raised the House of Worship in 'Is͟hqábád. Of this, Adib Taherzadeh relates:

> In this Tablet He intimates to the Vakílu'd-Dawlih the great dangers which have surrounded His person, and urges him to make arrangements, when and if it becomes necessary, for the election of the Universal House of Justice. To bring this about, He directs him to gather the Afnán and the Hands of the Cause in one place and establish this institution in accordance with the provisions of His Will and Testament.[198]

The members of the Commission were hard at work. One day they all inspected the building work on Mount Carmel. They took particular note of the vaults underneath the strong stone edifice.

'Soon after this visit', Hasan Balyuzi relates,

> they boarded the boat which had brought them from Constantinople and now lay anchored off Haifa. The sun was westering. The boat turned towards 'Akká. The whole populace of the two cities could see it set on this menacing course . . . The family of 'Abdu'l-Bahá and other Bahá'ís were in despair. But 'Abdu'l-Bahá, calm and serene, was walking all alone in the courtyard of His house. Here and there, at vantage points along the shores of 'Akká, anxious Bahá'ís were watching the movement of that boat of ill omen. The sun sank in the Mediterranean, and the boat kept its course. It came very close to 'Akká, but then, all of a sudden, changed direction and made for the open sea . . . When the news was brought to Him dusk had fallen, and He was still walking in His courtyard – with 'radiant acquiescence'.[199]

News came swiftly from Constantinople and it was grave. Sulṭán 'Abdu'l-Ḥamíd had narrowly escaped death. An assassin had planted a bomb on the path he took each Friday when returning, in pomp and circumstance, from his weekly visit to the mosque. The bomb had exploded prematurely. Some people were killed, others injured. When the members of the Commission arrived at Constantinople, a few days later, they found the Sulṭán and his court completely uninterested in the report they had brought from 'Akká. All were preoccupied with seeking out the revolutionaries in and around the capital.

As the weeks and months went by, Sulṭán 'Abdu'l-Ḥamíd became ever more preoccupied by the threat of revolution but he could not stem the rapidly-rising tide. In July 1908, following revolts in Monastir and Salonika, the Young Turks of the Committee of Union and Progress demanded that the Sulṭán restore the constitution he had suspended 30 years earlier or face being forcibly removed. The very next day the Sulṭán complied. At a stroke all the political and religious prisoners in his empire were set free. This naturally included 'Abdu'l-Bahá. But in 'Akká, so intense was the opposition aroused by the Covenant-breakers that the city officials sent a cable to Constantinople enquiring whether this applied to 'Abdu'l-Bahá also. The answer was affirmative.

The long imprisonment was at an end. 'Abdu'l-Bahá had entered the prison-city at 24 years of age. He was now, at 64 years of age, set free.

28

'The Most Joyful Tidings'

'Abdu'l-Bahá had so longed for the freedom to visit His Father's shrine at Bahjí. Now that He was able to visit Bahjí again, He resumed the work of tending to the flower beds He had planted there, close to the shrine. Every Friday and Sunday He would carry water for the plants, even when local officials and dignitaries accompanied Him, sometimes making as many as 60 trips from the nearest water tap to the garden. His physical frame was weak. The stresses of the last decade had affected His health and made Him prey to a number of ailments but this task of watering the garden was precious to Him, bringing Him joy and peace of heart.

Free at last, He was able to fulfil the task which Bahá'u-'lláh had given Him of laying to rest on Mount Carmel the earthly remains of the Báb. As Hasan Balyuzi relates:

On the morning of March 21st 1909, the day of Naw-rúz, 'Abdu'l-Bahá had the marble sarcophagus – gift of the Bahá'ís of Rangoon – carried up the mountain and placed in the vault. That evening He laid in the sar-cophagus the wooden casket which contained the insep-arable remains of the Báb and the disciple who had died with Him. A solitary lamp lit the scene, so poi-gnant and yet so exultant. The Báb had been cruelly maligned, cruelly wronged, cruelly put to death, His torn and smashed body had had no home for many long years. Now the heart of Carmel was receiving it forevermore. Of this event Zechariah had written: 'Thus speaketh the Lord of hosts, saying, Behold the man whose name is The Branch; and he shall grow up out of his place, and he shall build the temple of the Lord' . . .

With 'Abdu'l-Bahá on that same evening, in the vault of the Shrine which He had so hardly reared, were Bahá'ís of both the East and the West. There were veterans of the Faith, who had passed through its darkest days . . .[200]

Shoghi Effendi, who was 12 years old at the time, has written of the events of that evening:

When all was finished, and the earthly remains of the Martyr-Prophet of Shíráz were, at long last, safely deposited for their everlasting rest in the bosom of God's holy mountain, 'Abdu'l-Bahá, Who had cast aside His turban, removed His shoes and thrown off His cloak, bent low over the still open sarcophagus, His silver hair waving about His head and His face transfigured and luminous, rested His forehead on the border of the wooden casket, and, sobbing aloud, wept with such a weeping that all those who were present wept with Him. That night He could not sleep, so overwhelmed was He with emotion.[201]

To the Bahá'ís of the world He wrote:

The most joyful tidings is this, that the holy, the luminous body of the Báb . . . after having for sixty years been transferred from place to place, by reason of the ascendancy of the enemy, and from fear of the malevolent, and having known neither rest nor tranquillity has, through the mercy of the Abhá Beauty, been ceremoniously deposited, on the day of Naw-Rúz, within the sacred casket, in the exalted Shrine on Mt. Carmel . . . By a strange coincidence, on that same day of Naw-

Rúz, a cablegram was received from Chicago, announcing that the believers in each of the American centres had elected a delegate and sent to that city . . . and definitely decided on the site and construction of the Mashriqu'l-Adhkár.[202]

Less than a month later, on 13 April 1909, troops mutinied in Constantinople and in late April Sulṭán 'Abdu'l-Ḥamíd was deposed. He was to remain under close guard until his death nine years later.

A Bahá'í of 'Ishqábád, Áqá Mírzá Ja'far-i-Hadioff, now offered to pay for the construction of a pilgrim house close to the shrine. It was soon built. This house today welcomes pilgrims from all over the world to the shrine of the Báb.

After the entombment of the remains of the Báb, 'Abdu'l-Bahá moved from 'Akká to Haifa where a house was built for Him. Here the climate was far more healthy than in 'Akká but 'Abdu'l-Bahá suffered periodic bouts of illness, sometimes severe. He kept the knowledge of these illnesses from the Bahá'ís but His physician urged Him to travel to a different climate.

In mid-August 1910 'Abdu'l-Bahá went to Egypt. Isabella Brittingham, an American Bahá'í, received a letter from Sydney Sprague about this:

I have a very big piece of news to tell you. Abdul-Baha has left this Holy Spot for the first time in forty-two years, and has gone to Egypt . . . Everyone was astounded to hear of Abdul-Baha's departure, for no one knew until the very last minute that he had any idea of leaving. The afternoon of the day he left, he came to Mírzá Assad Ullah's home to see us and sat with us awhile beside a new well that has just been finished and said that he had come to taste the water. We did not realize that it was a good-bye visit. Then he took a carriage and went up the hill to the Holy Tomb (of the

Bab). That night, as usual, the believers gathered before the house of Abdul-Baha to receive that blessing, which every day is ours, of being in his presence, but we waited in vain, for one of the sons-in-law came and told us that Abdul-Baha had taken the Khedivial steamer to Port Said.[203]

'Abdu'l-Bahá stayed in Port Said for several weeks. Bahá'ís from Cairo visited Him there. Siyyid Asadu'lláh-i-Qumí, a Bahá'í who was to act as 'Abdu'l-Bahá's attendant during His forthcoming travels, relates the following:

> One day he called me to accompany him when taking a walk in the streets of the city. He said: 'Do you realize now the meaning of my statement when I was telling the friends that there was a wisdom in my indisposition?' I answered, 'Yes, I do remember very well.' He continued, 'Well, the wisdom was that I must always move according to the requirements of the Cause. Whatever the Cause requires for its promulgation, I will not delay in its accomplishment for one moment! Now, the Cause did require that I travel to these parts, and had I divulged my intention at that time, many difficulties would have arisen.[204]

After a month at Port Said, 'Abdu'l-Bahá boarded a ship sailing to Europe but was obliged to disembark at Alexandria as it very quickly became evident that His health was not yet good enough for such a strenuous journey. Here, in Alexandria, a remarkable and sudden change occurred. Egyptian and Persian journalists, who had been openly hostile to 'Abdu'l-Bahá on His arrival in Egypt, now began to seek interviews with Him and wrote articles in which they expressed their genuine admiration and respect. The Persian community of Alexandria actually invited 'Abdu'l-Bahá to attend their commemoration of the martyrdom of the Imám Ḥusayn during the month of Muḥarram. Hasan Balyuzi relates:

> He went and was received with every mark of respect. He gave a robe to the reciter of the heart-rending story of Karbilá, rewarding him richly for his talent and devotion. He also left money with the hosts to hold a commemorative meeting on His behalf and to feed the poor.[205]

In November 1910 Wellesley Tudor-Pole, an English admirer, visited 'Abdu'l-Bahá at Ramleh, near Alexandria, and wrote the following to the friends in England:

> Abdul-Baha's health had very greatly improved since his arrival from Port Said. He was looking strong and vigorous in every way. He spoke much of the work in America, to which he undoubtedly is giving considerable thought. He also spoke a good deal about the work that is going forward in different European centres as well as in London and he expects great things from England during the coming year.[206]

'Abdu'l-Bahá was hoping to leave for Europe in the early summer of 1911 but in May He moved to a small town near Cairo. Here, once again, the journalists of the country paid Him attention and accorded Him considerable respect. Here the Muftí of Egypt and the Khedive's principal religious advisor both called on 'Abdu'l-Bahá. He returned their calls. Then the Khedive himself met twice with 'Abdu'l-Bahá and treated Him with particular reverence.

Lord Kitchener too met with Him and was deeply impressed by His personality. Hasan Balyuzi summarizes the last months of the year that 'Abdu'l-Bahá spent in Egypt:

Indeed there were many, clerics, aristocrats, administrators, parliamentarians, men of letters, journalists and publicists, Arabs, Turks and Persians, who sought His presence. The poor and the deprived also had access to Him and went away happy.

His personal triumph resounding in Egypt, 'Abdu'l-Bahá turned His attention to Europe. On August 11th 1911, He boarded S.S. *Corsica*, bound for Marseilles.[207]

29

From Egypt to Britain

From Marseilles, 'Abdu'l-Bahá travelled to Thonon-Les-Bains on the southern shore of Lake Geneva. There he rested for some days. Horace Holley, an American Bahá'í, has left us this memorable account of entering the presence of 'Abdu'l-Bahá at Thonon-Les-Bains:

> I saw among them a stately old man, robed in a cream-coloured gown, his white hair and beard shining in the sun. He displayed a beauty of stature, an inevitable harmony of attitude and dress I had never seen nor thought of in men. Without having ever visualized the Master, I knew that this was He. My whole body underwent a shock. My heart leaped, my knees weakened, a thrill of acute, receptive feeling flowed from head to foot. I seemed to have turned into some most sensitive sense-organ, as if eyes and ears were not enough for this sublime impression. In every part of me I stood aware of 'Abdu'l-Bahá's presence. From sheer happiness I wanted to cry – it seemed the most suitable form of self-expression at my command. While my own personality was flowing away, a new being, not my own assumed its place. A glory, as it were from the summits of human nature poured into me, and I was conscious of a most intense impulse to admire . . . 'Abdu'l-Bahá answered questions and made frequent observations on religion in the West. He laughed heartily from time to time – indeed, the idea of asceticism or useless misery of any kind cannot attach itself to this fully-developed

personality. The divine element in Him does not feed at the expense of the human element, but appears rather to vitalize and enrich the human element by its own abundance, as if He had attained His spiritual development by fulfilling His social relations with the utmost ardour . . .[208]

From Thonon-Les-Bains the Master travelled to Britain, reaching London on 4 September 1911. Hippolyte and Laura Clifford Dreyfus-Barney had come from Paris to assist with translation from Persian to English. Lady Blomfield had prepared for the Master her home at 97 Cadogan Gardens 'in the hope that He might deign to sojourn there awhile'.[209] She has left us a vivid picture of His arrival:

He arrived, and who shall picture Him?

A silence as of love and awe overcame us, as we looked at Him; the gracious figure, clothed in a simple white garment, over which was a light-coloured Persian 'abá; on His head He wore a low-crowned táj, round which was folded a small, fine-linen turban of purest white; His hair and short beard were of that snowy whiteness which had once been black; His eyes were large, blue-grey with long, black lashes and well-marked eyebrows; His face was a beautiful oval with warm, ivory-coloured skin, a straight, finely-modelled nose, and firm, kind mouth. These are merely outside details by which an attempt is made to convey an idea of His arresting personality.

His figure was of such perfect symmetry, and so full of dignity and grace, that the first impression was that of considerable height. He seemed an incarnation of loving understanding, of compassion and power, of wisdom and authority, of strength, and of a buoyant youthfulness, which somehow defied the burden of His years; and such years!

One saw, as in a clear vision, that He had so wrought
all good and mercy that the inner grace of Him had
grown greater than all outer sign, and the radiance of
this inner glory shone in every glance, and word, and
movement as He came with hands outstretched.[210]

'Abdu'l-Bahá's first words in that house were, 'I am very
much pleased with you all. Your love has drawn me to
London. I waited forty years in prison to bring the Message
to you. Are you pleased to receive such a guest?'[211]

It was the custom at that time, in homes such as Lady
Blomfield's, to serve a large number of courses at dinner,
particularly when guests were present. After His first
dinner there, 'Abdu'l-Bahá said, 'The food was delicious
and the fruit and flowers were lovely, but would that we
could share some of the courses with those poor and
hungry people who have not even one.'[212]

At once, it was agreed by all present that

one substantial, plentiful dish, with salad, cheese,
biscuits, sweetmeats, fruits, and flowers on the table,
preceded by soup and followed by coffee or tea, should
be quite sufficient for any dinner. This arrangement
would greatly simplify life, both as to cookery and
service, and would undeniably be more in accordance
with the ideals of Christianity than numerous dishes
unnecessary and costly.[213]

'Abdu'l-Bahá had come to London with a secretary, Mírzá
Mahmúd, and one servant named Khusraw. Lady
Blomfield describes His daily routine:

He rose very early, chanted prayers, took tea, wrote
Tablets, and dictated others. He then received those
who flocked to see Him, some arriving soon after dawn,

patiently waiting on the door-steps until the door would be opened for their entrance.[214]

Oh, these pilgrims, these guests, these visitors! Remembering those days, our ears are filled with the sound of their footsteps – as they came from every country in the world! Every day, all day long, a constant stream . . .

Ministers and missionaries, Oriental scholars and occult students, practical men of affairs and mystics, Anglican-Catholics and Nonconformists, Theosophists and Hindus, Christian Scientists and doctors of medicine, Muslims, Buddhists, and Zoroastrians. There also called: politicians, Salvation Army soldiers, and other workers for human good, women suffragists, journalists, writers, poets, and healers, dressmakers and great ladies, artists and artisans, poor workless people and prosperous merchants, members of the dramatic and musical world, these all came; and none were too lowly, nor too great, to receive the sympathetic consideration of this holy Messenger . . .[215]

The Reverend R. J. Campbell, a liberal-minded minister, invited 'Abdu'l-Bahá to address his congregation at the City Temple church in central London. 'Abdu'l-Bahá had never given a public address anywhere. He opened with these words:

O noble friends; seekers after God!
Praise be to God! Today the light of Truth is shining upon the world in its abundance; the breezes of the heavenly garden are blowing throughout all regions; the call of the Kingdom is heard in all lands, and the breath of the Holy Spirit is felt in all hearts that are faithful. The Spirit of God is giving eternal life. In this wonderful age the East is enlightened, the West is fragrant, and everywhere the soul inhales the holy perfume.[216]

In His brief address, 'Abdu'l-Bahá brilliantly summarized the heart of the Bahá'í message in words of joyous exultation:

> The sea of the unity of mankind is lifting up its waves with joy, for there is real communication between the hearts and minds of men . . .
>
> This is a new cycle of human power . . . You are loosed from ancient superstitions which have kept men ignorant . . .
>
> The gift of God to this enlightened age is the knowledge of the oneness of mankind and of the fundamental oneness of religion. War shall cease between nations, and by the will of God the Most Great Peace shall come . . .
>
> There is one God; mankind is one; the foundations of religion are one. Let us worship Him, and give praise for all His great Prophets and Messengers who have manifested His brightness and glory.[217]

Before leaving the City Temple 'Abdu'l-Bahá was invited to write in the pulpit Bible. The words He wrote read, when translated:

> This book is the Holy Book of God, of celestial Inspiration. It is the Bible of Salvation, the noble Gospel. It is the mystery of the Kingdom and its light. It is the Divine Bounty, the sign of the guidance of God – Abdul-Baha Abbas.[218]

On 17 September, at the invitation of Archdeacon Wilberforce, 'Abdu'l-Bahá addressed the congregation of St John's, Westminster. The journal *The Christian Commonwealth* reported in its issue of 20 September:

All eyes were fixed on the leader of the Bahai movement. In his customary Eastern robe and headdress,
walking hand in hand with a leader of the West . . .

Down the aisle they passed to the bishop's chair,
which had been placed in front of the altar for Abdul
Baha. Standing at the lectern, Archdeacon Wilberforce
introduced the 'wonderful' visitor. He told of his life in
prison, of his sufferings and bravery, of his self-sacri-
fice, of his clear and shining faith . . . Then Abdul Baha
rose. Speaking very clearly, with wonderful intonations
in his voice and using his hands freely, it seemed to
those who listened almost as if they grasped his meaning, though he spoke in Persian . . .[219]

Both these churches were bombed in the Second World
War. The City Temple suffered a direct hit, was destroyed
and has been rebuilt.

The Lord Mayor of London invited 'Abdu'l-Bahá to call
on him at the Mansion House, which He did. He visited
a settlement of working women in Byfleet, a village in
Surrey. He spent a weekend in Bristol, staying at the
Clifton Guest House. There a reception was held for Him.
Around 90 prominent citizens of Bristol attended and
heard Him speak. He visited the home of Mr and Mrs
Jenner near Richmond Park and delighted in the green-
ness He saw there.

On 29 September He spoke to a gathering of 460
people invited by Lady Blomfield to bid Him farewell in
the hall of Passmore Edwards' Settlement in Tavistock
Place. He once again clearly and cogently spoke of Bahá'u-
'lláh:

His mission was to change ignorant fanaticism into
Universal love, to establish in the minds of his followers
the basis of the unity of humanity and to bring about
in practice the equality of mankind . . .

As the East and the West are illumined by one sun, so all races, nations, and creeds shall be seen as the servants of the One God. The whole earth is one home, and all peoples, did they but know it, are bathed in the oneness of God's mercy.[220]

'Abdu'l-Bahá's last public address of this visit was given to the Theosophical Society on 30 September. His departure was arranged for the morning of 3 October. Lady Blomfield relates of that morning:

'Abdu'l-Bahá sat calmly writing. We reminded Him that the hour to leave for the train was at hand. He looked up, saying: 'There are things of more importance than trains,' and He continued to write.

Suddenly in breathless haste a man came in, carrying in his hand a beautiful garland of fragrant white flowers. Bowing low before the Master, he said:

'In the name of the disciples of Zoroaster, The Pure One, I hail Thee as the "Promised Sháh Bahrám"!'

Then the man, for a sign, garlanded 'Abdu'l-Bahá, and proceeded to anoint each and all of the amazed friends who were present with precious oil, which had the odour of fresh roses.

This brief but impressive ceremony concluded, 'Abdu'l-Bahá, having carefully divested Himself of the garland, departed for the train.[221]

30

First Visit to France

'Abdu'l-Bahá reached Paris on 3 October. Hippolyte and Laura Dreyfus-Barney had found for Him a spacious, sunny apartment at 4 Avenue de Camoëns. From this avenue a flight of steps led to the Trocadero Gardens. Here, Lady Blomfield relates:

> . . . the Master often took solitary, restful walks. Sheltered in this modern, comfortable, Paris flat, He Whom we revered, with a secretary, servitors, and a few close friends, sojourned for an unforgettable nine weeks.[222]

Every morning 'Abdu'l-Bahá spoke to those who sought His presence. He spoke in Persian and His words were translated into French by Hippolyte and Laura Dreyfus-Barney. Lady Blomfield, with her two daughters and Miss Beatrice Marion Platt, had travelled from London to Paris and stayed there throughout His visit. Together they took down the addresses that He gave in Paris. The Master requested them to prepare an English version of these talks for publication and their compilation *Paris Talks* was published in London in 1912.

'The words of 'Abdu'l-Bahá can be put on to paper,' Lady Blomfield has written:

> but how describe the smile, the earnest pleading, the loving-kindness, the radiant vitality, and at times the

awe-inspiring authority of His spoken words? The
vibrations of His voice seemed to enfold the listeners
in an atmosphere of the Spirit and to penetrate to the
very core of being.[223]

The groups of people to whom 'Abdu'l-Bahá spoke were
more varied than those He had addressed in London. Paris
was, at that time, a very cosmopolitan city, a Mecca for
artists and a centre of intellectual thought. In addition,
there were many who had fled their own lands for various
reasons and were living in exile in Paris, amongst them a
number of Persians, formerly prominent in their homeland. Lady Blomfield describes those who came to see
'Abdu'l-Bahá as being:

> . . . of all nationalities and creeds, from the East and
> from the West, including Theosophists, agnostics,
> materialists, spiritualists, Christian Scientists, social
> reformers, Hindus, Súfís, Muslims, Buddhists, Zoroas-
> trians, and many others. Often came workers in various
> humanitarian societies, who were striving to reduce the
> miseries of the poor.[224]

One such was a man who had worked in equatorial Africa.
'O 'Abdu'l-Bahá,' he said,

> I have come from the French Congo, where I have been
> engaged in mitigating the hardships of some of the
> natives. For sixteen years I have worked in that country.

'Abdu'l-Bahá replied, 'It was a great comfort to me in the
darkness of my prison to know the work which you were
doing.'[225]

Horace Holley, who was present both in London and
in Paris that year, commented that 'As London emphasized
the social and spiritual aspects of Bahaism, so Paris re-

vealed its intellectual content and unparalleled power of definition.'[226]

It was in Paris that 'Abdu'l-Bahá said, when speaking of the relationship between science and religion:

> There is in existence a stupendous force, as yet, happily, undiscovered by man. Let us supplicate God, the Beloved, that this force be not discovered by science until spiritual civilization shall dominate the human mind. In the hands of men of lower material nature, this power would be able to destroy the whole earth.[227]

In Paris, as elsewhere, 'Abdu'l-Bahá counselled those He addressed to have faith and to work for harmony amongst the nations:

> Lift up your hearts above the present and look with eyes of faith into the future! Today the seed is sown, the grain falls upon the earth, but behold the day will come when it shall rise a glorious tree and the branches thereof shall be laden with fruit. Rejoice and be glad that this day has dawned, try to realize its power, for it is indeed wonderful![228]

In this most cosmopolitan of cities 'Abdu'l-Bahá laid great emphasis on kindliness, in particular to those who were away from their own native countries:

> Let not conventionality cause you to seem cold and unsympathetic when you meet strange people from other countries . . . Be kind to the strangers . . .
>
> Help to make them feel at home . . . ask if you may render them any service . . .
>
> What profit is there in agreeing that universal friendship is good, and talking of the solidarity of the human race as a grand ideal? Unless these thoughts are translated into the world of action, they are useless.[229]

Lady Blomfield relates that a Japanese ambassador to one of the European capitals was staying at the Hotel d'Jéna. Both he and his wife had learnt of 'Abdu'l-Bahá's presence in Paris. The ambassador's wife was anxious to meet the Master but was leaving Paris the next morning and, on account of a severe cold, was unable to leave the hotel. Lady Blomfield recounts:

> This was told to the Master, Who had just returned after a long, tiring day.
> 'Tell the lady and her husband that, as she is unable to come to me, I will call upon her.'[230]

This He proceeded to do, although it was already late, cold and raining. He brought joy to all and remained to speak with them of current world problems for more than an hour. The friends present marvelled that He, who had spent His life in the prison-city of 'Akká, had such an understanding of world issues and the power to state the appropriate solutions so simply.

One day Lady Blomfield received a letter threatening harm to 'Abdu'l-Bahá if He visited 'a certain country, for which I understand He proposes to set forth in the near future'.[231] When Lady Blomfield showed 'Abdu'l-Bahá this letter and expressed her fears for His safety, He smiled at her and replied:

> My daughter, have you not yet realized that never, in my life, have I been for one day out of danger, and that I should rejoice to leave this world and go to my Father?[232]

He then comforted her, assuring her and the other friends that such enemies had no power over His life but only that which was given them by God. Thus, when a group of

Bahá'ís were threatened in the nearby gardens by a sinister-looking man, they calmly told him, 'The Power that protects the Master protects also His other servants. Therefore we have no fear.'[233]

The man left and did not trouble them again.

A number of church leaders came to meet with 'Abdu'l-Bahá, some earnestly enquiring, others with minds already closed.

'One afternoon,' Lady Blomfield relates,

> a party of the latter type arrived. They spoke words of bigotry, of intolerance, of sheer cruelty in their bitter condemnation of all who did not accept their own particular dogma . . .
>
> The heart of 'Abdu'l-Bahá was saddened by this interview, which had tired Him exceedingly. When He referred to this visit there was a look in His eyes as if loving pity were blended with profound disapproval . . . Then He uttered these words in a voice of awe-inspiring authority:
>
> 'Jesus Christ is the Lord of Compassion, and these men call themselves by His Name! *Jesus is ashamed of them!*'
>
> He shivered as if with cold, drawing His *'abá* about Him, with a gesture as if sternly repudiating their misguided outlook.[234]

'Abdu'l-Bahá spoke in the homes of the Bahá'ís, at the Theosophist headquarters, at *L'Alliance Spiritualiste*, and to the congregation of Pastor Wagner's church. It was perhaps on His return from this church that, as Lady Blomfield recounts, He encountered a boisterous crowd in this very poor quarter of Paris:

> . . . amongst them a big man brandishing a long loaf of bread in his hand, shouting, gesticulating, dancing.

Into this throng walked 'Abdu'l-Bahá . . . The boisterous man with the loaf, suddenly seeing Him, stood still. He then proceeded to lay about him lustily with his staff of life, crying 'Make way, make way! He is my Father, make way!' The Master passed through the midst of the crowd, now become silent and respectfully saluting Him. 'Thank you, my dear friends, thank you,' He said, smiling round upon them.[235]

At His last meeting, held at 15 Rue Greuze, on 1st December 'Abdu'l-Bahá said:

The only real difference that exists between people is that they are at various stages of development . . . but one and all are the children of God. Love them all with your whole heart; no one is a stranger to the other, all are friends . . .

I in the East, and you in the West, let us try with heart and soul that unity may dwell in the world, that all the peoples may become one people, and that the whole surface of the earth may be like one country – for the Sun of Truth shines on all alike.[236]

The next day, 2 December, 'Abdu'l-Bahá left for Egypt.

Section V
1912

Howard Colby Ives

31

'The Utmost Longing
and Yearning to See You'

'Abdu'l-Bahá spent the winter in Egypt. He was physically
exhausted after visiting Britain and France but He was
already planning to start on a much more strenuous journey just as soon as He could regain His strength.

The Bahá'ís in North America were beseeching Him to
visit them. They raised £3,200 and sent Him the money.
They suggested that He might cross the Atlantic on the
Titanic, shortly to embark on her maiden voyage. 'Abdu'l-
Bahá returned their money and chose a smaller and slower
boat.

On 25 March He left Alexandria on the S.S. *Cedric*.
Shoghi Effendi, then 15 years old, was with Him. The ship
docked at Naples. Italian physicians there pronounced that
Shoghi Effendi and two of 'Abdu'l-Bahá's personal attendants were suffering from eye infections. This, the doctors
stated, disqualified them from entry into the United States.
They were obliged to return to Egypt.

On 11 April the *Cedric* docked in New York. Many
Bahá'ís had gathered at the dock. Amongst them was the
artist Juliet Thompson. She relates:

> The ship docked, but the Master did not appear. Sud-
> denly I had a great glimpse. In the dim hall beyond the
> deck, striding to and fro near the door, was One with

a step that shook you! Just that one stride, charged with
power, the sweep of a robe, a majestic head, turban
crowned – that was all I saw . . .[237]

'Abdu'l-Bahá requested the Bahá'ís to leave, promising
to meet them in the afternoon. On board He met with
press reporters who asked Him why He had come to
America. 'Abdu'l-Bahá replied that He had come to promote the establishment of universal peace and the oneness
of mankind. He wished to meet those in America who were
working for the cause of peace.

The Master chose to stay, at His own expense, at the
Hotel Ansonia. As in Britain and France, He refused to
accept any money from the believers and never requested
donations, nor would He accept any costly gifts that were
offered to Him. That same afternoon He met the Bahá'ís
at the home of Mr and Mrs Edward B. Kinney. Once again,
in the words of Juliet Thompson, we can catch a glimpse
of that occasion:

> . . . He was sitting in the centre of the dining room
> near a table strewn with flowers . . . At His knees stood
> the Kinney children, Sanford and Howard, and His
> arms were around them. He was very white and shin-
> ing. No words could describe His ineffable peace. The
> people stood about in rows and circles: several hundred
> in the big rooms, which all open into each other . . . We
> made a dark background for His Glory . . . Divinely He
> turned His head from one child to the other, one group
> to another . . . The very essence of compassion, the
> most poignant tenderness is in that turn of the head.[238]

The Master began His address with these words:

> After arriving today, although weary with travel, I had
> the utmost longing and yearning to see you and could

not resist this meeting. Now that I have met you, all my weariness has vanished, for your meeting is the cause of spiritual happiness.[239]

'Abdu'l-Bahá's first public address in New York was given at the Church of the Ascension on 14 April. The church was packed. There He spoke of the urgent need for international unity and conciliation.

On 19 April He spoke at Columbia University and the same night He visited the Bowery Mission where He spoke to about four hundred of the city's poorest, homeless people. 'Tonight I am very happy, for I have come here to meet my friends,' He began. 'I consider you my relatives, my companions; and I am your comrade.'[240]

He told them how Bahá'u'lláh had lived for two years, poor and homeless, in Iraq and that He often referred to Himself as *Darvísh*, which means 'the Poor One' and that He had been very proud of this title. After 'Abdu'l-Bahá's short address He stood at the doorway, shaking hands with each one of His listeners and placing a coin or two into each palm.

'Assuredly give to the poor!' He said later that evening, back in the Hotel Ansonia. 'If you give them only words, when they put their hands into their pockets they will find themselves none the richer for you.' He gave to a chambermaid the coins that remained. When she heard what 'Abdu'l-Bahá had been doing with the rest of the money, she said, 'I will do the same with this money. I too will give it.'[241]

On 20 April 'Abdu'l-Bahá travelled by train to Washington DC. There a wealthy believer, Mrs Agnes Parsons, had built a house in anticipation of His visit to that city. 'Abdu'l-Bahá had wished to stay in a rented house but, unwilling to disappoint Mrs Parsons, He agreed that He and one interpreter should stay in her house while the rest of His party occupied the rented house. The very same evening of the day He reached Washington, 'Abdu'l-Bahá spoke at the Orient-Occident-Unity Conference which was held at the Public Library Hall.

'May this American democracy,' He said, 'be the first nation to establish the foundation of international agreement. May it be the first nation to proclaim the universality of mankind. May it be the first to upraise the standard of the "Most Great Peace" . . .'[242]

Mrs Parsons spoke with 'Abdu'l-Bahá of a beloved artist friend who had lost his life in the *Titanic* disaster. 'Abdu'l-Bahá told her:

> Where one has been devoted to his work in life – art, or whatever it may be, it is regarded as worship and he is undoubtedly surrounded by the mercy of God.

'Abdu'l-Bahá then added:

> If one does you a service and at some other time a wrong, overlook the one for the other – think only of the good.[243]

He spoke to many groups, to Theosophists, to the Universalist Church, to students and faculty at Howard University, a leading African-American institution, to name but a few. On some days He had three or more separate engagements.

On 24 April, at the home of Mrs Andrew J. Dyer, He spoke these words:

> When the racial elements of the American nation unite in actual fellowship and accord, the lights of the oneness of humanity will shine, the day of eternal glory and bliss will dawn, the spirit of God encompass, and the divine favours descend . . . This is the blessing and

benefit of unity; this is the outcome of love. This is the sign of the Most Great Peace; this is the star of the oneness of the human world. Consider how blessed this condition will be. I pray for you and ask the confirmation and assistance of God in your behalf.[244]

Late one evening, He was invited by Alexander Graham Bell, the inventor of the telephone, to visit his home. He had already given three addresses that day in different locations. 'He was wonderfully exhilarated,' Hasan Balyuzi recounts:

> ... His voice could be heard, loud and clear, exclaiming: 'O Bahá'u'lláh! What hast Thou done! O Bahá'u-'lláh! May my life be sacrificed for Thee! O Bahá'u'lláh! May my soul be offered up for Thy sake! How full were Thy days with trials and tribulation! How severe the ordeals Thou didst endure! How solid the foundations Thou has finally laid, and how glorious the banner Thou didst hoist!'[245]

The next day a dinner party was given in His honour by the Turkish ambassador, Yúsuf Díyá Páshá. The ambassador referred to 'Abdu'l-Bahá as 'the Unique One of the age, who had come to spread His glory and perfection amongst us'. The Master's response was, 'I am not worthy of this.'[246]

During His stay in Washington 'Abdu'l-Bahá met with Theodore Roosevelt and on 27 April He had lunch with Lee McClung, the Treasurer of the United States. The same evening Mrs Parsons held a farewell reception for Him at her home. Three hundred of the capital's most distinguished citizens were present. The next morning, the day on which 'Abdu'l-Bahá was to leave Washington, a number of foreign ambassadors called on Him, amongst them James Bryce, the British Ambassador.

Mrs Parsons wished to provide 'Abdu'l-Bahá with a large sum of money to help pay some of the expenses He would incur travelling further west. 'Abdu'l-Bahá declined her offer and suggested that she give the money to the poor. As the train carried Him swiftly towards Chicago through green and beautiful countryside, 'Abdu'l-Bahá sorrowed that His Father had been shut away for so long from the verdant countryside and open spaces.

It was night when the train reached Chicago, a city especially dear to 'Abdu'l-Bahá's heart, for it was here that the call of Bahá'u'lláh had first been raised on the North American continent. A large number of Bahá'ís waited to greet the Master at the railway station. The convention of the Bahá'í Temple Unity had been convened in Chicago and was due to end its deliberations on the following day.

The next morning, 30 April, 'Abdu'l-Bahá first spoke at length to a group of journalists. He then addressed an interracial gathering at Hull House. Later He spoke at the fourth annual conference of the National Association for the Advancement of Colored People at Handel Hall. Finally, He addressed the Bahá'ís gathered for the concluding session of the convention of the Bahá'í Temple Unity. Besides this, He met both individuals and groups of people at His hotel.

The next morning He laid the foundation-stone of the Mother Temple of the West at Wilmette, on the shores of Lake Michigan. The stone He chose as the foundation-stone was a large stone brought to the site with great effort and difficulty by Mrs Nettie Tobin, a believer who had no money to spare and nothing else to offer.

At the ceremony, 'Abdu'l-Bahá said:

Thousands of Mashriqu'l-Adhkárs, dawning-points of praise and mention of God for all religionists will be built in the East and in the West, but this, being the first one erected in the Occident, has great importance.[247]

Day after day 'Abdu'l-Bahá spoke and visited and received visitors, showering upon all His tender love. Some followed Him, from meeting to meeting, in their cars. On 5 May, 'Abdu'l-Bahá said farewell to the Bahá'ís of Chicago with these words:

> Be in perfect unity. Never become angry with one another. Let your eyes be directed toward the kingdom of truth and not toward the world of creation. Love the creatures for the sake of God and not for themselves . . . Humanity is not perfect. There are imperfections in every human being, and you will always become unhappy if you look toward the people themselves . . . Therefore do not look at the shortcomings of anybody: see with the eye of forgiveness. The imperfect eye beholds imperfections. The eye that covers faults looks toward the Creator of souls.[248]

It was 6 May when 'Abdu'l-Bahá left Chicago. He spent one night in Cleveland and one in Pittsburgh. He then took a train back to Washington. It was a twelve-hour journey. His attendants urged Him to occupy a compartment alone so that might get some rest but He would not consent.

Back in Washington He stayed in a rented house near Mrs Parsons's residence. On 11 May He took the train to New York where an apartment had been rented for Him on Riverside Drive. That same afternoon He met with the believers there and told them:

> It is only three weeks that we have been away from the New York friends, yet so great has been the longing to see you that it seems like three months. We have had no rest by day or night since we left you; either travel-

ling, moving about or speaking; yet it was all so pleasantly done and we have been most happy. Praise be to God! everywhere and all the time it has been 'harakat', 'harakat', 'harakat' ('motion', 'motion', 'motion') . . .[249]

32

Laying a Strong Foundation

The next day, though greatly fatigued, 'Abdu'l-Bahá went to Montclair, New Jersey, to give an address and then spoke at a church in New York that same evening. The following day He was so exhausted that He had to stay in bed all day but insisted on attending an evening reception in His honour organized by the New York Peace Society. He told Juliet Thompson, who urged Him to remain in bed:

> 'I work by the confirmations of the Holy Spirit. I do not work by hygienic laws. If I did,' He laughed, 'I would get nothing done.'[250]

As chief speaker at the event, He told his listeners that there is no greater glory in this day than service to the cause of peace and that:

> The powers of earth cannot withstand the privileges and bestowals which God has ordained for this great and glorious century. It is a need and exigency of the time. Man can withstand anything except that which is divinely intended and indicated for the age and its requirements.[251]

Next He attended a Conference on Peace and Arbitration held at Lake Mohonk and spoke there. Back in New York He spoke to two church congregations on one day. His second address was given at the invitation of Howard Colby Ives, then pastor of the Brotherhood Church.

' . . . there was in that hall that evening', Colby Ives has written, 'an atmosphere of spiritual reality foreign to its past.'[252]

> And as I gazed at the Master as I faced Him from the audience, it was not so difficult to imagine a world transformed by the spirit of divine brotherhood. For He Himself was that spirit incarnate. His flowing 'abá, His creamlike fez, His silvery hair and beard, all set Him apart from the Westerners, to whom He spake. But His smile which seemed to embrace us with an overflowing comradeship; His eyes which flashed about the room as if seeking out each individual; His gestures which combined such authority and humility, such wisdom and humour, all conveyed to me, at least, a true human brotherhood which could never be content with plenty while the least of these little ones had less than enough, and yet still less content until all had that divine plenty only to be bestowed through the breaths of the Holy Spirit . . .[253]

'Trust in the favour of God,' 'Abdu'l-Bahá said that evening.

> Look not at your own capacities, for the divine bestowal can transform a drop into an ocean; it can make a tiny seed a lofty tree. Verily, divine bestowals are like the sea, and we are like the fishes in that sea. The fishes must not look at themselves; they must behold the ocean, which is vast and wonderful. Provision for the sustenance of all is in this ocean; therefore, the divine bounties encompass all, and love eternal shines upon all.[254]

'Abdu'l-Bahá went to Boston, to Cambridge and to Worcester. To the Unitarian Conference in Boston He spoke these words:

> Religion is the outer expression of the divine reality. Therefore, it must be living, vitalized, moving and progressive. If it be without motion and nonprogressive it is without the divine life; it is dead. The divine institutes are continuously active and evolutionary; therefore, the revelation of them must be progressive and continuous. All things are subject to reformation. This a century of life and renewal.[255]

Back in New York on 26 May 'Abdu'l-Bahá kept up the same pace of activity though He was at times extremely fatigued. He was now 70 years old. During a second visit to the Church of the Ascension on 2 June He was asked: 'What relation do you sustain to the Founder of your belief? Are you His successor in the same manner as the Pope of Rome?' 'Abdu'l-Bahá replied:

> I am the servant of Bahá'u'lláh the Founder and in this I glory. No honour do I consider greater than this and it is my hope that I may be confirmed in servitude to Bahá'u'lláh. This is my station.[256]

On 3rd June He went by train to Milford in Pennsylvania and stayed there one night. On the return journey His attendants saw Him weep as He gazed at the beautiful countryside through which the train sped.

'. . . once again', Hasan Balyuzi writes, 'the vivid contrast had forced the memory of His Father's sufferings and deprivations to plunge Him in deep sorrow.'[257]

On 8 June He was travelling again, this time to Philadelphia. Despite extreme fatigue, He spoke there in two churches. The Bahá'ís of Philadelphia were very active in teaching the Faith and all who heard 'Abdu'l-Bahá were most appreciative of His visit. On 11 June He told the Bahá'ís in New York:

> We have just returned from a visit to Philadelphia . . .
> The purpose in these movements here and there is a
> single purpose – it is to spread the light of truth in this
> dark world. On account of my age it is difficult to jour-
> ney. Sometimes the difficulties are arduous, but out of
> love for the friends of God and with desire to sacrifice
> myself in the pathway of God, I bear them in gladness.
> The purpose is the result which is accomplished – love
> and unity among mankind.[258]

In New York 'Abdu'l-Bahá moved to a house on West 78th Street belonging to one of the believers which had been newly rented for Him. Here He was to stay for the remainder of His visit to New York. It was a house whose door, Juliet Thompson states, was open at seven-thirty in the morning, or earlier, and kept wide open till midnight.

Here 'Abdu'l-Bahá spoke every day. Owing to the poor state of His health, Hasan Balyuzi writes:

> Reluctantly He had to institute a system whereby He
> would meet in private only those whom He had not
> previously met, or who had a particularly urgent prob-
> lem. All the rest He would meet together in His
> drawing-room.[259]

Hasan Balyuzi, quoting from the diary of Mírzá Maḥmúd-i-Zarqání, explains that 'Abdu'l-Bahá used to go to the market, with His attendants, to buy needed provisions, that He would Himself cook for His guests and supervise the kitchen arrangements.

Most of the time He had people sitting down at His table for luncheon or for dinner, and on the rare occasions when there was no guest He contented Himself with bread and cheese, so as not to put extra burdens on the members of His retinue.[260]

Besides the daily gatherings, meetings and interviews, He kept up a heavy schedule of visits to churches and groups and to the homes of the Bahá'ís. On 18 June a motion picture film was taken of Him at the MacNutt home. On the following day, 19 June, 'Abdu'l-Bahá made a significant declaration to the friends gathered at His house. He made very clear and explicit His own station as the Centre of the Covenant and named New York the City of the Covenant. Juliet Thompson gives us a glimpse of the Master on that day:

On His way down the stairs from His room He passed Lua and me, where we stood in the third-floor hall. We saw, and felt, as He walked down the upper flight, a peculiar power in His step – as though some terrific Force had possession of Him; a Force too strong to be caged in the body, sparking through, almost escaping His body, able to *sunder* it. I cannot begin to describe that indomitable step, its fearful majesty, or the strange flashing of His eyes. The sublime language of the Old Testament, words such as these: 'Who is *this* that cometh from Bozrah . . . that treadeth the wine-press in His fury?' faintly express what I saw as I watched the Master descending those stairs.[261]

'Abdu'l-Bahá addressed the assembled friends in these words:

To-morrow I wish to go to Montclair. To-day is the last day in which we gather together with you to say farewell to you. Therefore, I wish to expound for you an important question, and that question concerns the Covenant.

In former cycles no distinct Covenant has been made in writing by the Supreme Pen; no distinct personage had been appointed to be the Standard differentiating falsehood from truth, so that whatsoever He was to say was to stand as Truth and that which He repudiated was to be known as falsehood. At most, His Holiness Jesus Christ gave only an intimation, a symbol, and that was but an indication of the solidity of Peter's faith . . .

But in this dispensation of the Blessed Beauty, among its distinction is that He did not leave people in perplexity. He entered into a Covenant and Testament with the people. He appointed a Centre of the Covenant. He wrote with His own pen and revealed it in the Kitab-el-Akdas, the Book of Laws, the Book of the Covenant, appointing Him ('Abdu'l-Bahá) the Expounder of the Book. You must ask Him regarding the meanings of the texts of the verses. Whatsoever He says is correct. And outside of this, in numerous Tablets He (Bahá'u'lláh) has explicitly recorded it, with clear, sufficient, valid and forceful statements. In the Tablet of the Branch He explicitly states, 'Whatsoever the Branch says is right, or correct; and every person must obey the Branch with his life, with his heart, with his tongue. Without His will, not a word shall any one utter.' This is an explicit text of the Blessed Beauty. So there is no rescue left for anybody. No soul shall, of himself, speak anything. Whatsoever His ('Abdu'l-Bahá's) tongue utters, whatsoever His pen records, that is correct, according to the explicit text of Bahá'u'lláh in the Tablet of the Branch.

His Holiness Abraham covenanted with regard to Moses. His Holiness Moses was the Promised One of Abraham, and He covenanted with regard to His Holiness Christ, saying that Christ was the Promised One. His Holiness Christ covenanted with regard to His Holiness 'The Paraclete', which means His Holiness

Mohammed. His Holiness Mohammed covenanted as regards the Báb, whom He called 'My Promised One'. His Holiness the Báb, in all His books, in all His epistles, explicitly covenanted with regard to the Blessed Beauty, Bahá'u'lláh – that Bahá'u'lláh was the Promised One of His Holiness the Báb. His Holiness Bahá'u'lláh covenanted, not that I am the Promised One, but that 'Abdu'l-Bahá is the Expounder of the Book and the Centre of His Covenant, and that the Promised One of Bahá'u'lláh will appear after one thousand or thousands of years. This is the Covenant which Bahá'u'lláh took. If a person shall deviate, he is not acceptable at the Threshold of Bahá'u'lláh. In case of difference, 'Abdu'l-Bahá must be consulted. They must revolve around His good pleasure. After 'Abdu'l-Bahá, whenever the Universal House of Justice is organized, it will ward off differences . . .

I pray for you, and I am pleased with all of you, each one, one by one and I pray that God may aid and confirm you. From Montclair I will come back to you. New York is specialized, because I go away and I come back to it. The friends in New York must appreciate this. At present, farewell to you![262]

Lua Getsinger wrote of that day:

Those present will never forget that day, I am sure. Though He spoke the message very quietly and impressively, it went forth with such a power that I am sure the whole city of New York was affected by it, and I know, without any doubt, that every person present that day was touched with a spirit which in itself was recreative.[263]

On 20 June 'Abdu'l-Bahá went to Montclair. The midsummer heat in the city was oppressive and was affecting His health. He stayed at Montclair for a week, visiting Newark one night and meeting with the Bahá'ís and other visitors

every day. On 29 June He went by train to West Englewood, changing trains four times along the route. He had
invited all the friends from New York and the surrounding
area to be His guests at a Unity Feast held in a grove near
the house of Roy Wilhelm. Well over two hundred people
attended:

'Be happy and joyous', 'Abdu'l-Bahá told them, 'because
the bestowals of God are intended for you and the life of
the Holy Spirit is breathing upon you.'

> May you become as the waves of one sea, stars of the
> same heaven, fruits adorning the same tree, roses
> of one garden in order that through you the oneness
> of humanity may establish its temple in the world of
> mankind, for you are the ones who are called to uplift
> the cause of unity among the nations of the earth.[264]

The next day 'Abdu'l-Bahá was driven to Morristown where
He was invited to lunch at the home of the Persian Consul-
General, Mr Topakyan. There He met a number of distinguished local residents and was afterwards interviewed by
newspaper reporters.

'Abdu'l-Bahá spent three more weeks in New York. He
was determined to lay a strong foundation in that city for
the growth of the Cause. 'I desire', He told friends gathered at His house on 1 July, 'to make manifest among the
friends in America a new light that they may become a new
people, that a new foundation may be established and
complete harmony be realized; for the foundation of
Bahá'u'lláh is love.'[265]

33

New England and Canada

'Abdu'l-Bahá left New York on 23 July for Boston. On His first evening there He spoke at the Hotel Victoria on economics.

> The fundamentals of the whole economic condition are divine in nature and are associated with the world of the heart and spirit . . .
> . . . When the love of God is established, everything else will be realized. This is the true foundation of all economics. Reflect upon it. Endeavour to become the cause of the attraction of souls rather than to enforce minds.[266]

After two days in Boston 'Abdu'l-Bahá went to Dublin, an exclusive summer resort in New Hampshire. The resort was frequented by wealthy intellectuals from Washington DC and other large cities. In describing 'Abdu'l-Bahá's visit there, Howard Colby Ives invites us to:

> Picture, if you can, this Oriental, fresh from more than fifty years of exile and prison life, suddenly placed in an environment representing the proudest culture of the Western world. Nothing in His life, one would reasonably presume, had offered a preparation for such a contact . . .
> How, then, can it be explained that in this environment He not only mingled with these highest products of wealth and culture with no slightest embarrassment

to them or to Him, but He literally outshone them in their chosen field.

No matter what subject was brought up He was perfectly at home in its discussion, yet always with an undercurrent of modesty and loving consideration for the opinions of others.[267]

Mrs Parsons invited 'Abdu'l-Bahá to stay in a large house which she owned on her extensive estate. 'Abdu'l-Bahá accepted her invitation for His attendants, on condition that He would Himself meet all the expenses they incurred. He, however, chose to stay at the Inn, which was lower on the hillside and therefore warmer at night. After a day or two Mrs Parsons arranged a luncheon party at her house. She invited, as Hasan Balyuzi relates:

. . . some twenty people, all outstanding in various walks of life, to meet 'Abdu'l-Bahá. Culture, science, art, wealth, politics, achievement – all were represented. The hostess was eager that 'Abdu'l-Bahá should tell those leaders of society about Bahá'u'lláh and the Faith He had proclaimed to mankind. Probably the guests thought that they were in for a lecture. But 'Abdu'l-Bahá told them a story which made them laugh. He Himself laughed heartily, and again with them when they, encouraged by the lead He had given, also told amusing stories. 'Abdu'l-Bahá and his guests were full of mirth throughout that luncheon. It was 'good to laugh', He told them; 'laughter is a spiritual relaxation'.

At this point He referred to His years in prison. Life was hard, He said, tribulations were never far away, and yet, at the end of the day, they would sit together and recall events that had been fantastic, and laugh over them. Funny situations could not be abundant, but still they probed and sought them, and laughed. Joy was not, He told them, a by-product of material comfort and affluence. Were it so, dejection would have ruled every hour of their lives in those days, whereas their souls were joyful . . . Afterwards He asked His hostess whether she was pleased with Him.[268]

One day a tramp, very shabbily dressed, came along the street while 'Abdu'l-Bahá was dictating to a secretary in the grounds of the Inn. 'Abdu'l-Bahá stopped dictating and asked His secretary to fetch the tramp into the Inn grounds. Mr Balyuzi relates that

> He took the old man's dirt-crusted hands in His, and spoke to him with love and affection. It was as if He had known this weary, dejected tramp all His life. And then He saw how filthy and torn the old man's trousers were. At that hour of the day no one was about. 'Abdu'l-Bahá walked towards the porch of the Inn, wrapped His long-flowing 'abá round Himself, took off His own trousers, gave them to the old tramp, and told him: 'May God go with you.'[269]

Howard Colby Ives paints a memorable picture of a talk which 'Abdu'l-Bahá gave at the Unitarian Church in Dublin:

> What His subject was I do not recall, nor does a single word of His address remain with me. My memory is all of the quiet New England church; the crowded pews, and 'Abdu'l-Bahá on the platform. His cream-coloured robe; His white hair and beard; His radiant smile and courteous demeanour. And His gestures! Never a dogmatic downward stroke of the hand; never an upraised warning finger; never the assumption of teacher to the taught. But always the encouraging upward swing of hands, as though He would actually lift us up with them. And His voice! Like a resonant bell of finest timbre; never loud but of such penetrating quality that

the walls of the room seemed to vibrate with its music.[270]

On His last evening in Dublin 'Abdu'l-Bahá was invited by a friend of Mrs Parsons to dinner. She relates that before dinner was served, their host told a story from India which contained much description of killing. Then one of the guests asked 'Abdu'l-Bahá to tell them a story. Mrs Parsons wrote in her diary:

> I begged for the 'Story of Ios', which is the only story I ever heard of His telling. It is a pretty story with a moral which He of course told well, and the people liked it, but when it was finished He said [:] 'Now let me tell you an Arabian story! It isn't going to be a sermon.' This He did, to the accompaniment of peals of laughter, repeated again and again as climax after climax was reached. Needless to say, Abdul Baha brought out every subtle point in the brilliant story, and the mental picture of this beautiful Oriental telling the story with all the enthusiasm of the story tellers of old, is one never to be forgotten.
>
> On the way home when we were expressing our pleasure in the evening made delightful by Him, He said with the simplicity of a child, 'Now are you all pleased with me?' Oh that drive home! He was so unutterably kind, and made so happy these last moments at Dublin.[271]

From Dublin 'Abdu'l-Bahá went to Green Acre, a conference centre owned by the philanthropist and seeker after truth Sarah Farmer, set on the banks of the Piscataqua River in Maine. Only moments after His arrival 'Abdu'l-Bahá addressed the large crowd which had gathered to welcome Him. He then went to the sanatorium where Sarah Farmer was a patient and she accompanied Him back to Green Acre. 'Abdu'l-Bahá stayed at Green Acre for a week. He gave many talks to the Bahá'ís and spoke with many of the visitors staying at the Green Acre Fellowship. By His own example He demonstrated courtesy and consideration for all, no matter what their beliefs were.

One night a young man arrived at Green Acre. His appearance was, in Juliet Thompson's words, 'horrifying . . . From head to foot he was covered with soot. His blue eyes stared out from a dark gray face.'[272]

The young man was Fred Mortensen. He had spent much of his boyhood and young manhood in prison in Minneapolis where Albert Hall, a Bahá'í lawyer who had defended him, enabled him to obtain parole and told him of the Bahá'í Faith. Fred Mortensen rode the rods of the freight cars all the way from Minneapolis to Green Acre, for he had no money to buy a rail ticket and wanted more than anything in the world to meet 'Abdu'l-Bahá. Soon after Fred arrived at the Inn, where Ahmad Sohrab greeted his grimy appearance with cold distaste, 'Abdu'l-Bahá called for Fred, gave him a most warm welcome and then asked, 'Did you have a pleasant journey?' 'Of all the questions I wished to avoid,' Fred wrote later, 'this was the one!'

> I dropped my gaze to the floor – and again he put the question. I lifted my eyes to his and his were as two black, sparkling jewels, which seemed to look into my very depths. I knew he knew and I must tell, and as I answered I wondered what Ahmad thought – if I was a little unbalanced.
>
>   I answered: 'I did not come as people generally do, who come to see you.'
>   'How did you come?'
>   'Riding under and on top of the railway trains.'
>   'Explain how.'
>   Now as I looked into the eyes of 'Abdu'l-Bahá I saw they had changed and a wondrous light seemed to pour out. It was the light of love and I felt relieved and very

much happier. I explained to him how I rode on the trains, after which he kissed both my cheeks, gave me much fruit, and kissed the dirty hat I wore, which had become soiled on my trip to see him.[273]

When 'Abdu'l-Bahá left Green Acre for Malden, Massachusetts, He ordered Fred Mortensen to get into His automobile. The astonished Fred spent a week travelling with the Master before he left for home.

'The words of Bahá'u'lláh are my food, my drink and my life,' Fred later wrote. 'I have no other aim than to be of service in his pathway and to be obedient to his Covenant . . .'[274]

On His way to Malden 'Abdu'l-Bahá once more visited Sarah Farmer at the Portsmouth Sanitarium. While at Malden He spoke to three gatherings in nearby Boston and from there He headed north to Montreal, in Canada.

'Abdu'l-Bahá took only two attendants, Mírzá Maḥmúd-i-Zarqání and Ahmad Sohrab with Him for His brief visit to Canada. He only had time to visit Montreal and there He stayed at the home of May and Sutherland Maxwell. He arrived there on the evening of 30 August. The next day He was driven around the city and, as Hasan Balyuzi relates:

> . . . sighting the magnificent Roman Catholic Church of Notre Dame, He went in. When He came out, standing in the porch, He turned to those who were in His company and told them to take a lesson from that very church. It was the total self-abnegation of the apostles of Christ which had raised that splendorous edifice in a land far, far from the scene of their labours. Those disciples, said 'Abdu'l-Bahá, made a pact to go out into the wide world, preach the gospel, and accept every tribulation for the sake of their Master. They stood by

their pledge, and not a single one of them ever returned.[275]

On 1 September 'Abdu'l-Bahá spoke in the Church of the Messiah on the topic of the unity of humankind and the unity of religions, stating that with impartial love and wisdom God has sent His prophets and divine teachings, and warning of the dangers of prejudice. His address led to many visitors calling at the Maxwell home that same evening. Mr Balyuzi relates that:

> 'Abdu'l-Bahá spoke to them. So forceful was His speech, so emphatic His movement that His headgear fell off and He made no attempt to replace it. His head bared, His locks scattered round His head, He went on speaking for another half hour. Then He walked, through the thronged assemblage, upstairs to His room. But people could not tear themselves away, and 'Abdu'l-Bahá came back and spoke once again. Even then, there were individuals begging to be received by 'Abdu'l-Bahá in His room, and He received a good many.[276]

'Abdu'l-Bahá moved to the Hotel Windsor the next day but continued to speak at meetings held in the Maxwell home to the end of His stay in Montreal. He addressed two more public gatherings in the city. First He spoke at Coronation Hall to an audience described by *The Gazette*, a Montreal newspaper, as 'a socialistic and cosmopolitan gathering'.[277] To them He spoke on economic happiness and unfolded a scheme for dealing with the superfluous wealth of a nation. At St James Methodist Church He addressed a gathering of twelve hundred people. There He warned of the escalating arms race in Europe and of the necessity of establishing an international tribunal. Newspaper coverage of the Master's visit to Canada was remarkable for both the quantity of paragraphs devoted to His visit and the fine quality of the reporting.

'Abdu'l-Bahá was very weary by this time and was not well enough to leave Montreal as soon as He had planned but on 9 September He took a train to Buffalo. He had to change trains in Toronto and there He took a brief walk around Union Station and spoke to His companions of His great fatigue, wondering, Mr Balyuzi tells us, 'how He could go all the way to California; but go He must, for in the path of God troubles must rank as bounties, and toil as the greatest bestowal.'[278]

34

To the Western States

The believers in Buffalo took 'Abdu'l-Bahá to visit Niagara Falls and urged Him to rest there for a few days. He declined and after only two days in Buffalo He left for Chicago. There He stayed for four days at the home of Mrs Corinne True. Many, many people flocked to the True home to meet Him and on His last day there He spoke to members of the Theosophical Society. From Chicago He visited Kenosha in Wisconsin and on 16 September He left Chicago for Minneapolis. Here He was so exhausted that He could not accept the many invitations to speak that reached Him. He did, however, speak to the Commercial Club and at a Jewish Reform Temple. There He clearly affirmed the truth of the mission of Jesus Christ.

From Minneapolis He went to Lincoln, Nebraska, in order to visit William Jennings Bryan but could meet only with Mrs Bryan and her daughter as Bryan himself was away. Taking the train overnight, 'Abdu'l-Bahá reached Denver in Colorado on the following afternoon. After just two hours' rest 'Abdu'l-Bahá met with reporters and went directly to the home of a Bahá'í where a large gathering awaited Him. The following evening He spoke at the Second Divine Science Church.

'The supreme need of humanity', 'Abdu'l-Bahá said,

is cooperation and reciprocity. The stronger the ties of fellowship and solidarity amongst men, the greater will be the power of constructiveness and accomplishment in all the planes of human activity . . .

My highest hope and desire is that the strongest and most indissoluble bond shall be established between the American nation and the people of the Orient.[279]

After another full day of engagements, and to the great regret of His fellow guests at the Shirley Hotel, 'Abdu'l-Bahá left Denver. Mírzá Maḥmúd-i-Zarqání, the Master's chronicler, wrote of their last evening there:

Those men and women staying at the hotel who because of their wealth and pride had previously not deigned to look at us, now sought us out. Everyone was fascinated by the majesty and grandeur of 'Abdu'l-Bahá and gave their hearts to Him.[280]

'Abdu'l-Bahá travelled by train all the following day and into the night. By the early hours of the morning He was worn out from the constant travel and the jolting of the train along the tracks. At the urging of His attendants 'Abdu'l-Bahá alighted from the train and spent a day at Glenwood Springs. Mr Balyuzi relates:

During the entire eight months of that year 1912 when 'Abdu'l-Bahá travelled and sojourned in America, this September 28th was the only day He could be said to have rested and relaxed. He went to the mineral baths and had His lunch on the spacious lawn of the Colorado Hotel. And even on that day, as He stood by the cool stream and gazed at the verdant mountain, sorrow surged within Him, because He could not put aside the thought of the bleak prison-city and Bahá'u'lláh's incarceration inside its forbidding walls.[281]

While at Glenwood Springs a telegram reached Him telling of the serious deterioration in the condition of Thornton

Chase, already gravely ill in hospital. At midnight He took the train again. The following evening He stopped at Salt Lake City. There He stayed at the Kenyon Hotel and while in the city He ordered flower seeds for the gardens around the shrines in the Holy Land. At midnight on the eve of 1 October He reached San Francisco.

During His visit to that city the Master stayed in a house rented for him on California Street. On the day after He arrived, Dr David Starr Jordan, President of Leland Stanford Junior University, called and invited Him to speak at the university. 'Abdu'l-Bahá's first public address was at a Unitarian church on 6 October and on the following day He spoke at the Japanese Independent Church in Oakland. He spoke at Stanford on 8 October to an audience of over two thousand people. Faculty, students and administrators as well as prominent local leaders gathered to hear Him and the talk He delivered that day was, in Mr Balyuzi's words, 'one of the greatest, most powerful of His ministry'.[282]

Lua Getsinger, who was in the audience, wrote later that same day to Agnes Parsons:

> We have had a most wonderful day with 'Abdu'l-Bahá here. This morning He spoke to fifteen hundred students – introduced by Dr Jordan. His subject was international peace and such splendid attention was paid Him! Not a murmur not a distracting move – during the hour and fifteen minutes that he addressed them. When He finished they cheered and cheered until he arose – and then the *whole audience* rose – and the students gave the college yell! It was perfectly splendid.[283]

After lunching with Dr Jordan, 'Abdu'l-Bahá spent the rest of the day in Palo Alto and gave an address there in the evening at the local Unitarian church. On 10 October He spoke at the Open Forum, a gathering of agnostics and freethinkers, and two days later He spoke to a Jewish congregation of about two thousand, amongst whom were leaders of the Jewish community. He spoke of Abraham and Moses and of the special destiny of the Jewish people. He explained in lucid simplicity that the basic teachings of all the different Messengers of God are in harmony, as all derive from the one source. The secondary teachings, He went on to explain, are subject to change as human society gradually evolves. Then, He declared:

> The basis of the law was promulgated by Christ. That same foundation of religion was promulgated by Muḥammad. Since all the Prophets called on the people to accept this reality, the purpose of all the Prophets has been the same.[284]

'Abdu'l-Bahá spoke boldly and clearly of the divine missions of both Jesus Christ and Muḥammad and at the end there was not a word of dissent. That evening, the Master told the gathered friends that no one had ever before spoken in a synagogue affirming that Jesus Christ was the Word of God and Muḥammad the Messenger of God.

The renowned philanthropist Mrs Phoebe Hearst, who had led the little group of American pilgrims to 'Akká in 1898, came into San Francisco to invite 'Abdu'l-Bahá and His attendants to visit her home near Pleasanton. Mrs Hearst had been sorely wounded by a number of believers who had imposed on her great generosity and she no longer considered herself to be a Bahá'í. However, she had arranged for a large house party of prominent citizens to be her guests so that they might meet with 'Abdu'l-Bahá. The Master accepted her invitation and Mrs Hearst came again on 13 October to escort Him to her home.

In the three days that He spent there, 'Abdu'l-Bahá made no reference to the Faith except at Mrs Hearst's request. On His departure, the Master asked to speak to her large household staff and gave each one a gift of two guineas as a memento of His visit.

While in San Francisco 'Abdu'l-Bahá visited Oakland several times. After one such visit it was found that His signet ring was missing. After this 'Abdu'l-Bahá personally signed every Tablet that He wrote or dictated.

The Master found it necessary to keep a very close eye on some of those in His company, particularly His relative Dr Amínu'lláh Faríd, who was acting as a translator but whose 'erratic and damaging behaviour . . . was causing Him great concern and sorrow'.[285] Dr Faríd was secretly soliciting money from the American friends.

The Bahá'ís of Portland and Seattle longed for 'Abdu'l-Bahá to visit them but the Master, greatly saddened, told them that He could not do this. He had to make haste to return home. War had already broken out in the Balkans and war in Europe was imminent.

In October of that year, Greece, Bulgaria and Serbia and Montenegro buried their differences, fearful that the Young Turks now in power in Constantinople would revive Ottoman strength in the Balkans. They made a joint declaration of war and determined to drive the Turks out of the Balkans. War in the Balkans meant enforced conscription and severe hardships in the Holy Land. Palestine was under the control of the new Turkish government which would use all the resources at its command against the new nations of the Balkans.

'Abdu'l-Bahá had yet to reach Los Angeles, where Thornton Chase had recently passed away. On 18 October the Master travelled to Los Angeles to the cemetery where Thornton Chase, the first American believer, was buried.

He could not, He said, accept any invitations to give addresses. Time was too short. He needed to hurry back to the Holy Land.

The cemetery was outside the city and 'Abdu'l-Bahá took a tram car there. ' Alighting', Mr Balyuzi relates,

> He walked very quietly into the cemetery until He approached the grave of Thornton Chase, when He remarked on the beauty of the surroundings. Then, leaning against a tree, He stood silently before that resting-place of the first Bahá'í of the Christian West. He asked for some flowers and, with great care and loving attention, He arranged them on the grave. Then, still facing the grave, He turned in the direction of 'Akká and chanted the Tablet of Visitation – the Tablet which is read in the Shrines of the Báb and Bahá'u'lláh. Following that, He chanted a prayer for Thornton Chase and spoke of the services which that dedicated man had rendered to the Faith . . . At the conclusion of His visit, 'Abdu'l-Bahá knelt on the ground and kissed the grave of Thornton Chase.[286]

So exhausted was 'Abdu'l-Bahá that night that He could not eat. A throng of people were waiting for Him at His hotel and the next day more came – believers, enquirers and journalists. On the night of 21 October 'Abdu'l-Bahá took the train back to San Francisco. Mrs Helen Goodall had reserved sleeping berths for all the party but 'Abdu'l-Bahá could not sleep; His mind was too occupied. After one final visit to Oakland, 'Abdu'l-Bahá left for a brief visit to Sacramento. There He spoke twice at the Hotel Sacramento.

'Abdu'l-Bahá told those who had gathered to hear Him:

> The issue of paramount importance in the world today is international peace. The European continent is like

an arsenal, a storehouse of explosives ready for igni-
tion, and one spark will set the whole of Europe aflame,
particularly at this time when the Balkan question is
before the world. Even now war is raging furiously in
some places . . . Therefore the greatest need in the
world today is international peace . . . It is time for the
abolition of warfare, the unification of nations and
governments . . . It is time for cementing together the
East and the West.

Inasmuch as the Californians seem peace loving and
possessed of great worthiness and capacity, I hope that
advocates of peace may daily increase among them . . .
May the first flag of international peace be upraised in
this state . . .

. . . Let us cooperate in love and through spiritual
reciprocity enjoy eternal happiness and peace.[287]

35

Farewell to North America

On 26 October 'Abdu'l-Bahá left Sacramento by train for Denver. Here He stayed for only 24 hours but gave two addresses in that time. At midnight He boarded the train for Chicago but would not book a sleeping-berth. The next night, however, He told His attendants that they had endured enough mortification and asked them to book sleepers for the whole party. When His attendants suggested that He alone have a sleeper, 'Abdu'l-Bahá firmly rejected this plan, insisting on equal treatment for all.

On 31 October the Bahá'ís of Chicago met the train and welcomed 'Abdu'l-Bahá to their city for the third time. He stayed again at the Hotel Plaza but could accept very few of the many invitations to speak that now flooded in. His stay was to be a short one. At two of the meetings with the friends He warned of the activities of those who had broken the Covenant of Bahá'u'lláh.

> Bahá'u'lláh has not left any possible room for dissension . . . in this day the Blessed Perfection has declared, 'This person is the Expounder of My Book and all must turn to Him.' The purpose is to ward off dissension and differences among His followers.[288]

On 3 November, His last day in Chicago, 'Abdu'l-Bahá spoke at the hotel in the morning, then spoke at the Englewood Church and at a Congregational church and in the evening attended a farewell Feast in His honour. The next day He took the train for Washington DC, stopping for one night in Cincinnati where the friends had arranged a banquet for Him at the Grand Hotel. After a second address in the hotel the following morning, He took the noon train to Washington. On the evening of the same day He spoke at the Universalist Church.

The war between Turkey and the Balkan confederation was much in His thoughts and on the following day He quoted to the friends a number of the warnings and prophecies Bahá'u'lláh had made about the future of the Ottoman Empire.

'The purpose of these quotations', 'Abdu'l-Bahá explained,

> is to show that Bahá'u'lláh's great endeavour in the East was to unify mankind . . . preparing the way for international peace and establishing the foundations of happiness and welfare . . . But, alas, the commands and guidance of the Blessed One have been neglected and ignored. Day by day they have followed their own devices and imaginations, until now this fire of war is raging most furiously.[289]

On 8 November 'Abdu'l-Bahá spoke at the Eighth Street Temple, affirming the divine origin of Christianity and Islam. Mrs Agnes Parsons was present and has left this account of the evening:

> The Rabbi after much music, gave a long description of a Jewish play depicting the life of the Rothchilds. Abdul Baha then spoke on the oneness of the foundation of spiritual truth, as taught by all the prophets. He spoke first of the wonderful achievement of Abraham, and Moses, gave an extraordinary survey of Jewish history, leading up to the coming of another great

Prophet of God. 'His Holiness Jesus Christ'! This produced a stir among the people, and an effort was made by the Rabbi through Dr F[areed] to stop the address, but Abdul Baha went blandly on, asking for their closest attention. After having finished His message, He went quickly out of the Tabernacle, and the Rabbi arose to make a few closing remarks.

He said[:] 'We are not accustomed here to the mention of other prophets than our own, but people of culture all over the world listen to others with ideas different from their own. They may be right and we may be wrong.' During the latter part of Abdul Baha's address many people left the Church [sic] & many of those who remained were restless. It was a very wonderful demonstration of the power of God that Abdul Baha was able to stay and finish His message.[290]

The next day the Rabbi called on 'Abdu'l-Bahá and spent a long time with Him going over the same ground. At the end, as Mr Balyuzi relates, the Rabbi commented, 'I believe that what you have said is perfectly true, but I must ask one thing of you. Will you not tell the Christians to love us a little more?'

'Abdu'l-Bahá replied that He had advised them to do so and would continue to give this counsel.[291]

On 9 November a banquet attended by about three hundred was held at Rauscher's Hall where 'Abdu'l-Bahá presented flowers and sweets to each table and then spoke words of love and encouragement to the guests. Among His final words that evening were:

I hope that each one of you may become a shining light even as these electric lights are now brilliant in their intensity. Nay, may each one of you be a luminary like unto a sparkling star in the heaven of the divine Will. This is my supplication at the throne of God. This is my hope through the favours of Bahá'u'lláh.[292]

Two meetings were held on 10 November, 'Abdu'l-Bahá's last day in the capital, the first at the house He was renting and in the evening at the home of Joseph and Pauline Hannen. By the evening 'Abdu'l-Bahá was so exhausted that He had to rest on a couch while receiving individuals and groups and talking with them. That night, in the capital city of the United States, a country riven by racial divisions, 'Abdu'l-Bahá chose to speak of Bahá'u'lláh's African steward, Isfandíyár. He recounted the story of this remarkable man on whom Bahá'u'lláh had relied for the smooth running of His large household and in whom He had placed so much trust:

> If a perfect man could be found in the world, that man was Isfandíyár . . . Whenever I think of Isfandíyár, I am moved to tears, although he passed away fifty years ago. He was the faithful servant of Bahá'u'lláh and was entrusted with His secrets.[293]

On the evening of 23 November a banquet was held at the Great Northern Hotel.

' . . . endeavour that your attitudes and intentions here tonight be universal and altruistic in nature,' 'Abdu'l-Bahá counselled the gathered friends.

> Consecrate and devote yourselves to the betterment and service of all the human race. Let no barrier of ill feeling or personal prejudice exist between these souls, for when your motives are universal and your intentions heavenly in character, when your aspirations are centred in the Kingdom, there is no doubt whatever that you will become the recipients of the bounty and good pleasure of God.[294]

On a number of occasions during 'Abdu'l-Bahá's travels the American friends had begged Him to accept financial contributions towards His travelling expenses. On each occasion the Master had politely but firmly refused these offers, asking instead that the friends give their money to the poor and needy. Once again, on 30 November, as the day of His departure from them drew near, gifts were brought to Him. Once again, 'Abdu'l-Bahá gently refused to accept their gifts.

'I am very thankful for your services,' He told them.

> Indeed you served me well, showed me great hospitality. Day and night you rose up to serve; you strove hard to disseminate the fragrances of God. I shall never forget your services because you have no purpose other than to seek the good-pleasure of God, and look for no station save entry into the Kingdom of God. Now you have brought gifts for the members of my family. These gifts are exquisite and most acceptable; but better than all these gifts are the gifts of the love of God to be preserved in the treasure-houses of the hearts. These gifts are evanescent, but those gifts are everlasting. These jewels should be kept in boxes and vaults, and in the end they perish. But those jewels remain in the treasure-houses of the hearts, and shall remain in the world of God forevermore. In my home they do not use diamond rings. They do not keep rubies. That home is free of such allurements. Now I have accepted these gifts, but I leave them in trust with you to sell them and send the money for the Mashriqu'l-Adhkár in Chicago.[295]

When the Bahá'ís still begged 'Abdu'l-Bahá to accept these gifts, He again refused, saying that He preferred to take on their behalf jewels that belonged to the treasuries of hearts.

On 5 December 'Abdu'l-Bahá boarded the S.S. *Celtic*. On board the ship, He spoke at length to those who had gathered to bid him farewell:

These are my final words of exhortation . . . you must manifest the greatest kindness and love toward the nations of the world . . .

. . . It is the wish of our heavenly Father that every heart should rejoice and be filled with happiness, that we should live together in felicity and joy . . .

Beware lest ye offend any heart, lest ye speak against anyone in his absence, lest ye estrange yourselves from the servants of God. You must consider all His servants as your own family and relations. Direct your whole effort toward the happiness of those who are despondent, bestow food upon the hungry, clothe the needy, and glorify the humble. Be a helper to every helpless one, and manifest kindness to your fellow creatures in order that ye may attain the good pleasure of God. This is conducive to the illumination of the world of humanity and eternal felicity for yourselves. I seek from God everlasting glory in your behalf; therefore this is my prayer and exhortation.[296]

The friends disembarked and the ship sailed. Juliet Thompson wrote in her diary:

It was death to leave that ship. I stood on the pier with May Maxwell, tears blurring my sight. Through them I could see the Master in the midst of the group of Persians waving a patient hand to us. It waved and waved, that beautiful patient hand, till the Figure was lost to sight.[297]

Section VI
1912–14

Hippolyte Dreyfus

36

Return to Britain

On 13 December the S.S. *Celtic* reached Liverpool where a number of Bahá'ís from London, Paris and the north of England were waiting to welcome 'Abdu'l-Bahá. While in Liverpool, the Master stayed at the Adelphi Hotel. He spoke to a gathering of Theosophists and addressed the congregation of Pembroke Chapel before taking the train for London on 16 December.

In London He once again stayed at the home of Lady Blomfield in Cadogan Gardens where, as on His previous visit, a constant stream of people from all walks of life arrived at all hours. Professor Edward Granville Browne, who had met with Bahá'u'lláh in 'Akká, now visited 'Abdu'l-Bahá more than once, Lady Blomfield relates, 'speaking in Persian with the Master, Who was delighted to see him, and talked over many things'.[298]

Mrs Pankhurst, a leading suffragist, came also and was, Lady Blomfield reports, 'much cheered by her interview, for the Master told her to continue her work steadfastly, for women would very shortly take their rightful place in the world'.[299]

Mrs Pankhurst, while speaking with the Master, referred to Him as a prophet and Hasan Balyuzi relates that the Master's response was: 'Oh, no! I am a man, like you.'[300] 'Abdu'l-Bahá firmly advised a number of suffragettes who called on Him against the use of violence, whatever the circumstances.

One day, a wretched-looking tramp knocked at the door after walking 30 miles to reach Cadogan Gardens. He had been about to put an end to his own life but, after glimpsing a picture of 'Abdu'l-Bahá in a newspaper, felt drawn to seek His presence first. Mr Balyuzi relates:

> 'Abdu'l-Bahá Himself opened the door to the wretched tramp, His hand extended, His welcome warm and affectionate . . . The tramp, his head bowed, sat on a low chair next to 'Abdu'l-Bahá, Who took his hand and stroked his matted hair, and spoke to him: 'Be happy! Be happy! Do not be filled with grief when humiliation overtaketh thee. The bounty and power of God is without limit for each and every soul in the world.' . . .
>
> When the man rose to go, he was no longer a dejected tramp. To Lady Blomfield he said: 'Please write down for me His words. I have attained all I expected, and even more.'[301]

One day, Lady Blomfield relates, a woman called without an appointment and asked to see the Master:

> 'I am sorry,' answered the over-zealous friend who met her in the hall, 'but He is occupied now with most important people, and cannot be disturbed.'
>
> The woman turned away, feeling too humble to persist in her appeal, but, oh! so bitterly disappointed. Before she had reached the foot of the stairway, she was overtaken by a breathless messenger from 'Abdu'l-Bahá.
>
> 'He wishes to see you, come back! He has told me to bring you to Him.'
>
> We had heard His voice from the door of His audience room speaking with authority:
>
> 'A heart has been hurt. Hasten, hasten, bring her to me!'[302]

Ḥájí Amín, the veteran and distinguished Bahá'í who had attained the presence of Bahá'u'lláh in the public bath house in 'Akká, now arrived from Paris. On his first attempt to leave Paris and reach the Master in London, being unable to speak English, French or any other European language, Ḥájí Amín had found himself, inexplicably, back in the French capital. His second attempt was successful. "'Abdu'l-Bahá laughingly told him that no doubt the Ḥájí could not forsake the delights of Paris and had to hurry back there."[303]

Men of rank and position sought 'Abdu'l-Bahá's presence, amongst them Lord Lamington, a former governor of Bombay. The Maharajah of Jalawar was another eminent guest. On 20 December Mushíru'l-Mulk, the Persian Minister in London, came to pay his respects and to hear of the Master's travels in America. Prince Jalálu'd-Dawlih, who had been governor of Yazd in 1903 when the Bahá'ís of that province had been sorely persecuted, came too. Now a broken man, exiled from his homeland, he came seeking forgiveness for his part in the fierce persecution of Bahá'ís which had taken place during his governorship. The prince threw himself at 'Abdu'l-Bahá's feet but the Master would not permit him to thus humiliate himself.

On 20 December 'Abdu'l-Bahá went to see a performance of *Eager Heart*, a play about the birth of Jesus written by Alice Buckton. It was the first time that the Master had been to the theatre and He wept openly. On 24 December He spent a long time talking with reporters about the purpose of His travels in the West. That night, when He sat down to dinner, 'Abdu'l-Bahá said playfully that He was not hungry but that 'He had to come to the dinner table because Lady Blomfield was very insistent; two despotic monarchs of the East had not been able to command Him and bend His will, but the ladies of America and Europe, because they were free, gave him orders.'[304]

On the evening of Christmas Day 'Abdu'l-Bahá visited a Salvation Army hostel and spoke to five hundred needy people gathered there. He thoroughly inspected the hostel's sleeping accommodation. He also inspected a children's home and attended a Christmas party given for poor children. Much moved by what He had seen, 'Abdu'l-Bahá gave generously to the hostel and to the children. He showered upon the children wherever He went in London such loving attention that some thought Him to be Father Christmas and sang a song in His praise.

On 29 December 'Abdu'l-Bahá spoke at a Methodist church in London and on 31 December He visited Oxford. There He spoke at Manchester College at the invitation of Dr T. K. Cheyne, an eminent scholar of biblical studies. Although it was the holiday period, a large audience gathered to hear him. Lady Blomfield was present when the Master met with Dr Cheyne. She later wrote:

> The meeting between 'Abdu'l-Bahá and the dear, revered higher critic, Dr. T. K. Cheyne, was fraught with pathos . . .
> 'Abdu'l-Bahá embraced the Doctor with loving grace, and praised his courageous steadfastness in his life's work, always striving against increasing weakness, and lessening bodily health. Through those veiling clouds the light of the mind and spirit shone with a radiant persistence. The beautiful loving care of the devoted wife for her gifted, invalid husband touched the heart of 'Abdu'l-Bahá. With tears in His kind eyes He spoke of them to Mrs Thornburgh-Cropper and myself on our way back to London.[305]

On 6 January 'Abdu'l-Bahá left London for Edinburgh at the invitation of Dr and Mrs Alexander Whyte. Dr Whyte was a well-known academic and a prominent minister of the United Free Church of Scotland. His wife had met the Master while travelling in Palestine in 1906. 'Abdu'l-Bahá stayed at the home of Dr and Mrs Whyte in Charlotte Square with one interpreter while the rest of His attendants stayed at a nearby hotel. The very same evening that He arrived in Edinburgh, 'Abdu'l-Bahá met a number of the city's eminent citizens at the Whyte's home. The next day He visited the Outlook Tower museum and met there Professor Sir Patrick Geddes, a pioneer of educational and social reform. After being driven along the Royal Mile in the city and being shown other notable landmarks, 'Abdu'l-Bahá spoke to a packed meeting organized by the Esperanto Society at the Freemasons' Hall. Some three hundred people who could not get into the hall had to stand outside. 'Abdu'l-Bahá spoke on the need for an international auxiliary language and Sir Patrick Geddes gave the evening's vote of thanks.

Visitors and enquirers now began to flock to Charlotte Square, just as they had done to Cadogan Gardens. On 8 January a large group of university students from Egypt, India and Japan arrived. Dr Whyte was profoundly moved by this gathering of varied peoples in his own house. 'Dear Master!' he said. 'In my time I have had many meetings in this house, but never have I seen a gathering like this. It reminds me of the words of St Paul that God "hath made of one blood all nations of men" . . .'[306]

On 8 January the Master spoke at a meeting organized by the Outlook Tower Society over which Sir Patrick Geddes presided. The meeting was fully reported in the leading newspaper, the *Scotsman*. On 9 January 'Abdu'l-Bahá spoke to a crowded meeting of Theosophists. He was exhausted when He arrived at the meeting but, Lady Blomfield writes:

> Then, seeming to gather strength, He arose, and with
> voice and manner of joyous animation, and eyes aglow,
> He paced the platform with a vigorous tread, and spoke
> with words of great power.[307]

The next day 'Abdu'l-Bahá left for London. On 11 January
He spoke at the Caxton Hall. On 14 January He was the
guest of honour at a dinner party at the Persian Legation.
His days in London were as busy this time as on earlier
occasions. When He spoke in a church in the East End of
London, Lady Blomfield noted in her diary that the 'congregation seemed spell-bound by the power which spread
like an atmosphere from another, higher world'.[308]

On 15 January 'Abdu'l-Bahá left London for Bristol.
There He stayed at the Clifton Guest House. This guest
house belonged to Mr and Mrs Tudor-Pole, who had
organized a public meeting for that same evening. Near
to one hundred eminent citizens of Bristol came to hear
'Abdu'l-Bahá's address. The very next day He returned to
London. On 18 January 'Abdu'l-Bahá went to Woking in
Surrey where, after taking lunch with a number of Muslim
and Christian leaders, He was scheduled to speak at the
mosque. So large was the crowd that gathered to hear Him
– Indian, Turkish, Egyptian as well as British – that He had
to deliver His address in the courtyard of the mosque. The
following day He was the luncheon guest of a leading
cleric, Dr. R. J. Campbell, who invited a number of other
clergy to meet Him. In the evening He was the guest of
honour at a dinner given for Him by a Rajput prince.

On 20 January 'Abdu'l-Bahá attended an afternoon
reception in His honour given by Dr Felix Moscheles and
in the evening He spoke at the Higher Thought Centre.
The next day He left for Paris.

37

Second Visit to the Continent

In Paris 'Abdu'l-Bahá stayed in a rented apartment in the Rue St Didier. On this visit He had few public engagements and devoted much of His time to those Bahá'ís who had come from Persia and other countries in the hope of seeing Him.

Only a week after 'Abdu'l-Bahá's arrival in Paris the Persian Minister called on Him and on the same evening 'Abdu'l-Bahá returned the call. In those years there were many political emigres and aristocrats of Persian origin living in Paris. Many of these people called upon 'Abdu'l-Bahá to seek His counsel. Young Persians studying in Paris came too. To all He gave generously of His time and energies. Tea was served daily from a samovar in His drawing room and He offered meals each day to those Eastern visitors who had come so far to see Him.

He was seldom without visitors. An ex-válí of Beirut, Rashíd Páshá, notorious for his earlier hostility towards the Master, came to pay a most respectful call. 'Abdu'l-Bahá received him with kindness in His own room and returned his call the same evening.

In His drawing-room 'Abdu'l-Bahá spoke at length on the history of Persia and assured His listeners that their country had a bright future. He also recalled many incidents from His life in Palestine. He was oppressed by the materialism of Parisian society. Work was made for man, He said, and not man for work. The stark contrast seen in

Europe between the lives of the wealthy and the great needs of the poor saddened Him. 'Abdu'l-Bahá was weary. He was not sleeping well and suffered from occasional fevers.

On 12 February He was invited to address the Paris Esperantists and the next evening He spoke to the Theosophists. On 17 February He spoke at the homes of three Bahá'í families and the same night visited Pasteur Monnier's Theological Seminary. On 21 February He spoke at the Salle de Troyes, at a meeting arranged by *L'Alliance Spiritualiste*. On 26 February He was sick with a heavy cold and could scarcely speak, yet He continued to receive visitors even while resting in bed. His public engagements, His visits to Bahá'í homes, even His own talks in Rue St Didier had to be halted. On 9 March Professor and Mrs Browne visited Him and He spoke to them for an hour. The effort greatly tired Him.

On 19 March He moved to a hotel in Rue Lauriston and there celebrated Naw-Rúz with a number of luncheon guests. Later that day He gave an address at the Iranian Legation and spoke at the home of Hippolyte and Laura Dreyfus-Barney the same evening.

For some weeks the Bahá'ís of Germany had been pleading for the Master to visit their communities. Professor and Mrs Stark, living in Budapest, wrote also, extending an invitation for 'Abdu'l-Bahá to visit them. By 30 March, 'Abdu'l-Bahá had recovered His strength sufficiently to start out for Stuttgart in Germany. He did not notify the Bahá'ís in Stuttgart that He was coming for He wanted His arrival in Germany to be a surprise. He loved the German Bahá'ís very much and praised their excellent qualities.

'Abdu'l-Bahá arrived in Stuttgart unannounced with four Persian attendants late in the evening on 1 April and booked into the Hotel Marquardt. As soon as He had registered at the hotel, He let one of His attendants telephone the Bahá'ís. Thrilled at this news, some of them came at once and more the next morning, to the great astonishment of the hotel staff. On 3 April 'Abdu'l-Bahá addressed a large meeting at the City Museum. He began His address with these words:

> I came from a distant land. I have travelled twenty thousand miles until I came to you in Stuttgart. Forty years I was a prisoner. I was young when I was put into prison and my hair was white when the prison doors opened . . . Now I am here in order to be united with you, in order to meet you. My purpose is that perchance you may illumine the world of humanity . . .[309]

He went on to state that the religions of the day consisted of differing dogmas which are the cause of discord and hatred.

> Religion must be the basis of all good fellowship. Think of the turmoil that today exists in the Balkans . . . The Balkan states have become a volcano. All this ruin originates from the prejudices created by the different dogmas, called forth by superstitions and race prejudices.
>
> . . . mankind today has forgotten what constitutes true religion. Each nation and each people today hold to some definite dogma.
>
> . . . These traditions and these dogmas are like the husks surrounding the kernel. We must release the kernel from the husk.[310]

The Master visited Esslingen where a particularly joyous meeting was held with 80 adults and 50 children present. He was persuaded to visit Bad Mergentheim, a hundred miles from Stuttgart. There He heard nightingales singing in the beautiful spa garden. Never, He said, since leaving Persia had He heard so many nightingales singing in such beautiful surroundings but He would not stay more than one night. Back in Stuttgart He maintained a busy schedule until His departure for Budapest on 8 April.

There were no Bahá'ís in Budapest at that time. 'Abdu'l-Bahá stayed at the Ritz Hotel and through the hospitality of Mr and Mrs Stark He met a considerable number of leaders of thought, including the oriental scholar Professor Arminius Vambéry. Professor Vambéry was 82 years old and unwell. 'Abdu'l-Bahá visited him at his home on two occasions.

The hectic schedule of public addresses, visits and visitors continued unabated. On 15 April 'Abdu'l-Bahá developed the symptoms of a severe cold and could not leave for Vienna until 19 April. In Vienna He stayed at the Grand Hotel. His first visit was to the Turkish Ambassador, a man renowned for his fanatical religious views who was captivated by the presence of the Master. The next day 'Abdu'l-Bahá was the guest of both the Persian minister and the Turkish ambassador. While in Vienna He addressed the Theosophists of that city three times. He left Vienna on 24 April, arriving back in Stuttgart in the early hours of the 25th.

The Bahá'ís of Stuttgart had arranged for and advertised a public address for the evening of 25 April at the City Museum. The cold 'Abdu'l-Bahá was still suffering from had settled onto His chest and that afternoon His condition worsened. The doctors consulted advised Him to stay indoors and to use His voice as little as possible. 'Abdu'l-Bahá chose to ignore their advice. Mr Balyuzi recounts that:

While Wilhelm Herrigel was giving a talk in His stead, He walked into the hall, to the utmost delight and surprise of the audience, and using His full voice delivered a discourse on the need of world peace and the power that can guarantee it . . . The next day, to questions about His health, He answered that the previous night's venture, although considered very risky, had proved the right medicine for Him.[311]

'Abdu'l-Bahá maintained a less hectic schedule for the remainder of His time in Stuttgart and was sufficiently recovered to leave for Paris on 1 May. 'Abdu'l-Bahá knew that He must return soon to the Holy Land. In the Balkans the conflict that had broken out the previous October had finally ended in April 1913 with the virtual eviction of the Turks from the area. The peace that followed was an uneasy one, as the Balkan League powers began to quarrel amongst themselves over the spoils of war.

On this final visit to Paris 'Abdu'l-Bahá stayed first at the Hotel California near the Bibliothèque Nationale. Visitors came daily as before but 'Abdu'l-Bahá was often not well enough to visit the Bahá'ís in their homes. He did manage to keep up His practice of taking a walk out of doors each day. One day some Persian notables took Him by car to the race course at Longchamps but 'Abdu'l-Bahá did not stay there long. He preferred walking, He said, to sitting in a car.

He spoke to the Bahá'ís about the Covenant on several occasions. 'Some people have imagined,' He said, 'that the Blessed Perfection has taken relations between father and son into account. They do not know that He has instituted the power of the Covenant for the propagation of the Cause of God and for the victory of His Word.'[312]

In late May 'Abdu'l-Bahá moved to the hotel in Rue Lauriston. He was so tired that He was in great need of a few days' rest on His own before the Bahá'ís and others found out where He was. Letters came for Him constantly and on 1 June a visitor from the Holy Land brought the news that there were many pilgrims waiting there for 'Abdu'l-Bahá's return. On 6 June 'Izzat Páshá, once a prominent figure in the regime of the deposed Sulṭán 'Abdu'l-Ḥamíd, gave a dinner party in 'Abdu'l-Bahá's honour.

'On June 12th', Mr Balyuzi relates,

> at 8 a.m. 'Abdu'l-Bahá left His hotel for the station. There he spoke with the Bahá'ís who had come to say farewell, urging them to be united at all times. At noon His train left for Marseilles, which it reached twelve hours later. He stayed the night at a hotel next to the station, and boarded the P. & O. steamer, *Himalaya*, at 9 a.m. the next morning.

'Abdu'l-Bahá's historic tour of the West was over.[313]

38

In Egypt and the Holy Land

In Port Said 'Abdu'l-Bahá welcomed the pilgrims and other guests in a large tent pitched on the roof of His hotel. Letters continued to pour in from East and West and there was a constant stream of visitors. Yet 'Abdu'l-Bahá found the time to answer the letters sent to Him and the Tablets from these months are in His own handwriting. The recurrent fevers had not left Him but neither had His sense of humour. At a time, He told His guests, when others were fleeing the heat of Egypt for Paris, He had come from Paris to Egypt.

On 27 June a Bahá'í from <u>Sh</u>íráz gave a dinner for all the Bahá'ís in Port Said. Seventy came and ate in the shade of 'Abdu'l-Bahá's tent. 'Abdu'l-Bahá Himself served the food and then gave sweets to all present. On 11 July 'Abdu'l-Bahá moved to Ismá'ílíyyah for the oppressive heat of Port Said was affecting Him adversely. Though the climate was less humid, the Master's feverish condition worsened. On 17 July He moved to Ramlih near Alexandria. There He rented three houses, one for the eminent Bahá'í scholar Mírzá Abu'l-Faḍl, who was seriously ill. The climate of Ramlih suited the Master and His health improved. Mr Balyuzi relates that:

> One morning, around six o'clock, 'Abdu'l-Bahá went to the house where His secretaries lived, to find most of the residents still asleep. He Himself had already

attended to His correspondence and other matters, and had written several Tablets.[314]

On 1 August the Greatest Holy Leaf arrived from Haifa with Shoghi Effendi and Ḍiyá'iyyíh Khánum, 'Abdu'l-Bahá's eldest daughter. On 17 August 'Abbás Ḥilmí Páshá, the Khedive of Egypt, visited Him. Deputies of the Turkish parliament sought audiences, as did academic staff of the Syrian Protestant College in Beirut. And all the time there were more letters arriving. Mr Balyuzi recounts:

> Individual Bahá'í's, and particularly the Bahá'ís of the East, wrote to Him on every conceivable subject; one would ask His advice about purchasing a piece of land, another would request a name for a child newly-born; one would ask Him whether to marry, another whether to make a certain journey. He always had misunderstandings to resolve, feelings to soothe. Bahá'í groups, communities, and spiritual assemblies, as more of them came into being, also took more and more of His time, for counsel, advice and guidance. His correspondence was not limited to the Bahá'ís. Many were the people, not His adherents, who wrote to Him and had replies.[315]

During the summer and early autumn of 1913 the Master's health was greatly restored but as winter approached, once again, He was increasingly troubled by fever and insomnia. These symptoms were greatly aggravated by the increasingly erratic behaviour of Dr Faríd, who had already caused much stress during 'Abdu'l-Bahá's Western journeys. A few days' rest at Abúqír brought no relief and 'Abdu'l-Bahá decided to return to the Holy Land. He took ship on 2 December and on 5 December arrived back in Haifa. There He sent His attendants on ahead, asking them to ensure that the Bahá'ís did not gather to greet Him as He left the ship. At nightfall, He disembarked.

Emogene Hoagg, an American pilgrim who was in Haifa at that time, wrote:

> The home coming of Abdul-Baha, after an absence of three years and four months, was a real festival. Such excitement and happiness as reigned in the holy household can only be imagined . . . In Abdul-Baha's house, there is a very large central room around which are the other rooms, and in it Persian rugs were spread and tables placed upon which were fruits and sweets.
>
> . . . When 'Abdul-Bahá's voice was heard as he entered, the moment was intense – and as he passed through to his room, all heads were bowed. In a few moments he returned to welcome all. He sat in a chair at one end of the room, and most of the believers sat on the floor. 'Abdul-Baha was tired so remained but a short time, and after a prayer chanted by his daughter Zia Khanum, went to his room.
>
> Then the ladies vacated so that the men might enter. To see the faces of those sturdy, earnest men – faces that spoke the fervour of their faith, the earnestness and resoluteness of their purpose – was something to remember. I am sure not an eye was dry . . . He welcomed them, and seating himself on the floor, spoke to them a short time, after which he retired.[316]

The next morning, 'Abdu'l-Bahá went up the mountain to the shrine of the Báb. 'The Bahá'ís of the Holy Land and the pilgrims', Mr Balyuzi relates,

> had already gathered there and lined the pathway which led to the Shrine. 'Abdu'l-Bahá beckoned to them to enter the eastern foreroom of the inner shrine; He, all alone, entered the western foreroom.[317]

After two days in Haifa 'Abdu'l-Bahá went to 'Akká by train. A large crowd of people, Bahá'ís and others, including prominent citizens of the Haifa-'Akká area, escorted Him into the city which had held Him prisoner for so long.

Some six weeks later, on 21 January 1914, Mírzá Abu'l-Faḍl passed away in Cairo. 'Abdu'l-Bahá grieved deeply at this loss. 'Abdu'l-Bahá told the friends:

> Today very sad news has been received. He was indeed a very glorious personage. In every way he was un-equalled . . . he was in the utmost severance, in the utmost firmness and steadfastness in the Cause of God. He was detached from all things . . . He was my partner and participant in the servitude of the holy threshold.
>
> During the days of sorrow, he was my consolation. I had perfect confidence in him. Every written criticism of the Cause I used to refer to him and he wrote the answer . . .
>
> A great wisdom necessitated his passing. There is nothing to do but to exercise patience . . .
>
> All the friends of God should gather together and pray at the holy tomb of the Báb and I will pray here.

Section VII

1914–21

*The House
of 'Abbúd*

39

Outbreak of Conflict

In these early months of 1914 the shadows of impending war grew ever deeper. '. . . the surface of the Continent [Europe] was now strewn with powder', the historian and military tactician Captain B. H. Lidell Hart has written, 'and everywhere the air was heavy with fatalism.'[318]

Pilgrims and other visitors continued to arrive in Haifa. Frequently fatigued and burdened by so many cares, 'Abdu'l-Bahá wrote sometime during those early months of 1914:

> Friends! The time is coming when I shall be no longer with you. I have done all that could be done. I have served the Cause of Bahá'u'lláh to the utmost of my ability. I have laboured night and day, all the years of my life. O how I long to see the loved ones taking upon themselves the responsibilities of the Cause! . . . I am straining my ears toward the East and toward the West, toward the North and toward the South that haply I may hear the songs of love and fellowship chanted in the meetings of the faithful. My days are numbered, and, but for this, there is no joy left unto me . . .
>
> Ah me I am waiting, waiting, to hear the joyful tidings that the believers are the very embodiment of sincerity and truthfulness, the incarnation of love and amity, the living symbols of unity and concord. Will they not gladden my heart? Will they not satisfy my yearning? Will they not manifest my wish? Will they not

fulfil my heart's desire? Will they not give ear to my call?[319]

By June the threat of war was acute. 'Abdu'l-Bahá could not permit any more pilgrims to visit the Holy Land. Those who were already present were instructed to leave at once. The Master consoled them with these words:

> Indeed, I am deeply grieved, but I do not say good-bye to you because there is a complete connection among the hearts, and among the souls there is unity and agreement . . . When the heart is engaged with the friends there is no separation, especially if you go in service to the Cause of God . . .[320]

By the mid-point of the year Dr Faríd's defection and his defiant unwillingness to accept 'Abdu'l-Bahá as the Centre of the Covenant was out in the open. He was already travelling and speaking in Europe and planned to visit Britain. 'Abdu'l-Bahá despatched two young Bahá'ís, one still a student at the Syrian Protestant College, to counter Dr Faríd's activities in Europe. Laura and Hippolyte Dreyfus-Barney left to counter the effects of Dr Faríd's attempts to divide the American believers.

At 11 a.m. on 28 June a Slav nationalist shot and killed the Archduke Franz Ferdinand, heir to the Austro-Hungarian Empire, in Sarajevo. By a cruel irony, as Lidell Hart recounts, the Serb nationalists slew the one man of influence in Austria sympathetic to their cause. Austria took this event as the excuse to attempt to regain control of Serbia and at precisely 11 a.m. on 28 July declared war on Serbia.

'The rush to the abyss', Lidell Hart relates, 'now gathered unbrakable speed – driven by the motor of "military necessity" . . . Desire for war, and fear of being caught at a disadvantage, reacted on each other.'[321]

In July Edward Getsinger passed through the Holy Land on his way home to the United States from India. In the autumn of that same year he wrote a graphic account of the conditions he observed there in July:

The entire population of Syria is in a state of lamentation. Turkey is mobilizing, and all men between the ages of twenty and forty-five are called to the colours, or rather forced to go to the front. Hardly six months have passed since the soldiers of the Balkan Army returned here, and now they must again join their regiments. But this time every available man is taken, by force if necessary . . .

Food of all kinds has doubled in price, and within two months there will be a famine in Syria. The Government has confiscated eighty per cent of all food stuffs in sight both for man and beast, is taking sheep by the thousands, and for this pays no money whatever . . .

The officers have taken all bread winners, leaving the women and children without means of support, and in some cases with a meagre supply of food stored for winter use. Even in these cases the soldiers have broken into the very homes of the bereft and taken this small store. The merchants have had their shops cleared of stores and been given a receipt, which means bankruptcy. All horses and wagons are taken . . .

The farming section everywhere is devoid of men, and their women and children are hastening to the villages and cities for protection from the marauding bands of Bedouins who are making night raids upon the defenceless homes. Thus the cities are being crowded and no food for anyone, nor money with which to purchase it at famine prices . . .

The poor women, weeping with their children, sit for hours at the doors of the well-to-do, begging for bread, and this is rapidly becoming a luxury. A few

ships are arriving at these ports now where formerly ten
to fifty arrived weekly . . .

. . . During the Balkan War, at the end of one year
the conditions were not as bad as they are now, at the
end of one month.[322]

At the end of July, mobilization of troops began in both
Russia and Germany. On 29 July the British naval fleet left
its Portsmouth base for Scapa Flow in the Orkney Islands.
On 3 August Germany declared war on France and on 4
August invaded Belgium, demanding free passage for her
troops. Britain then issued an ultimatum to Germany
demanding that she respect Belgian neutrality. The German government ignored this ultimatum and by 11 p.m.
that same night Britain too was at war.

On the Western front, the cumbrous armies of Germany, France and Britain lumbered into place and were
soon locked into opposing lines. Russia, urged on by her
French and British allies to relieve the intense German
pressure in the West, invaded East Prussia in mid-August.
The German army defeated the invaders at Tannenburg
where the Russian army suffered very heavy loss of life. In
the West, the First Battle of the Marne took place in September. French forces weakened the German line and
British forces pierced it but, as Lidell Hart explains, the
slow pace of British action after the battle proved fatal to
any chance of converting the German retreat into a disaster. The way was thereby paved for four years of hideous
trench warfare in which thousands of young men were to
slaughter each other. The military history of the next four
years thus became a grim struggle to break this deadlock
either by forcing a way through the barrier or by somehow
finding a way around it.

The German government now strove to relieve the
pressure again brought to bear on it by Russia. A principal

aim of this strategy was to bring Turkey into the war on the German side, for an alliance with Turkey would block Russia's southern supply route through the Black Sea. Throughout the previous century, Britain had been the leading ally of the weakening Ottoman Empire. Ever since 1908, when the Young Turks had overthrown the Sulṭán, Germany had worked to gain a dominating influence in Constantinople. Understandably, the new rulers of Turkey hated the very thought of an alliance with Britain, the former Ottoman rulers' strongest ally.

At the end of October, Turkey's provocative military action both in the Caucasus and on the Sinai peninsula forced Britain, France and Russia to declare war on the Turkish government. In response, Turkey declared war against the Anglo-French-Russian entente on 14 November.

40

'A Reign of Terror'

'Abdu'l-Bahá now made plans to move the Bahá'ís from the Haifa area. Lady Blomfield recounts that those Bahá'ís who were merchants had lost all their goods and stores to the government and that 'the friends, in spite of the reassurances of the Master that no guns would be turned on Haifa, were living in constant fear, and the children, having heard terrible stories which were being told everywhere, grew quite ill, always looking round and about with frightened eyes'.[323]

'Abdu'l-Bahá decided to accept the hospitality offered to the Bahá'í community by the Shaykh of the Druze village Abú-Sinán. Bahá'u'lláh had once spent three months amongst these Druze people, who lived two hours inland from 'Akká. The Shaykh now offered his own house to the Master and His family and other Bahá'í families were warmly welcomed in other Druze homes. They lived under the strictest economy but the pure air and simple food and the freedom from constant dread of bombardment restored their spirits.

Lua Getsinger arrived in the Holy Land from India on 3 December 1914. Exhausted after her pioneer work in India, she stayed in the Holy Land as a guest of 'Abdu'l-Bahá until late August of 1915. A letter written by her on 1 January from Abú-Sinán states:

I am glad to write you of the very good health of the
Beloved Master and family at the above mentioned
place of safety in which I found them on my arrival
Dec. 3rd . . .

　. . . The Master spends most of His time in Acca
where He is the Light and Hope of all the troubled
people who without him would be in the depths of
despair indeed![324]

In mid-December the Turkish government attacked with
force on two fronts, against Russia in the Caucasus and
against Britain in the Sinai peninsula. The latter assault
was an attempt to cut Britain's link with the East through
the Suez Canal. A few weeks later, as part of the strategy
of finding some way around the deadlock in Europe,
British forces took Basra at the head of the Gulf waters and
also deposed the Khedive of Egypt. All this provoked great
fear in the Holy Land.

Lady Blomfield relates that 'Haifa, which was still under
Turkish rule, was panic-stricken. Most of the inhabitants
fled inland, fearing bombardment by the Allies.'[325]

'Abdu'l-Bahá opened a dispensary at Abú-Sinán and
engaged a doctor to serve all who needed medical help. He
arranged for schooling for the Bahá'í children although
much of His own time was spent in Haifa and 'Akká where
there was great need of His counsel and of the corn which
He had stored, foreseeing the current hardships. Lady
Blomfield tells us:

'Abdu'l-Bahá had taught the friends to grow nourishing
vegetables, which, with the corn from His village of
'Adasíyyih – where there were marvellous crops – kept
many from perishing of hunger . . .
　Sometimes the Governor of 'Akká, or the Comman-
dant, the Chief Magistrate, the Mufti, or the Páshá,
would come to visit 'Abdu'l-Bahá, staying one or two

nights, as guests of the village. All consulted Him on many questions regarding the feeding or otherwise caring for the people during this time of difficulty . . .[326]

On 19 January, a pilgrim arrived in Haifa from Sh̲íráz. Mírzá Faḍlu'lláh had come from Persia to the Holy Land via India, a circuitous route but the only one possible. His was the last visit by any pilgrim for many months.

During this time, the sole occupant of the pilgrim house in Haifa was Ḥájí Mírzá Ḥaydar-'Alí. For five months, Lady Blomfield relates, there was no word from any part of the world.

The relative inactivity of these months, the absence of pilgrims and the cessation of correspondence with the outside world did not suit 'Abdu'l-Bahá. He wished, He said one day, that He had gone to India where He might be occupied in spreading the teachings.

Early in 1915 the Holy Land and all of Syria came under the control of Jamál Pás̲h̲á. As commander of the 4th Army Corps, his mission was to overrun the Suez Canal and drive the British out of Egypt. Mr Balyuzi writes:

> With him came a reign of terror . . . Throughout 1915 and into the following year, Jamál Pás̲h̲á was bringing Arab nationalists to trial in his military courts. Thirty-four of them were executed, and many more were deported. Mírzá Muḥammad-'Alí and his associates, long discredited and cowed into silence, now found fresh opportunities to plot against 'Abdu'l-Bahá.[327]

The Covenant-breakers carried to the new military governor their lying tales, informing him that 'Abdu'l-Bahá was opposed to the military regime. They even gave to him the tent which Bahá'u'lláh Himself had used.

'During the last days of January and the first of Feb.'
Lua Getsinger later wrote to the friends in America,

the Beloved was in great danger; several nights he kept
sleepless watch preparing Himself and certain members of the Household for what seemed inevitable . . .
I was called to Haifa to make some statements concerning the matter, and when informed by the Master of all
that was pending I could but marvel at His gentleness
in dealing with its source, His patient fortitude, and His
kindness to all concerned. Three of the Holy Leaves
were in Haifa – having gone there with me. A telegram
came, and the Master sent us all in great haste back to
Abou Senan . . . None of us knew the contents of the
telegram nor its portents. He remained with Ahmad
Sohrab in Haifa to meet alone what He alone knew
might befall Him. In a few days it was reported in Acca
that He was to be arrested and sent to Damascus. The
friends and inhabitants of that place as well as Abou
Senan were plunged into consternation and despair . . .

The next morning 'Abdu'l-Bahá went to Acca where
He remained a short time, quieting, helping and reas-
suring the people; then, without sending any word he
came to Abou Senan! Oh, how we rejoiced to see Him!
His smiling face, His clear, consoling voice, His loving
solicitude dawned all suddenly like a glowing Sun in
the midst of our darkness . . .[328]

Two days later the Master called Lua to Him and spoke to
her for nearly an hour. Among many things He said:

I have been in great danger and am still like one sitting
under a suspended sword which may fall at a moments
notice! For myself I do not care, and am ready for any
sacrifice and yearn for the cup of martyrdom – but I am
thinking of those whom I must leave, their helplessness
when I am gone so cries out to me before I go that for
their sakes I hope to be spared yet a little while. Still,

I am prepared – and I now prepare you for a day will come when I shall go suddenly from the midst of all and you will see me no more.[329]

The next day, Lua wrote, 'He left us as unexpectedly as He came, returning to Acca, Haifa.'[330]

In early summer locusts descended on the Holy Land. Lua wrote on 11 June:

. . . a dire famine stares the people in the face for a year to come, on account of the locusts which have come in such vast swarms as to darken the sun and still they come! Everything has been consumed save a few wheat fields and we are praying that they may remain unmolested otherwise there will be no bread even for a single soul.[331]

41

'The Fire of War and Carnage'

Jamál Páshá, once encamped near 'Akká, demanded to see 'Abdu'l-Bahá and the Master went, on a donkey, to see him. Mr Balyuzi relates that Jamál Páshá received the Master courteously:

> . . . but told Him that He was a religious mischief-maker, which was the reason He had been put under restraint in the past. It happened that, in the days of 'Abdu'l-Ḥamíd, Jamál Páshá himself had been known as a political mischief-maker. So 'Abdu'l-Bahá now replied that mischief-making was of two kinds: political and religious; and then, pointing at the arrogant Páshá, He said that so far the political mischief-maker had not caused any damage, and it was to be hoped that the religious mischief-maker would not do so either.[332]

In 1915, while the huge armies were deadlocked on the Western front, the centre of gravity of the war operations moved eastward. This followed a decision made in January by the Allies: 'to prepare for a naval expedition in February to bombard and take the Gallipoli peninsula, with Constantinople as its objective.'

A naval bombardment of Turkish coasts began in late February. On 25 April the Allies launched a land attack on the Gallipoli peninsula in an attempt to gain control of the Dardanelles Strait. In late May, Italy, which had been an ally of Germany and Austria since 1882, declared war on

Austria while avoiding an open breach with Germany. The Italians soon found themselves struggling in trenches against determined Austrian defenders.

In May, 'Abdu'l-Bahá decided that conditions were calm enough, despite the continuing conflict, to allow the Bahá'ís to return to Haifa. On 5 May they left Abú-Sinán. Dr Mu'ayyad, who had run the clinic in the Druze village, left for Persia. News had just come from Persia of the martyrdom of Shaykh 'Alí-Akbar-i-Qúchaní, a distinguished teacher and scholar. He was shot while shopping in the bazaar of his home town. A cable sent at this time by the Master to a believer in Mashhad reads: '[May] My life be a sacrifice unto 'Alí-Akbar. I am well. 'Abbás.'[333]

Soon after their return to Haifa, coastal areas were bombarded by the French fleet. The bombardments were always localized and the French commanders sent word on shore before they began so that the local people could stay away from the target areas. Still, Lua wrote to the friends:

> . . . the bombardments were terrifying though of short duration. It was wonderful to see the Master at such times sitting unmoved, watching from the window, as I beheld him on two occasions; His marvellous Face wearing the expression of one who knew and knows what needs must be and all the reasons why . . .
>
> During the first bombardment which destroyed the railroad bridge near Acca He was sitting thus. I was standing near Him gazing intently upon His countenance, trying to read and understand all that it expressed, when He turned and said with quiet determination, 'I must go at once to Acca. My place is there before the cannons striking such terror to the hearts of the people now fleeing away in all directions. They are afraid, I must gather them. They are helpless and hopeless. I must rescue and assure them.' And before the firing ceased He was ready to start out . . . I stood

watching Him descend the little hill upon which the house is situated, to mount His donkey waiting on the rocky path below . . .[334]

The Gallipoli campaign dragged on. It was, Lidell Hart writes, 'A sound and farsighted conception, marred by a chain of errors in execution almost unrivaled even in British history.'[335] Casualties were appallingly heavy. In July the Allies abandoned their efforts.

In August the British took Búshihr, on the Persian Gulf coast, the same port where the Báb had once lived and worked. In September the Allies began a fresh offensive on the Western front. In the ensuing battles they lost 242,000 men and the Germans 141,000. Further south, Italy was taking heavy casualties; she lost 280,000 men between May and December of 1915. In October an Austro-German force attacked Serbia. With the help of Bulgaria, Serbia was overrun, though the Serbian armies were able to retreat into the mountains of Albania. This conquest of Serbia, as Lidell Hart explains, 'relieved Austria of danger on her southern frontier and gave Germany free communication and control over a huge central belt from the North Sea to the Tigris'.[336]

In Haifa, with the Bahá'ís back in their homes, the regular weekly gatherings were once again held in the Master's house. In the latter half of 1915, with war raging on several fronts, 'Abdu'l-Bahá shared with those gathered the stories of some 80 early believers, most of whom had died many years earlier. These short, poignant biographies, each one of which was spoken by 'Abdu'l-Bahá, were in 1924 compiled into a book and published in Haifa. Fifty years later the work was translated into English by Marzieh Gail and published as *Memorials of the Faithful*.

As Marzieh Gail writes in her introduction:

'Abdu'l-Bahá was present at many of these scenes, yet
time after time He effaces Himself to focus on some
companion, often on one so humble that the passing
years would surely have refused him a history.[337]

This book, Marzieh Gail notes:

> . . . is more than the brief annals of early Bahá'í disci-
> ples; it is, somehow, a book of prototypes; and it is a
> kind of testament of values endorsed and willed to us
> by the Bahá'í Exemplar, values now derided, but – if
> the planet is to be made safe for humanity – indispens-
> able. These are short and simple accounts, but they
> constitute a manual of how to live, and how to die.[338]

Also in these months 'Abdu'l-Bahá began to compile a
short volume on the lives of the Báb and the two heralds
of the new dispensation, Shaykh Aḥmad and Siyyid Káẓim,
for the Bahá'í youth who met at the pilgrim house. These
discourses were published in Cairo in 1919.

The Covenant-breakers were taking every opportunity
the war provided them to poison the mind of Jamál Páshá
against 'Abdu'l-Bahá. Mírzá Jalál, a son-in-law of 'Abdu'l-
Bahá, related the following account to Lady Blomfield:

> At the beginning of the year 1916, at about seven
> o'clock one morning, 'Abdu'l-Bahá sent me for His
> faithful coachman. 'Tell Isfandíyár to have my carriage
> brought, and you and Khusraw be ready to accompany
> me to Nazareth in half an hour.' We did as He com-
> manded . . .[339]

That day, Mírzá Jalál relates, 'Abdu'l-Bahá was not well and
was very tired, but Jamál Páshá was in Nazareth and the
Master was determined to meet him. The journey took

until seven in the evening, when 'Abdu'l-Bahá took a room at the German Hotel in Nazareth.

'The next day', Mírzá Jalál continues,

> the Master was invited to lunch at the home of one of the notables . . . one of the Fahúm family. On that day Jamál Páshá, and nearly two hundred of the war leaders, were present at the lunch where the Master sat down at one o'clock and arose from the table at four.
>
> During all those hours 'Abdu'l-Bahá was speaking in Turkish on philosophical and scientific subjects, and on heavenly teachings. So intense was His utterance that all stopped eating while they listened to His blessed words.
>
> . . . Jamál Páshá, who had been His great enemy because of false accusations, had not paid the proper respect to 'Abdu'l-Bahá when He had first arrived. Now, however, having heard the Master speak so learnedly and wisely, he was most deferential and full of all kinds of politeness. When the time came for the Master to rise, Jamál Páshá most courteously held the Beloved's arm to assist Him to leave the table, and himself led the way to the reception room, and seated the Master comfortably.
>
> Finally, after answering more questions, and giving wondrous light on many subjects, the Master arose to bid farewell to His host. Jamál Páshá accompanied Him out of the house, and to the bottom of the steps, and would have gone further with the Master, but was thanked with great kindness and urged by 'Abdu'l-Bahá to return. This was that Jamál Páshá who was not accustomed to rise from his seat to pay respect to any one . . . 'Abdu'l-Bahá was excessively fatigued, and remained that night at the German Hotel at Nazareth. The next day, His work of making a friend of an old enemy having been accomplished, He returned to Haifa.[340]

For the moment, the efforts of the Covenant-breakers were stalled.

42

'Black Darkness Enshrouds All Regions . . .'

In late December of 1915 a conference of leaders of the Allies took place in France. There, France, Britain, Russia and Italy adopted the principle of a simultaneous general offensive in 1916. It would take months of preparation to launch these offensives but in February, Germany itself took the offensive in a drive towards Verdun. The centre of gravity of the war began to swing back once more to the Western front. Russia made desperate efforts to prepare for a fresh offensive in the East but was woefully ill-prepared and was forced into action by the German offensive. In March the Russians launched a costly and unsuccessful attack at Lake Narocz. It was broken off as soon as possible and preparations continued for a larger offensive timed to coincide with a Western offensive on the Somme planned for July. In the East, also in March, British forces under Sir Percy Sykes landed a small force at Bandar 'Abbás on the southern coast of Persia at the entrance to the Gulf and pushed north-east towards Kirmán and then north-west towards Yazd.

The believers in Persia continued to suffer persecution through the years of war. Iran was formally a neutral country during the struggle surging around her but, as Mr Balyuzi writes:

None of the belligerents respected her declared neutrality. Her own people adopted active partisan attitudes, the majority favouring Turkey and Germany. German and Turkish, Russian and British agents were everywhere. Russia and Turkey fought their battles in the north and the north-west of the country, each side receiving substantial aid from the Iranians . . . The central government was powerless. Bandits and highwaymen, as long as they did not get in the way of the belligerents, had the freedom of the roads and caravan routes.[341]

In March 1916 'Abdu'l-Bahá began to write the Tablets of the Divine Plan, a series of fourteen letters addressed to the North American believers, charging them with the mission of taking the message of Bahá'u'lláh to every part of the planet.

'O ye heavenly heralds', these letters begin:

These are the days of Naw-Rúz. I am always thinking of those kind friends! I beg for each and all of you confirmation and assistance from the threshold of Oneness, so that those gatherings may become ignited like unto candles, in the republics of America . . .[342]

These letters, Mr Balyuzi relates, 'are no less than 'Abdu'l-Bahá's charter for the teaching of the Faith of Bahá'u'lláh throughout His Dispensation'.[343]

Eight of these letters were revealed between 26 March and 22 April 1916. In each of these 'Abdu'l-Bahá exhorts the believers to spread the fragrance of the divine teachings throughout the world and gives them a planetary vision of the many countries, territories and islands where they must travel and teach. The scope and vision of the letters are breathtaking and only in the last of these eight letters is there any mention of the war which was then raging.

In the letter to the believers of the United States and Canada, revealed at Bahjí on 19 April 1916, we can glimpse something of the agony at the carnage of war which filled the Master's soul on the eve of the Riḍván Festival:

> O God, my God! Thou seest how black darkness is enshrouding all regions, how all countries are burning with the flame of dissension, and the fire of war and carnage is blazing throughout the East and the West. Blood is flowing, corpses bestrew the ground, and severed heads are fallen on the dust of the battlefield . . .
>
> O Lord! Draw up the people from the abyss of the ocean of hatred and enmity, and deliver them from this impenetrable darkness . . .
>
> O Lord! Hearts are heavy and souls are in anguish. Have mercy on these poor souls and do not leave them to the excesses of their own desires.
>
> O Lord! Make manifest in Thy lands humble and submissive souls, their faces illumined with the rays of guidance, severed from the world, extolling Thy Name, uttering Thy praise, and diffusing the fragrance of Thy holiness amongst mankind.[344]

The first five of these letters were sent to the United States and were published in *Star of the West* magazine in September of 1916.

In June, still ill-prepared and ahead of the Allies' plan of action, Russian troops attacked the Austrians in response to desperate appeals from Italy to prevent Austria reinforcing its Trentino attack.

> Without warning, because without any special concentration of troops, Brusilov's troops advanced against the

Austrian Fourth Army near Luck, and the Austrian Seventh Army in the Bukovina, whose resistance collapsed at the first shock. In three days Brusilov took 200,000 prisoners.

... Brusilov's offensive continued for three months with fair success, but reserves were not at hand for immediate exploitation, and before they could be moved down from the north the Germans were patching up the holes. His later efforts were never so dangerous, but they absorbed all the available Russian reserves, and his ultimate loss of 1,000,000 casualties completed the virtual ruin of Russia's military power.[345]

This last effort of the collapsing Russian regime had several significant consequences. It stopped the Austrian attack on Italy, compelled the Germans to withdraw vital troops from the Western front and led to Rumania, which had only been waiting for a favourable opportunity, to enter the war on the Allies' side. It also led to the replacement of Falkenhayn as supreme commander in chief of the German army by Hindenburg, with Ludendorff as his strategic planner.

In July British and French forces launched their long-planned massive onslaught against German forces both north and south of the River Somme. The campaign dragged on with terrible casualties on both sides until December. In December Rumania was defeated by an Austro-German force and the year ended in an atmosphere of gloom and disappointment for the Allies.

The offensive measures planned by the Entente for 1917 were hindered by the increasing weakness of the French army. So many of her men had already died that the supplies of fresh troops were almost exhausted. The Russian army was almost completely spent and the Russian people were clamouring for peace. In March open revolution broke out and the Tsar was forced to abdicate. A

Provisional Government attempted to continue the war effort but without success. In the spring of 1917 the Entente was perilously near to defeat.

The isolation of the Holy Land was complete at this time. Lady Blomfield writes:

> During these very difficult and dangerous days of the war 'Abdu'l-Bahá was desirous of sending a Tablet to the friends in Ṭihrán, there to be copied and despatched to the Bahá'ís in different parts of the world.[346]

This was an extremely difficult assignment. But an Arabian Bahá'í, named Ḥájí Ramaḍán, stepped forward to undertake the task.

Ḥájí Ramaḍán was 75 years old, almost blind, without wife or dependents and had given away his shop and property to his sons-in-law. 'Abdu'l-Bahá accepted his offer to walk to Ṭihrán with a letter. The letter began:

> What though the doors be closed, the roads and the ways barred, and the usual means of communication be no longer existing, yet the streams of union and nearness of heart flow on without ceasing in the ecstasy of spiritual communion.[347]

The journey took Ḥájí Ramaḍán 45 days and after a short rest he hurried back to Haifa. Through Kirmánsháh and Baghdád he went, disguised as pedlar, with gold in the bottom of his pedlar's bags and letters sewn into his cloak. As Lady Blomfield recounts, he 'laid the gold and the letters with which he had been entrusted, intact, at the feet of the Master!'

> 'Behold by what poor and humble children of God are great events served,' said 'Abdu'l-Bahá, embracing him.

After some rest this gallant friend again started on a mission, but alas! he never arrived. And no tidings of the fate of brave and loving Ḥájí Ramaḍán ever reached the friends. From time to time others were sent to seek him, but all in vain.[348]

43

An Ominous Threat

Between 2 February and 8 March 1917 'Abdu'l-Bahá revealed six more Tablets to the North American believers, expanding and reinforcing the instructions given in the eight Tablets of the previous year. Altogether, some 120 territories and islands are mentioned by name in the Tablets of the Divine Plan.

By the spring of 1917 the people of Palestine were suffering severely from the mismanagement of the Ottoman authorities and from increasing food shortages. Locusts once again descended on the growing crops. Hardships and scarcities increased daily. 'Abdu'l-Bahá, foreseeing that famine would soon result,

> . . . arose to alleviate suffering. There were properties and lands in the Jordan Valley and beyond, at Samrah and 'Adasíyyih, and by the shores of the Sea of Galilee (Lake Tiberias), which 'Abdu'l-Bahá could cultivate for food.[349]

This new responsibility took the Master to Tiberias frequently, a journey which He found difficult when the weather was hot.

In March 1917 British forces advancing slowly up through Mesopotamia took Baghdád. In the Atlantic arena, the ruthless submarine attacks of the Germans against neutral American ships and an attempt to incite Mexico to act against the United States, pushed President Wilson to declare war on Germany on 6 April 1917, but it would be many months before the United States, unprepared for war, could make up for the loss of Russia in the East. By early August Austro-German forces were on the frontiers of Russia itself. In April the British forces struggling to take Gaza were defeated. This reversal led to General Allenby being appointed to take Gaza and lead an offensive into Palestine. This offensive was delayed by the need to withdraw most of his troops to fight in France but reinforcements were dispatched to him from India and Mesopotamia.

By September of 1917 General Allenby was ready to attack. Using the tactics of surprise and speed, he began to roll back the Turkish forces. Jamál Páshá was still in control of the northern parts of Palestine but Allenby pushed swiftly north. By 14 November the Turkish forces were driven apart and the port of Jaffa was taken. Allenby then wheeled his forces to the right for an advance inland towards Jerusalem and on 9 December took control of the Holy City. His advance further north was delayed while the necessary military preparations were made.

The ceaseless efforts of the Covenant-breakers to use the crisis of the war for their own ends continued unabated. So venomous were the reports they now fed to Jamál Páshá that the Turkish commander began threatening to crucify 'Abdu'l-Bahá and all His family on the slopes of Mount Carmel.

Major Tudor-Pole, the British believer whom 'Abdu'l-Bahá had visited in Bristol during His Western journey, took part in the attack on Jerusalem but after it, in his own words:

. . . being temporarily incapacitated for active service, was transferred to Intelligence, first at Cairo and later at Ludd, Jaffa and Jerusalem . . .

Meanwhile, the news reaching me concerning 'Abdu'l-Bahá's imminent danger became more and more alarming. I tried to arouse interest in the matter among those who were responsible for Intelligence Service activities . . .

At this time chance brought me into touch with an officer whose social and political connexions in London were strong. Through his courtesy and interest I was enabled to get an urgent message through to the British Foreign Office.[350]

At the same time, Major Tudor-Pole contacted Lady Blomfield in London. As she recounts:

In the spring of 1918, I was much startled and deeply disturbed by a telephone message: ''Abdu'l-Bahá in serious danger. Take immediate action.' It came from an authoritative source. There was not a moment to be lost . . .

I went at once to Lord Lamington. His sympathetic regard for 'Abdu'l-Bahá, his understanding of the ramifications and 'red tape' necessary for 'immediate action' were of priceless value . . .

That very evening a cable was sent to General Allenby with these instructions, 'Extend every protection and consideration to 'Abdu'l-Bahá, His family and His friends, when the British march on Haifa.'[351]

Major Tudor-Pole continues:

This despatch passed through my hands in Cairo *en route* for Army Headquarters at Ludd . . . and Intelligence was requested to make urgent enquiry. In due course this demand for information reached the Headquarters of Intelligence at the Savoy Hotel, Cairo, and ultimately (when enquiries elsewhere had proved fruitless) was passed to me for action. As a result, General Allenby was provided with full particulars in regard to 'Abdu'l-Bahá . . . and the history of the Movement of which He was the Master.

Allenby at once issued orders to the General Commanding Officer in command of the Haifa operations to the effect that immediately the town was entered, a British guard was to be posted at once around 'Abdu'l-Bahá's house, and a further guard was to be placed at the disposal of His family and followers. Means were found for making it known within the enemy lines that stern retribution would follow any attempt to cause death or injury to the great Persian Master or to any of His household . . .[352]

Once Allenby was ready to push further north, his advance was swift. During the advance towards Haifa, Major Tudor-Pole recounts:

. . . field batteries were placed in position on high ground immediately to the south-east of Mount Carmel, the intention being to shell Haifa at long range over Mount Carmel itself. Some of the Eastern Bahá'ís living on the northern slopes of Mount Carmel becoming agitated, went to 'Abdu'l-Bahá's residence and expressed fear as to the tragic course of possible events . . . 'Abdu'l-Bahá calmed His excited followers and called them to prayer. Then He told them that all would be well, and that no British shells would cause death or damage to the population or to Haifa and its environs. As a matter of historical fact, the range of the field batteries in question was inaccurate . . .[353]

Once the assault on the town began, the shells fired passed right over the town and fell into the sea. Allenby took Haifa several days before it was thought possible for him to do so and that same day, Lady Blomfield relates:

. . . he sent a cablegram to London which caused everybody to wonder, and especially filled the hearts of the Bahá'ís in all the world with deep gratitude to the Almighty Protector.

The cable of General Allenby was as follows: 'Have to-day taken Palestine. Notify the world that 'Abdu'l-Bahá is safe.'[354]

'Akká, too, fell without bloodshed, an event that the Master had also confidently foretold. Major Tudor-Pole later learnt that:

> Very early one morning, two British Army Service soldiers, who had lost their bearings in the night, found themselves at the gates of 'Akká, believing erroneously that the town was already in British hands. However, the Turkish rear-guard troops had been secretly evacuated only eight hours earlier, and the Mayor of the town, seeing British soldiers outside the gates, came down and presented them with the keys of the town in token of surrender! It is credibly stated that the dismayed Tommies, being unarmed, dropped the keys and made post haste for the British lines![355]

44

In the First Months of Peace

The very day after Haifa was taken by the British, the Governor of Jerusalem, Lt Col (later Sir) Ronald Storrs called on the Master. The governor had met 'Abdu'l-Bahá both in Haifa and in Egypt, where, as he himself writes:

> . . . I had the honour of looking after him and of presenting him to Lord Kitchener, who was deeply impressed by his personality, as who could fail to be?
> The war separated us again until Lord Allenby, after his triumphant drive through Syria, sent me to establish the Government at Haifa and throughout that district. I called upon 'Abbás Effendi on the day I arrived and was delighted to find him quite unchanged.[356]

Lady Blomfield writes of these first days of peace:

> We learned that when the British marched into Haifa there was some difficulty about the commissariat. The officer in charge went to consult the Master.
> 'I have corn,' was the reply.
> 'But for the army?' said the astonished soldier.
> 'I have corn for the British Army,' said 'Abdu'l-Bahá.[357]

Major Tudor-Pole reached the Haifa area on 20 November 1918, only a week after the armistice agreement was signed in Europe and the war officially ended.

'Captain [later Major] Tudor-Pole surprised and gladdened us', Shoghi Effendi, then acting as 'Abdu'l-Bahá's secretary, records,

> with his unexpected arrival from Egypt . . . The Beloved has been sojourning for a month and a half at Acca, visiting almost daily the Tomb of his father and offering his thanksgivings for the bounty, care and protection of the Blessed Perfection . . .[358]

Tudor-Pole wrote of his own visit:

> . . . The Master was standing at the top [of the stairway] waiting to greet me with that sweet smile and cheery welcome for which he is famous. For seventy-four long years Abdul-Baha has lived in the midst of tragedy and hardship, yet nothing has robbed or can rob him of his cheery optimism, spiritual insight and keen sense of humour.
>
> He was looking little older than when I saw him seven years ago, and certainly more vigorous than when in England after the exhausting American trip. His voice is as strong as ever, his step virile, his hair and beard are (if possible) more silver-white than before . . .
>
> After lunch Abdul-Baha drove me out to the Garden Tomb of Baha'o'llah . . . He approached the Tomb in complete silence, praying with bent head – a wonderfully venerable figure in his white turban and flowing grey robe.
>
> On reaching the portal to the Tomb itself, the Master prostrated himself at length, and kissed the steps leading to the inner chamber. There was a majestic humility about the action that baffles description . . .
>
> . . . Then I went to pay my respects to the Military Governor . . .
>
> . . . I returned to the prison house and spent the evening with the Master, supping with him and answering his questions about the new administration.

Then I slept in the room next Abdul-Baha's (which was Baha'o'llah's before him) – simple attics with stone floors and practically no furniture. Abdul-Baha still gives away all money, and lives the life of poverty himself.

Before breakfast the house was filled with believers who had come to receive the morning blessing.

I had brought Abdul-Baha letters from all parts of the world, and he spent the morning dictating replies for me to take away. I gave him the Persian camel-hair cloak, and it greatly pleased him, for the winter is here, and he had given away the only cloak he possessed. I made him promise to keep this one through the winter anyway, and I trust he does.

At lunch we had another long talk; then came the leave-taking and the Master's blessing. He sent greetings by me to all his friends in Egypt, Europe, England and America!

As I drove off on my return to Haifa, I caught a glimpse of the Master, staff in hand, wending his way through the awful Acca slums, on his way to attend the local Peace celebrations . . . He stands out a majestic figure . . .[359]

Major Tudor-Pole was able to help Laura and Hippolyte Dreyfus-Barney to reach Haifa very soon after the war ended. In December, Ahmad Sohrab left Haifa for the United States carrying with him the Tablets of the Divine Plan which had been hidden, during the most dangerous days of the war, in the vaults under the shrine of the Báb on Mount Carmel.

Letters from believers all over the world now began to arrive in great numbers and 'Abdu'l-Bahá was much occupied in replying. Pilgrims too were arriving from both East and West. Shoghi Effendi, now 21 years old and acting as 'Abdu'l-Bahá's secretary, noted, at the end of January that nearly one hundred letters had recently been revealed for the American believers alone. As soon as the war had ended the American believers had begun to beseech 'Abdu'l-Bahá to visit them again. The believers of Chicago sent out a petition asking for signatures and over a thousand believers signed the supplication for 'Abdu'l-Bahá to visit their shores again.

Between 26 and 30 April 1919, during the annual meeting of the Bahá'í Temple Unity, the Tablets of the Divine Plan were presented and read to the American Bahá'ís. A number of American believers began to make preparations to travel and teach in response to the exhortations given in these Tablets. In May the Master wrote to the American believers that their unity and constancy would be the magnet that would draw Him to America again.

45

'An Almost Incredible
Amount of Work'

In the Holy Land itself relief work was set in hand to assist those displaced or suffering as a result of the recent struggles. 'Abdu'l-Bahá gave generously to the local relief fund. Lord Lamington, who was supervising relief work in the Holy Land from his headquarters in Damascus, called on 'Abdu'l-Bahá twice in July. On his second visit, 'Abdu'l-Bahá said that, if circumstances permitted, He would visit 'Ishqábád, then Japan and India. Many years later, in a letter to Lady Blomfield, Lord Lamington recalled his memories of the Master in these words:

> There was never a more striking instance of one who desired that mankind should live in peace and goodwill and have love for others by the recognition of their inherent divine qualities.
> At Haifa, in 1919, I well remember seeing a white figure seated by the roadside; when he arose and walked the vision of a truly holy and saintly man impressed itself on me. I think it was on this occasion that he took his signet ring from off his finger and gave it to me.[360]

The work of 'Abdu'l-Bahá increased daily as contacts with the believers were restored. Shoghi Effendi wrote in a letter at this time:

My head is in a whirl, so busy and so eventful was the day. No less than a score of callers from prince and pasha to a simple private soldier have sought interview with 'Abdu'l-Bahá.[361]

And in another:

The Beloved from morn till eve, even at midnight is engaged in revealing Tablets, in sending forth his constructive, dynamic thoughts of love and principles to a sad and disillusioned world.[362]

Beyond the Holy Land, 'Abdu'l-Bahá gave great encouragement to the founders of the Save the Children Fund. Lady Blomfield was closely associated with this organization which was founded by Eglantyne Jebb in 1919. In a letter to one of those working for this organization, 'Abdu'l-Bahá wrote:

My hope is that thou mayest be confirmed in the great cause (of saving children), which is the greatest service to the world of mankind. For the poor children are perishing from hunger and their condition is indeed pitiable. This is one of the evils of the war.[363]

To another worker for the Fund He wrote:

. . . praise be unto God, such an Association has been formed (for the relief of destitute children and orphans) in which almost every nation and every religion is represented.[364]

On 4 November 1919 Dr John Esslemont, a physician from Britain, arrived in Haifa. 'Abdu'l-Bahá had invited him to bring the manuscript of a book he was writing on the Faith. 'Abdu'l-Bahá intended to have the manuscript translated into Persian so that He could amend it where necessary. Dr Esslemont has given us the following account of those days in his well-known work *Bahá'u'lláh and the New Era*:

> During the winter of 1919–20 the writer had the great privilege of spending two and a half months as the guest of 'Abdu'l-Bahá at Haifa and intimately observing His daily life. At that time, although nearly seventy-six years of age, He was still remarkably vigorous, and accomplished daily an almost incredible amount of work. Although often very weary He showed wonderful powers of recuperation, and His services were always at the disposal of those who needed them most. His unfailing patience, gentleness, kindliness and tact made His presence like a benediction. It was His custom to spend a large part of each night in prayer and meditation. From early morning until evening, except for a short siesta after lunch, He was busily engaged in reading and answering letters from many lands and in attending to the multitudinous affairs of the household and of the Cause. In the afternoon He usually had a little relaxation in the form of a walk or a drive, but even then He was usually accompanied by one or two, or a party, of pilgrims with whom He would converse on spiritual matters, or He would find opportunity by the way of seeing and ministering to some of the poor. After His return He would call the friends to the usual evening meeting in His salon. Both at lunch and supper He used to entertain a number of pilgrims and friends, and charm his guests with happy and humorous stories as well as precious talks on a great variety of subjects. 'My home is the home of laughter and mirth,' He declared, and indeed it was so. He delighted in gathering together people of various races, colours, nations and religions in unity and cordial friendship around His hospitable board. He was indeed a loving father not only to the little community at Haifa, but to the Bahá'í community throughout the world.[365]

In December 1919 'Abdu'l-Bahá revealed a Tablet which He addressed to the Central Organization For a Durable Peace at The Hague, a group of progressive thinkers from a number of European countries. In this Tablet He writes at length of the prerequisites for a just and lasting peace between the nations:

> . . . although the League of Nations has been brought into existence, yet it is incapable of establishing Universal Peace. But the Supreme Tribunal which . . . Bahá'u'lláh has described will fulfil this sacred task with the utmost might and power.[366]

On 27 April 1920, at the Twelfth Annual Convention of the Bahá'í Temple Unity, held in Chicago, several designs for the House of Worship at Wilmette were considered by the assembled delegates and Louis Bourgeois's striking design was chosen by a majority vote.

On the very same afternoon, a Knighthood of the British Empire was conferred on 'Abdu'l-Bahá in recognition of the work He had done during the war in the Holy Land to relieve famine and distress. 'Abdu'l-Bahá accepted the honour as the gift of a 'just king' but chose never to use the title. Lady Blomfield tells us more of this occasion:

> The dignitaries of the British crown from Jerusalem were gathered in Haifa, eager to do honour to the Master, Whom every one had come to love and reverence for His life of unselfish service. An imposing motor-car had been sent to bring 'Abdu'l-Bahá to the ceremony. The Master, however, could not be found. People were sent in every direction to look for Him, when suddenly from an unexpected side He appeared, alone, walking His kingly walk, with that simplicity of greatness which always enfolded Him.

The faithful servant, Isfandíyár, whose joy it had been for many years to drive the Master on errands of mercy, stood sadly looking on at the elegant motor-car which awaited the honoured guest.

'No longer am I needed.'

At a sign from Him, Who knew the sorrow, old Isfandíyár rushed off to harness the horse, and brought the carriage out at the lower gate, whence 'Abdu'l-Bahá was driven to a side entrance of the garden of the governorate of Phoenicia.

So Isfandíyár was needed and happy.[367]

In the spring of 1920 Shoghi Effendi left Haifa, first for Paris and then to study at Balliol College in Oxford. In April 1920 Hyde and Clara Dunn arrived in Australia and in July Martha Root set out for South America. In September work began on breaking ground for the foundation for the House of Worship in Wilmette and in December of 1920 the first All-India Convention of Bahá'ís was held in Bombay.

Pilgrims and visitors continued to arrive in Haifa. In 1921 Fujita came from the United States and Luṭfu'lláh Hakím from London to assist 'Abdu'l-Bahá, chiefly with the reception of the many pilgrims. There was much going on in Haifa, as Mr Balyuzi relates:

A house close to 'Abdu'l-Bahá's house had been prepared for pilgrims from the West. Mrs Emogene Hoagg looked after the pilgrims there during the summer of 1921. A little above 'Abdu'l-Bahá's house, land was purchased on the other side of the road for the building of a Western Pilgrim house in the future.[368]

'Abdu'l-Bahá was now 77 years old.

Section VIII

1921

'Abdu'l-Bahá's bed

46

The Passing of 'Abdu'l-Bahá

In the early part of 1921, 'Abdu'l-Bahá's health was not good. In March He stayed for a while at Tiberias. Back in Haifa, He spent some nights on Mount Carmel near the shrine of the Báb. He was on Mount Carmel on the evening of the anniversary of the martyrdom of the Báb. There He revealed a prayer in honour of a relative of the Báb who had recently passed away. In this prayer are the words:

> O Lord! My bones are weakened, and the hoar hairs glisten on My head . . . and I have now reached old age, failing in My powers . . . No strength is there left in Me wherewith to arise and serve Thy loved ones . . . O Lord, My Lord! Hasten My ascension unto Thy sublime Threshold . . . and My arrival at the Door of Thy grace beneath the shadow of Thy most great mercy . . .[369]

Sometime in October the Master recounted to His family a striking dream:

> I seemed to be standing within a great temple, in the inmost shrine, facing the east, in the place of the leader himself. I became aware that a large number of people were flocking into the temple: more and yet more crowded in, taking their places in rows behind me, until there was a vast multitude. As I stood I raised loudly the

'Call to Prayer'. Suddenly the thought came to me to go forth from the temple.

When I found myself outside I said within myself, 'For what reason came I forth, not having led the prayer? But it matters not: now that I have uttered the call to prayer, the vast multitude will of themselves chant the prayer.'[370]

At the end of October a Turkish friend, Dr Sulaymán Rafat Bey, who was a guest in the Master's house, received news of the sudden death of his brother. In comforting him, 'Abdu'l-Bahá whispered these words:

'Sorrow not, for he is only transferred from this plane to a higher one; I too shall soon be transferred, for my days are numbered.' Then patting him gently on the shoulder he looked him in the face and said, 'And it will be in the days that are shortly to come.'[371]

In that same week He revealed a Tablet for the friends in America which contains this prayer:

Yá Bahá'i'l-Abhá! (O Thou the Glory of Glories) I have renounced the world and the people thereof, and am heart-broken and sorely afflicted because of the un-faithful. In the cage of this world, I flutter even as a frightened bird, and yearn every day to take my flight unto Thy Kingdom.

Yá Bahá'i'l-Abhá! Make me to drink of the cup of sacrifice and set me free. Relieve me from these woes and trials, from these afflictions and troubles. Thou art He that aideth, that succoureth, that protecteth, that stretcheth forth the hand of help.[372]

A few weeks later, as Shoghi Effendi and Lady Blomfield relate:

. . . the Master came in from the solitary room in the garden, which he had occupied of late, and said:–

'I dreamed a dream and behold the Blessed Beauty (Bahá'u'lláh) came and said unto me, 'Destroy this room!'

The family, who had been wishing that he would come and sleep in the house, not being happy that he should be alone at night, exclaimed, 'Yes, Master, we think your dream means that you should leave that room and come into the house.' When he heard this from us, he smiled meaningly as though not agreeing with our interpretation. Afterwards we understood that by the 'room' was meant the temple of his body . . .[373]

In November 'Abdu'l-Bahá wrote His last Tablet to the Bahá'ís of America. He had been much occupied in guiding the believers there through the many problems that arose as construction of the House of Worship in Chicago began. An added burden came from the activities of the Covenant-breakers. During the years of isolation brought about by the war, they had exerted every effort to divide the American Bahá'í community.

'O ye friends of God!' 'Abdu'l-Bahá wrote.

'Abdu'l-Bahá is day and night thinking of you and mentioning you . . . Every morning at dawn I supplicate the Kingdom of God and ask that you may be filled with the breath of the Holy Spirit . . .

In America, in these days, severe winds have surrounded the Lamp of the Covenant, hoping that this brilliant Light may be extinguished, and this Tree of Life may be uprooted. Certain weak, capricious, malicious and ignorant souls have been shaken . . . Every day they seek a pretext and secretly arouse doubts, so that the Covenant of Bahá'u'lláh may be completely annihilated in America.

O friends of God! Be awake, be awake; be vigilant, be vigilant . . .[374]

A wedding was planned for Khusraw, a trusted household servant, for late November. On 25 November, which was a Friday, 'Abdu'l-Bahá spoke these words to His daughters:

The wedding of Khusraw must take place today. If you are too much occupied, I myself will make the necessary preparations, for it must take place this day.[375]

That day 'Abdu'l-Bahá attended the noonday prayer at the mosque. As was the custom, the poor of the neighbourhood were waiting for Him after the prayers.

This day, as usual, he stood, in spite of very great fatigue, whilst he gave a coin to every one with his own hands.
    After lunch he dictated some Tablets, his last ones, to Ruhi Effendi. When he had rested he walked in the garden. He seemed to be in a deep reverie.[376]

Later in the evening of Friday He blessed the bride and bridegroom who had just been married. He also attended the usual meeting of the friends in His own audience chamber.

On Saturday, 26 November, 'Abdu'l-Bahá rose early and drank tea with the friends, as was His custom. Then, as Shoghi Effendi and Lady Blomfield relate:

He asked for the fur-lined coat which had belonged to Bahá'u'lláh. He often put on this coat when he was cold or did not feel well, he so loved it. He then withdrew to his room, lay down on his bed and said, 'Cover me up. I am very cold. Last night I did not sleep well, I felt cold. This is serious, it is the beginning.'

After more blankets had been put on, he asked for
the fur coat he had taken off to be placed over him.
That day he was rather feverish. In the evening his
temperature rose still higher, but during the night the
fever left him. After midnight he asked for some tea.[377]

On Sunday He seemed better but was persuaded to remain
on the sofa in His room. That day a feast was to be held
on the occasion of the anniversary of the declaration of the
Covenant, hosted by a Parsi pilgrim who had recently
arrived from India. 'Abdu'l-Bahá sent all the friends up to
the shrine of the Báb where the feast was held.

He asked His sister and all the family to have tea with
Him in His room. After tea the Muftí of Haifa and the
head of the Municipality, together with another visitor,
called and were received by Him. They stayed for about an
hour.

He spoke to them about Bahá'u'lláh, related to them
his second dream, showed them extraordinary kindness
and even more than his usual courtesy. He then bade
them farewell, walking with them to the outer door in
spite of their pleading that he should remain resting
on his sofa.[378]

Next, the head of the local police, an Englishman, arrived.
'Abdu'l-Bahá received him warmly and gave him a gift
of some silk hand-woven Persian handkerchiefs. Then
'Abdu'l-Bahá's four sons-in-law and Ruhi Effendi came to
see Him after returning from the feast held on the mountain. They told the Master that the giver of the feast was
unhappy because 'Abdu'l-Bahá had not been there:
'But I was there,' 'Abdu'l-Bahá told them,

though my body was absent, my spirit was there in your
midst. I was present with the friends at the Tomb. The

friends must not attach any importance to the absence
of my body. In spirit I am, and shall always be, with the
friends, even though I be far away.[379]

On that same evening 'Abdu'l-Bahá asked after the health
of each member of the Household, of the pilgrims and of
the friends in Haifa. 'Very good, very good' was His reply
when He learnt that all were well.

Shoghi Effendi and Lady Blomfield relate that this was
'Abdu'l-Bahá's very last utterance concerning His friends.
He went to bed at eight that evening after taking a little
food and assuring His family that He was quite well. He
asked all the family to go to bed and rest but two of His
daughters stayed with Him.

Shoghi Effendi and Lady Blomfield have left us this
account of the next hours:

That night the Master had gone to sleep very calmly,
quite free from fever. He awoke about 1.15 a.m., got
up and walked across to a table where he drank some
water. He took off an outer garment, saying: 'I am too
warm.' He went back to bed and when his daughter
Ruha Khanum, later on, approached, she found him
lying peacefully and, as he looked into her face, he
asked her to lift up the net curtains, saying:
'I have difficulty in breathing, give me more air.'
Some rose water was brought of which he drank, sitting
up in bed to do so, without any help. He again lay
down, and as some food was offered him, he remarked
in a clear and distinct voice:
'You wish me to take some food, and I am going?'
He gave them a beautiful look. His face was so calm,
his expression so serene, they thought him asleep . . .
His long martyrdom was ended![380]

Early on Monday morning November 28th the news
of this sudden calamity had spread over the city, caus-

ing an unprecedented stir and tumult, and filling all hearts with unutterable grief.

The next morning, Tuesday November 29th the funeral took place; a funeral the like of which Haifa, nay Palestine itself, had surely never seen; so deep was the feeling that brought so many thousands of mourners together, representative of so many religions, races and tongues.[381]

The funeral procession was headed by a guard of honour

consisting of the City Constabulary Force, followed by the Boy Scouts of the Moslem and Christian communities holding aloft their banners, a company of Moslem choristers chanting their verses from the Quran, the chiefs of the Moslem community headed by the Mufti, a number of Christian priests, Latin, Greek and Anglican, all preceding the sacred coffin, upraised on the shoulders of his loved ones. Immediately behind it came the members of his family . . .[382]

The High Commissioner of Palestine, Sir Herbert Samuel, was there. The Governor of Jerusalem, the Governor of Phoenicia, the chief officials of the Government and the consuls of various countries who were resident in Haifa were also there. These high officials walked immediately behind the family of 'Abdu'l-Bahá. Behind them came the heads of the different religious communities and the notables of Palestine and behind them

. . . Jews, Christians, Moslems, Druses, Egyptians, Greeks, Turks, Kurds, and a host of his American, European and native friends, men, women and children, both of high and low degree, all, about ten thousand in number, mourning the loss of their Beloved One.[383]

The day was cloudless. There was no sound in all the town of Haifa and its surrounding countryside through which the funeral procession passed

> . . . save only the soft, slow, rhythmic chanting of Islam in the Call to Prayer, or the convulsed sobbing moan of those helpless ones, bewailing the loss of their one friend, who had protected them in all their difficulties and sorrows, whose generous bounty had saved them and their little ones from starvation through the terrible years of the 'Great Woe' . . .
>
> As they slowly wended their way up Mount Carmel, the Vineyard of God, the casket appeared in the distance to be borne aloft by invisible hands, so high above the heads of the people was it carried.[384]

It took two hours for the procession to reach the garden of the shrine of the Báb. There the coffin was placed upon a plain table covered with a white linen cloth. Representatives of the various denominations now stepped forward, one by one:

> . . . some on the impulse of the moment, others prepared, raised their voices in eulogy and regret, paying their last homage of farewell to their loved one. So united were they in their acclamation of him, as the wise educator and reconciler of the human race in this perplexed and sorrowful age, that there seemed to be nothing left for the Bahá'ís to say.[385]

The nine speakers having delivered their funeral orations,

> . . . then came the moment when the casket which held the pearl of loving servitude passed slowly and triumphantly into its simple, hallowed resting place.[386]

Appendix 1
List of Names

'Abdu'l-Bahá
  eldest surviving son of Bahá'u'lláh and Ásíyih Khánum, born in Ṭihrán in May 1844

Abu'l Faḍl, Mírzá
  foremost Bahá'í scholar in the time of Bahá'u'lláh and 'Abdu'l-Bahá

Ali-Kuli Khan
  a young Bahá'í of Káshán who worked in 'Abdu'l-Bahá's household as a translator and travelled to the United States to assist Mírzá Abu'l Faḍl. He married Florence Breed, an American Bahá'í, and worked in the diplomatic service of Iran.

Ásíyih Khánum
  mother of 'Abdu'l-Bahá, honoured by Bahá'u'lláh with the title Navváb. A noblewoman of Yalrúd who married Bahá'u'lláh in 1835.

Báb
  Prophet-Herald of the Bahá'í Faith who was martyred in 1850

Badí'u'lláh
son of Bahá'u'lláh and Mahd-i-Ulyá who broke the Covenant of Bahá'u'lláh

Bahá'u'lláh
Founder-Prophet of the Bahá'í Faith, Father of 'Abdu'l-Bahá

Bahíyyih Khánum
sister of 'Abdu'l-Bahá, next to Him in age, given the title 'The Greatest Holy Leaf' by Bahá'u'lláh

Ḍíyá'iyyih Khánum
eldest daughter of 'Abdu'l-Bahá

Ḍíyá'u'lláh
son of Bahá'u'lláh and Mahd-i-'Ulyá who broke the Covenant

Faríd, Dr Amín
a nephew of 'Abdu'l-Bahá who accompanied Him on His Western travels and then broke the Covenant

Gawhar Khánum
third wife of Bahá'u'lláh, mother of one daughter. Both mother and daughter broke the Covenant.

Ḥaydar-'Alí, Ḥájí Mírzá
a Bahá'í of Iṣfahán who travelled widely and suffered greatly for the Faith. Given the name 'Angel of Carmel' by 'Abdu'l-Bahá.

Ḥusayn-i-Ashchí
a Bahá'í youth from Káshán who served Bahá'u'lláh as a cook in Adrianople and later in 'Akká

Isfandíyár
household steward, much trusted African servant of Bahá'u'lláh while He lived in Persia

Isfandíyár
faithful servant of 'Abdu'l-Bahá in the Holy Land

Ján, Mírzá Áqá
amanuensis of Bahá'u'lláh for many years, he broke the Covenant after the passing of Bahá'u'lláh

Mahd-i-'Ulyá
second wife of Bahá'u'lláh, mother of Muḥammad-'Alí and three other surviving children, all of whom broke the Covenant

Majdu'd-Dín
nephew of Bahá'u'lláh, son of Mírzá Músá who broke the Covenant

Mihdí, Mírzá
younger brother of 'Abdu'l-Bahá, who joined the exiles in Baghdád and died after falling through a skylight in the Most Great Prison in 1870

Muḥammad, Siyyid
a Bábí who was jealous of Bahá'u'lláh's prestige. He schemed with Mírzá Yaḥyá to destroy Bahá'u'lláh's authority. He was murdered in 'Akká in 1872.

Muḥammad-'Alí
half-brother of 'Abdu'l-Bahá, he did not accept the leadership of 'Abdu'l-Bahá and worked to destroy 'Abdu'l-Bahá's authority

Muḥammad Qulí, Mírzá
half-brother and loyal follower of Bahá'u'lláh, uncle of 'Abdu'l-Bahá, shared in exile and imprisonment

Munavvar Khánum
daughter of 'Abdu'l-Bahá

Munírih Khánum
wife of 'Abdu'l-Bahá, she bore Him nine children, five of whom died in infancy

Músá Áqáy-i-Kalím, Mírzá
loyal brother of Bahá'u'lláh, uncle of 'Abdu'l-Bahá, shared exile and imprisonment, died in 'Akká in 1887

Nabíl-i-A'ẓam (Mullá Muḥammad-i-Zarandí)
a Bahá'í who compiled *The Dawn-Breakers*, an account of the early days of the Bahá'í Revelation. He drowned himself in the sea shortly after the passing of Bahá'u'lláh.

Rúḥá Khánum
daughter of 'Abdu'l-Bahá, she helped Him with His vast correspondence

Ṭáhirih
the only woman amongst the Letters of the Living, the Báb's first disciples, martyred in 1852

Túbá Khánum
daughter of 'Abdu'l-Bahá who related her memories
of her childhood to Lady Blomfield

Vaḥíd
outstanding religious teacher who became a Bábí and
was martyred in 1850

Yaḥyá, Mírzá
younger half-brother of Bahá'u'lláh, uncle of 'Abdu'l-
Bahá, he never acknowledged Bahá'u'lláh's leadership, died on Cyprus in 1912

Yúnis Khán-i-Afrúkhtih, Dr
a loyal secretary of 'Abdu'l-Bahá who wrote down his
memoirs of that time

Appendix 2
Qájár and Ottoman Rulers

Qájár Rulers of Persia during the
Life of 'Abdu'l-Bahá

Muḥammad Sháh   1834–48

Náṣiri'd-Dín Sháh   1848–96 (assassinated)

Muẓaffaru'd-Dín Sháh 1896–1907

Muḥammad-'Alí Sháh 1907–9 (abdicated)

Aḥmad Sháh   1909–25 (deposed)

Qájár dynasty ended   1925

Ottoman Rulers during the
Life of 'Abdu'l-Bahá

Sulṭán 'Abdul-Majíd   1839–61

Sulṭán 'Abdu'l-'Azíz   1861–76 (deposed)

Sulṭán Murád V   1876 (deposed)

Sulṭán 'Abdu'l-Ḥamíd 1876–1909 (deposed)

Muḥammad V   1909–18

Muḥammad VI   1918–22

Sultanate abolished   1922

Appendix 3

A Few Dates

1844   *23 May* The Báb declares His mission to Mullá Ḥusayn in S͟híráz

1844   Birth of 'Abdu'l-Bahá in Ṭihrán

1852   Bahá'u'lláh is imprisoned in the Síyáh-C͟hál

1853   Bahá'u'lláh and His family exiled to Bag͟hdád

1863   Bahá'u'lláh and His family exiled to Constantinople

1863   Bahá'u'lláh and His family exiled to Adrianople

1868   Bahá'u'lláh and His family exiled to 'Akká

1868–70   The exiles are imprisoned in the citadel of 'Akká

1870   Death of Mírzá Mihdí, the Purest Branch

1870 The exiles are moved to the house of 'Údí <u>Kh</u>ammár

1872 Marriage of 'Abdu'l-Bahá and Munírih <u>Kh</u>ánum

1892 Passing of Bahá'u'lláh

1901 A strict confinement in 'Akká reimposed

1908 'Abdu'l-Bahá is released from imprisonment

1910 'Abdu'l-Bahá visits Egypt

1911 'Abdu'l-Bahá visits Britain and France

1912 'Abdu'l-Bahá visits the United States and Canada

1912–13 'Abdu'l-Bahá visits Britain, Europe and Egypt again

1921 Passing of 'Abdu'l-Bahá

Bibliography

'Abdu'l-Bahá. *Memorials of the Faithful*. Wilmette, Ill.: Bahá'í Publishing Trust, 1971.

— *The Promulgation of Universal Peace*. Wilmette, Ill.: Bahá'í Publishing Trust, 1982.

— *The Secret of Divine Civilization*. Wilmette, Ill.: Bahá'í Publishing Trust, 1957.

— *Some Answered Questions*. Wilmette, Ill.: Bahá'í Publishing Trust, 1981.

— *Tablets of the Divine Plan*. Wilmette, Ill.: Bahá'í Publishing Trust, 1977.

— *The Will and Testament of 'Abdu'l-Bahá*. Wilmette, Ill.: Bahá'í Publishing Trust, 1971.

Bahá'í Revelation, The. London: Bahá'í Publishing Trust, 1955.

Bahá'í World, The. vol. 13. Haifa: The Universal House of Justice, 1970.

Bahá'í Year Book. vol. 1. New York City: Bahá'í Publishing Committee, 1926.

Bahá'u'lláh. *The Kitáb-i-Aqdas*. Haifa: Bahá'í World Centre, 1992.

— *Tablets of Bahá'u'lláh*. Wilmette, Ill.: Bahá'í Publishing Trust, 1988.

Balyuzi, H. M. *'Abdu'l-Bahá*. Oxford: George Ronald, 1971.

— *The Báb*. Oxford: George Ronald, 1973.

— *Bahá'u'lláh, The King of Glory*. Oxford: George Ronald, 1980.

— *Eminent Bahá'ís in the Time of Bahá'u'lláh: with some Historical Background*. Oxford: George Ronald, 1985.

Barber, Noel. *The Sultans*. New York: Simon and Schuster, 1973.

Barkhordar Nahai, Gina. *Cry of the Peacock*. New York: Crown Publishers Inc., 1991.

Blomfield, Lady [Sara Louise]. *The Chosen Highway*. Wilmette, Ill.: Bahá'í Publishing Trust, no date.

Browne, Edward G. 'Introduction', *A Traveller's Narrative*. Cambridge: Cambridge University Press, 1891.

Chase, Thornton. *In Galilee*. Los Angeles: Kalimát Press, 1985.

Diary of Juliet Thompson, The. Los Angeles: Kalimát Press, 1983.

Esslemont, J. E. *Bahá'u'lláh and the New Era*. London: Bahá'í Publishing Trust, 1974.

Faizi, A. Q. *A Gift of Love offered to the Greatest Holy Leaf*. Comp. and ed. by Gloria Faizi. 1982.

Furútan, 'Alí-Akbar. *Stories of Bahá'u'lláh*. Oxford: George Ronald, 1986.

Gail, Marzieh. *Summon Up Remembrance*. Oxford: George Ronald, 1987.

Ḥaydar-'Alí, Ḥájí Mírzá. *Stories from the Delight of Hearts: The Memoirs of Ḥájí Mírzá Ḥaydar-'Alí*. Los Angeles: Kalimát Press, 1980.

Hollinger, Richard, ed. *'Abdu'l-Bahá in America: Agnes Parsons' Diary*. Los Angeles: Kalimát Press, 1996.

Honnold, Annamaire. *Vignettes from the Life of 'Abdu'l-Bahá*. Oxford: George Ronald, rev. ed. 1991.

Ives, Howard Colby. *Portals to Freedom*. London: George Ronald, 1967.

Kazemzadeh, Firuz. *Russia and Britain in Persia, 1864–1914. A Study in Imperialism*. New Haven and London: Yale University Press, 1968.

Lidell Hart, Captain B.H. *The Real War 1914–1918*. Boston and Toronto: Little, Brown and Company, 1930.

Maḥmúd-i-Zarqání. *Maḥmúd's Diary*. Oxford: George Ronald, 1998.

Maxwell, May. *An Early Pilgrimage*. Oxford: George Ronald, 1976.

Metelmann, Velda Piff. *Lua Getsinger: Herald of the Covenant*. Oxford: George Ronald, 1997.

Momen, Moojan. *The Bábí and Bahá'í Religions, 1844–1944. Some Contemporary Western Accounts*. Oxford: George Ronald, 1981.

Nabíl-i-A'ẓam. *The Dawn-Breakers: Nabíl's Narrative of the Early Days of the Bahá'í Revelation*. Wilmette, Ill.: Bahá'í Publishing Trust, 1970.

Nakhjavání, Bahíyyih. *Four on an Island*. Oxford: George Ronald, 1983.

Phelps, Myron H. *The Master in 'Akká.* Los Angeles: Kalimát Press, 1985.

Rabbaní, Rúḥíyyih. *The Priceless Pearl.* London: Bahá'í Publishing Trust, 1969.

Ruhe, David. S. *Door of Hope.* Oxford: George Ronald, 1983.

Rutstein, Nathan. *Corinne True: Faithful Handmaid of 'Abdu'l-Bahá.* Oxford: George Ronald, 1987.

Shoghi Effendi. *God Passes By.* Wilmette, Ill.: Bahá'í Publishing Trust, rev. edn. 1974.

— *The World Order of Bahá'u'lláh.* Wilmette, Ill.: Bahá'í Publishing Trust, 1991.

Star of the West. Rpt. Oxford: George Ronald, 1984.

Stockman, Robert. *The Bahá'í Faith in America,* vol. 1. Wilmette, Ill.: Bahá'í Publishing Trust, 1985.

Taherzadeh, Adib. *The Covenant of Bahá'u'lláh.* Oxford: George Ronald, 1992.

— *The Revelation of Bahá'u'lláh,* vol. 1. Oxford: George Ronald, 1974.

— *The Revelation of Bahá'u'lláh,* vol. 2. Oxford: George Ronald, 1977.

— *The Revelation of Bahá'u'lláh,* vol. 3. Oxford: George Ronald, 1983.

— *The Revelation of Bahá'u'lláh,* vol. 4. Oxford: George Ronald, 1987.

References

1. Taherzadeh, *Revelation of Bahá'u'lláh*, vol. 2, p. 394.
2. Taherzadeh, *Covenant of Bahá'u'lláh*, p. 102.
3. Blomfield, *Chosen Highway*, p. 40.
4. Honnold, *Vignettes*, p. 69.
5. 'Abdu'l-Bahá, quoted in *Star of the West*, vol. 13, no. 10, p. 272.
6. Quoted in Blomfield, *Chosen Highway*, p. 22.
7. ibid.
8. Quoted in Nabíl, *Dawn-Breakers*, p. 285n.
9. ibid. p. 441.
10. Quoted in Balyuzi, *'Abdu'l-Bahá*, p. 13.
11. Quoted in Blomfield, *Chosen Highway*, pp. 40–1.
12. Quoted in Balyuzi, *'Abdu'l-Bahá*, pp. 9–10.
13. Faizi, *Gift of Love*, pp. 14–15.
14. 'Abdu'l-Bahá, *Promulgation*, p. 426.
15. Quoted in Blomfield, *Chosen Highway*, pp. 42–3.
16. Phelps, *Master in 'Akká*, p. 17.
17. Quoted in Balyuzi, *'Abdu'l-Bahá*, p. 10.
18. ibid. pp. 11–12.
19. Shoghi Effendi, *God Passes By*, p. 240.
20. Shoghi Effendi, *God Passes By*, p. 109.
21. Phelps, *Master in 'Akká*, pp. 19–20.
22. ibid. pp. 20–2.
23. Quoted in Blomfield, *Chosen Highway*, p. 45.
24. Balyuzi, *'Abdu'l-Bahá*, p. 13.
25. Quoted in Phelps, *Master in 'Akká*, p. 25.
26. Quoted in Blomfield, *Chosen Highway*, p. 53.
27. Phelps, *Master in 'Akká*, pp. 28–9.
28. Quoted in Phelps, *Master in 'Akká*, pp. 29–30.
29. Furútan, *Stories of Bahá'u'lláh*, p. 25.
30. ibid. pp. 25–6.

31. Quoted in Taherzadeh, *Covenant of Bahá'u'lláh*, p. 138.
32. ibid. pp. 103–4.
33. Quoted in *Diary of Juliet Thompson*, p. 171.
34. Quoted in Shoghi Effendi, *God Passes By*, p. 150.
35. Blomfield, *Chosen Highway*, p. 82.
36. Balyuzi, *'Abdu'l-Bahá*, p. 17.
37. 'Abdu'l-Bahá, *Memorials of the Faithful*, p. 146.
38. Quoted in Phelps, *Master in 'Akká*, pp. 39–41.
39. Quoted in Balyuzi, *King of Glory*, p. 179.
40. 'Abdu'l-Bahá, in *Star of the West*, vol. 13, no. 10, p. 278.
41. Quoted in Phelps, *Master in 'Akká*, pp. 41–2.
42. Quoted in *Star of the West*, vol. 13, no. 10, pp. 277–8.
43. Quoted in Phelps, *Master in 'Akká*, p. 42.
44. Quoted in Shoghi Effendi, *God Passes By*, p. 161.
45. Quoted in Phelps, *Master in 'Akká*, p. 47.
46. Quoted in Shoghi Effendi, *God Passes By*, p. 161.
47. Quoted in Phelps, *Master in 'Akká*, pp. 47–8.
48. ibid. p. 48.
49. Quoted in Shoghi Effendi, *God Passes By*, p. 169.
50. Taherzadeh, *Covenant of Bahá'u'lláh*, pp. 126–7.
51. Shoghi Effendi, *God Passes By*, p. 241.
52. ibid.
53. Quoted in ibid. p. 171.
54. ibid. pp. 170–1.
55. Quoted in Shoghi Effendi, *World Order of Bahá'u'lláh*, p. 135.
56. Quoted by Blomfield, *Chosen Highway*, p. 62.
57. Taherzadeh, *Revelation of Bahá'u'lláh*, vol. 2, p. 406.
58. ibid. pp. 406–7.
59. ibid. p. 408.
60. Quoted in Phelps, *Master in 'Akká*, p. 69.
61. ibid. p. 70.
62. 'Abdu'l-Bahá, *Memorials of the Faithful*, pp. 145, 147.
63. ibid. pp. 146–7.
64. Quoted in Phelps, *Master in 'Akká*, pp. 70–2.
65. Quoted in Blomfield, *Chosen Highway*, p. 63.
66. ibid. p. 66.

67. 'Abdu'l-Bahá, *Memorials of the Faithful*, pp. 59–60.
68. Quoted in Blomfield, *Chosen Highway*, p. 65.
69. 'Abdu'l-Bahá, *Memorials of the Faithful*, p. 60.
70. Quoted in Blomfield, *Chosen Highway*, p. 66.
71. Quoted in Phelps, *Master in 'Akká*, pp. 75–6.
72. Quoted in ibid. p. 78.
73. ibid. pp. 80–1.
74. Taherzadeh, *Revelation of Bahá'u'lláh*, vol. 3, pp. 18–19.
75. *Star of the West*, vol. 4, no. 5, p. 89.
76. Quoted in Shoghi Effendi, *God Passes By*, p. 186.
77. 'Abdu'l-Bahá, *Memorials of the Faithful*, p. 20.
78. Quoted in Phelps, *Master in 'Akká*, pp. 84–5.
79. Balyuzi, *'Abdu'l-Bahá*, p. 25.
80. Quoted in Blomfield, *Chosen Highway*, p. 64.
81. Taherzadeh, *Revelation of Bahá'u'lláh*, vol. 3, p. 65.
82. ibid. p. 66.
83. ibid. pp. 66–7.
84. Quoted in Balyuzi, *'Abdu'l-Bahá*, p. 35.
85. *Star of the West*, vol. 4, no. 5, p. 89.
86. ibid.
87. Quoted in Taherzadeh, *Revelation of Bahá'u'lláh*, vol. 3, pp. 70–1.
88. ibid. p. 71.
89. Quoted in ibid. p. 207.
90. Quoted in Balyuzi, *King of Glory*, pp. 311–13.
91. ibid. p. 311.
92. Quoted in ibid. p. 209.
93. ibid. p. 222.
94. Balyuzi, *'Abdu'l-Bahá*, p. 33.
95. Shoghi Effendi, *God Passes By*, p. 191.
96. Balyuzi, *'Abdu'l-Bahá*, pp. 36–7.
97. Bahá'u'lláh, *Kitáb-i-Aqdas*, para. 121.
98. ibid. para. 174.
99. Balyuzi, *King of Glory*, p. 340.
100. Quoted in Blomfield, *Chosen Highway*, p. 84.
101. ibid. p. 85.
102. ibid. pp. 85–6.
103. ibid. p. 87.

104. ibid.
105. Quoted in Balyuzi, *King of Glory*, p. 348.
106. Quoted in Blomfield, *Chosen Highway*, pp. 87–8.
107. Quoted in Balyuzi, *King of Glory*, p. 348.
108. Quoted in Blomfield, *Chosen Highway*, p. 89.
109. 'Abdu'l-Bahá, *Secret of Divine Civilization*, p. 6.
110. Quoted in Esslemont, *Bahá'u'lláh and the New Era*, pp. 33–5.
111. Quoted in Ḥaydar-'Alí, *Stories from the Delight of Hearts*, pp. 105–6.
112. Quoted in Gail, *Summon Up Remembrance*, p. 235.
113. Quoted in Blomfield, *Chosen Highway*, p. 90.
114. Quoted in ibid. pp. 100–3.
115. Quoted in Shoghi Effendi, *World Order*, p. 136.
116. Quoted in Balyuzi, *'Abdu'l-Bahá*, pp. 4–5.
117. Quoted in Taherzadeh, *Covenant of Bahá'u'lláh*, p. 139.
118. ibid. p. 141.
119. Quoted in Balyuzi, *'Abdu'l-Bahá*, p. 44.
120. ibid.
121. Quoted in Taherzadeh, *Covenant of Bahá'u'lláh*, pp. 139–40.
122. Quoted in Shoghi Effendi, *God Passes By*, p. 250.
123. Shoghi Effendi, *God Passes By*, p. 221.
124. Quoted in Blomfield, *Chosen Highway*. p. 105.
125. Taherzadeh, *Covenant of Bahá'u'lláh*, pp. 148–9.
126. Quoted in Blomfield, *Chosen Highway*, p. 106.
127. Taherzadeh, *Covenant of Bahá'u'lláh*, p. 149.
128. Quoted in *Chosen Highway*, pp. 106–7.
129. Ḥaydar-'Alí, *Stories from the Delight of Hearts*, pp. 120–1.
130. Taherzadeh, *Covenant of Bahá'u'lláh*, p. 149.
131. Bahá'u'lláh, *Tablets*, p. 219.
132. ibid. pp. 221–2.
133. ibid. p. 223.
134. Ḥaydar-'Alí, *Stories from the Delight of Hearts*, p. 121.
135. Quoted in Blomfield, *Chosen Highway*, pp. 109–10.
136. ibid. p. 110.
137. ibid. pp. 110–11.

138. Ḥaydar-'Alí, *Stories from the Delight of Hearts*, p. 121.
139. Quoted in Balyuzi, *'Abdu'l-Bahá*, p. 53.
140. Phelps, *Master in 'Akká*, pp. 8–10.
141. Quoted in Blomfield, *Chosen Highway*, p. 112.
142. Taherzadeh, *Covenant of Bahá'u'lláh*, p. 201.
143. Quoted in Blomfield, *Chosen Highway*, p. 112.
144. ibid. p. 114.
145. ibid. pp. 114–15.
146. Quoted in Shoghi Effendi, *God Passes By*, p. 250.
147. Quoted in Balyuzi, *'Abdu'l-Bahá*, p. 64.
148. Taherzadeh, *Covenant of Bahá'u'lláh*, p. 178.
149. 'Abdu'l-Bahá, quoted in ibid.
150. 'Abdu'l-Bahá, quoted in Shoghi Effendi, *World Order of Bahá'u'lláh*, p. 133.
151. Quoted in Stockman, *Bahá'í Faith in America*, vol. 1, pp. 136–7.
152. ibid. pp. 144–5.
153. Quoted in Balyuzi, *'Abdu'l-Bahá*, p. 69.
154. ibid.
155. Quoted in ibid. p. 70.
156. ibid.
157. Maxwell, *Early Pilgrimage*, pp. 10–11.
158. ibid. pp. 12–13.
159. 'Abdu'l-Bahá, quoted in ibid. p. 15.
160. ibid. pp. 15–16.
161. ibid. p. 18.
162. ibid. pp. 18–19.
163. ibid. pp. 30–1.
164. ibid. p. 30.
165. ibid. p. 29.
166. ibid. pp. 34–5.
167. ibid. pp. 34–8.
168. ibid. pp. 39–40.
169. ibid. pp. 41–3.
170. ibid. p. 30.
171. 'Abdu'l-Bahá, quoted in Gail, *Summon Up Remembrance*, pp. 108–9.
172. ibid. p. 109.

173. 'Abdu'l-Bahá, quoted in Shoghi Effendi, *God Passes By*, pp. 275–6.
174. 'Abdu'l-Bahá, quoted in Balyuzi, *King of Glory*, pp. 364.
175. Phelps, *Master in 'Akká*, p. 131.
176. ibid. p. 2.
177. ibid. pp. 2–3.
178. ibid. p. 3.
179. ibid. pp. 4–6.
180. ibid. p. 7.
181. ibid. p. 118.
182. Metelmann, *Lua Getsinger*, 89–90.
183. Balyuzi, *'Abdu'l-Bahá*, p. 114.
184. 'Abdu'l-Bahá, *Some Answered Questions*, p. xvii.
185. Quoted in Gail, *Summon Up Remembrance*, p. 226.
186. 'Abdu'l-Bahá, quoted in ibid. p. 242.
187. 'Abdu'l-Bahá, quoted in ibid. p. 227.
188. ibid. p. 235.
189. Quoted in ibid. pp. 235–6.
190. Quoted in Rutstein, *Corinne True*, p. 58.
191. Chase, *In Galilee*, p. 27.
192. ibid. pp. 23–4.
193. Taherzadeh, *Covenant of Bahá'u'lláh*, p. 235.
194. 'Abdu'l-Bahá, *Will and Testament*, p. 19.
195. ibid. p. 23.
196. Bahá'u'lláh, *Kitáb-i-Aqdas*, para. 37.
197. Taherzadeh, *Covenant of Bahá'u'lláh*, p. 233.
198. ibid. p. 241.
199. Balyuzi, *'Abdu'l-Bahá*, pp. 121–2.
200. Balyuzi, *'Abdu'l-Bahá*, p. 129.
201. Shoghi Effendi, *God Passes By*, p. 276.
202. 'Abdu'l-Bahá, quoted in ibid. p. 276.
203. Quoted in Balyuzi, *'Abdu'l-Bahá*, p. 134.
204. ibid. p. 135.
205. ibid. p. 137.
206. Quoted in ibid. p. 138.
207. ibid. p. 139.
208. Quoted in 'Horace Hotchkiss Holley', *Bahá'í World*, vol. 13, p. 851.

209. Blomfield, *Chosen Highway*, p. 149.
210. ibid. pp. 149–50.
211. 'Abdu'l-Bahá, quoted in ibid. p. 150.
212. ibid. p. 156.
213. ibid.
214. ibid.
215. ibid. pp. 150–1.
216. 'Abdu'l-Bahá, in *Bahá'í Revelation*, p. 280.
217. ibid. pp. 280–1.
218. Quoted in Balyuzi, *'Abdu'l-Bahá*, p. 145.
219. Quoted in ibid. p. 146.
220. 'Abdu'l-Bahá, quoted in ibid. pp. 153–4.
221. Blomfield, *Chosen Highway*, pp. 173–4.
222. ibid. p. 179.
223. ibid. p. 181.
224. ibid. p. 180.
225. ibid. p. 181.
226. Quoted in Balyuzi, *'Abdu'l-Bahá*, p. 159.
227. 'Abdu'l-Bahá, quoted in Blomfield, *Chosen Highway*, p. 184.
228. 'Abdu'l-Bahá, quoted in Balyuzi, *'Abdu'l-Bahá*, p. 164.
229. ibid. pp. 160–1.
230. Blomfield, *Chosen Highway*, p. 183.
231. ibid. p. 184.
232. ibid.
233. ibid. p. 185.
234. ibid. pp. 182–3.
235. ibid. p. 180.
236. 'Abdu'l-Bahá, quoted in Balyuzi, *'Abdu'l-Bahá*, pp. 167–8.
237. *Diary of Juliet Thompson*, p. 233.
238. ibid. pp. 234–6.
239. 'Abdu'l-Bahá, *Promulgation*, p. 3.
240. ibid. p. 32.
241. Balyuzi, *'Abdu'l-Bahá*, p. 178.
242. 'Abdu'l-Bahá, quoted in ibid. p. 179.
243. Hollinger, *Agnes Parsons' Diary*, pp. 12–13.
244. 'Abdu'l-Bahá, *Promulgation*, p. 57.

245. Balyuzi, *'Abdu'l-Bahá*, p. 183.
246. ibid. pp. 183–4.
247. 'Abdu'l-Bahá, *Promulgation*, p. 71.
248. 'Abdu'l-Bahá, quoted in Balyuzi, *'Abdu'l-Bahá*, pp. 188–9.
249. ibid. pp. 190–1.
250. *Diary of Juliet Thompson*, p. 285.
251. 'Abdu'l-Bahá, *Promulgation*, p. 125.
252. Ives, *Portals to Freedom*, p. 83.
253. ibid. pp. 86–7.
254. 'Abdu'l-Bahá, *Promulgation*, p. 131.
255. ibid. p. 140.
256. Balyuzi, *'Abdu'l-Bahá*, pp. 207–8.
257. ibid. p. 208.
258. 'Abdu'l-Bahá, *Promulgation*, pp. 183–4.
259. Balyuzi, *'Abdu'l-Bahá*, p. 213.
260. ibid. p. 223.
261. *Diary of Juliet Thompson*, p. 315.
262. 'Abdu'l-Bahá, quoted in Metelmann, *Lua Getsinger*, pp. 165–6.
263. ibid. p. 164.
264. 'Abdu'l-Bahá, *Promulgation*, pp. 214–15.
265. ibid. p. 218.
266. ibid. pp. 238–9.
267. Ives, *Portals to Freedom*, pp. 115–16.
268. Balyuzi, *'Abdu'l-Bahá*, pp. 31–2.
269. ibid. p. 239.
270. Ives, *Portals to Freedom*, p. 127.
271. Hollinger, *Agnes Parsons' Diary*, pp. 114–15.
272. *Diary of Juliet Thompson*, p. 359.
273. Quoted in Balyuzi, *'Abdu'l-Bahá*, pp. 250–1.
274. ibid. p. 251.
275. Balyuzi, *'Abdu'l-Bahá*, p. 260.
276. ibid. pp. 263–4.
277. ibid. p. 264.
278. ibid. p. 265.
279. 'Abdu'l-Bahá, *Promulgation*, pp. 238–42.
280. Maḥmúd-i-Zarqání, *Maḥmúd's Diary*, p. 290.
281. Balyuzi, *'Abdu'l-Bahá*, pp. 283–4.

282. ibid. p. 288.
283. Metelmann, *Lua Getsinger*, p. 176.
284. 'Abdu'l-Bahá, quoted in Maḥmúd-i-Zarqání, *Maḥmúd's Diary*, p. 320.
285. Balyuzi, *'Abdu'l-Bahá*, p. 230.
286. ibid. pp. 309–10.
287. 'Abdu'l-Bahá, *Promulgation*, pp. 376–80.
288. ibid. p. 382.
289. ibid. p. 399.
290. Hollinger, *Agnes Parsons' Diary*, pp. 131–2.
291. Balyuzi, *'Abdu'l-Bahá*, p. 323.
292. 'Abdu'l-Bahá, *Promulgation*, p. 421.
293. ibid. p. 426.
294. ibid. p. 448.
295. 'Abdu'l-Bahá, quoted in Balyuzi, *'Abdu'l-Bahá*, pp. 336–7.
296. 'Abdu'l-Bahá, *Promulgation*, p. 469.
297. *Diary of Juliet Thompson*, p. 393.
298. Blomfield, *Chosen Highway*, p. 153.
299. ibid. p. 155.
300. Balyuzi, *'Abdu'l-Bahá*, p. 347.
301. ibid. pp. 345–6.
302. Blomfield, *Chosen Highway*, p. 159.
303. Balyuzi, *'Abdu'l-Bahá*, p. 347.
304. ibid. p. 351.
305. Blomfield, *Chosen Highway*, pp. 168–9.
306. Quoted in Balyuzi, *'Abdu'l-Bahá*, p. 368.
307. Blomfield, *Chosen Highway*, p. 172.
308. ibid. p. 168.
309. 'Abdu'l-Bahá, quoted in Balyuzi, *'Abdu'l-Bahá*, p. 381.
310. ibid.
311. ibid. pp. 389–90.
312. ibid. p. 392.
313. ibid. p. 395.
314. ibid. p. 400.
315. ibid. p. 401.
316. *Star of the West*, vol. 4, no. 17, pp. 288–90.
317. Balyuzi, *'Abdu'l-Bahá*, p. 403.

318. Lidell Hart, *Real War*, p. 22.
319. 'Abdu'l-Bahá, quoted in *Bahá'í Year Book*, vol. 1, p. 31.
320. 'Abdu'l-Bahá, quoted in Balyuzi, *'Abdu'l-Bahá*, pp. 406–7.
321. Lidell Hart, *Real War*, p. 28.
322. Quoted in Metelmann, *Lua Getsinger*, pp. 294–5.
323. Blomfield, *Chosen Highway*, p. 189.
324. Metelmann, *Lua Getsinger*, pp. 291–2.
325. Blomfield, *Chosen Highway*, p. 189.
326. ibid. pp. 190–2.
327. Balyuzi, *'Abdu'l-Bahá*, p. 412.
328. Metelmann, *Lua Getsinger*, pp. 314–15.
329. ibid. p. 315.
330. ibid.
331. ibid. p. 311.
332. Balyuzi, *'Abdu'l-Bahá*, p. 413.
333. ibid. p. 416.
334. Metelmann, *Lua Getsinger*, p. 313.
335. Lidell Hart, *Real War*, p. 124.
336. ibid. p. 138.
337. Quoted in 'Abdu'l-Bahá, *Memorials of the Faithful*, p. xii.
338. ibid. p. xi.
339. Quoted in Blomfield, *Chosen Highway*, p. 202.
340. ibid. pp. 204–5.
341. Balyuzi, *'Abdu'l-Bahá*, pp. 416–17.
342. 'Abdu'l-Bahá, *Tablets of the Divine Plan*, p. 5.
343. Balyuzi, *'Abdu'l-Bahá*, p. 425.
344. 'Abdu'l-Bahá, *Tablets of the Divine Plan*, pp. 53–4.
345. Lidell Hart, *Real War*, pp. 203–4.
346. Blomfield, *Chosen Highway*, p. 206.
347. ibid. pp. 207–8.
348. ibid. p. 207.
349. Balyuzi, *'Abdu'l-Bahá*, p. 418.
350. Quoted in ibid, pp. 426–7.
351. Blomfield, *Chosen Highway*, p. 219.
352. Quoted in Balyuzi, *'Abdu'l-Bahá*, pp. 427–8.
353. ibid. pp. 428–9.

354. Blomfield, *Chosen Highway*, pp. 219–20.
355. Quoted in Balyuzi, *'Abdu'l-Bahá*, p. 429.
356. Quoted in Blomfield, *Chosen Highway*, p. 227.
357. ibid. p. 210.
358. Quoted in Balyuzi, *'Abdu'l-Bahá*, p. 432.
359. ibid. pp. 431–2.
360. Quoted in Blomfield, *Chosen Highway*, p. 221.
361. Quoted in Rabbaní, *Priceless Pearl*, p. 28.
362. ibid.
363. Quoted in Balyuzi, *'Abdu'l-Bahá*, p. 512.
364. ibid. p. 513.
365. Esslemont, *Bahá'u'lláh and the New Era*, pp. 61–2.
366. Quoted in Balyuzi, *'Abdu'l-Bahá*, p. 438.
367. Blomfield, *Chosen Highway*, pp. 214–15.
368. Balyuzi, *'Abdu'l-Bahá*, p. 448.
369. 'Abdu'l-Bahá, quoted in Balyuzi, *'Abdu'l-Bahá*, p. 452.
370. Quoted in *Bahá'í Year Book*, vol. 1, p. 19.
371. Balyuzi, *'Abdu'l-Bahá*, p. 458.
372. ibid.
373. *Bahá'í Year Book*, vol. 1, p. 19.
374. 'Abdu'l-Bahá, quoted in Balyuzi, *'Abdu'l-Bahá*, pp. 450–1.
375. ibid. p. 458.
376. ibid. pp. 458–9.
377. ibid. pp. 460–1.
378. ibid. p. 461.
379. ibid. pp. 461–2.
380. ibid. p. 462.
381. *Bahá'í Year Book*, vol. 1, p. 23.
382. Balyuzi, *'Abdu'l-Bahá*, p. 465.
383. ibid.
384. ibid.
385. ibid. pp. 465–6.
386. ibid. p. 474.

1875 abdul-Baha – "Secret of Devine
      Pg 79   Civilization"
Baha'u'llah – country world of Soul ... Pg 81